# The Winter's Tale

# THE WINTER'S TALE

## A Guide to the Play

### JOAN LORD HALL

*Greenwood Guides to Shakespeare*

**GREENWOOD PRESS**
Westport, Connecticut • London

**Library of Congress Cataloging-in-Publication Data**

Hall, Joan Lord.
 The winter's tale : a guide to the play / Joan Lord Hall.
  p. cm. — (Greenwood guides to Shakespeare)
 Includes bibliographical references and index.
 ISBN 0–313–32818–8 (alk. paper)
 1. Shakespeare, William, 1564–1616. Winter's tale. 2. Tragicomedy.
 I. Title. II. Series.
 PR2839.H26   2005
  822.3'3—dc22       2005012730

British Library Cataloguing in Publication Data is available.

Library of Congress Catalog Card Number: 2005012730
ISBN: 0–313–32818–8

First published in 2005

Greenwood Press, 88 Post Road West, Westport, CT 06881
An imprint of Greenwood Publishing Group, Inc.
www.greenwood.com

Printed in the United States of America

The paper used in this book complies with the
Permanent Paper Standard issued by the National
Information Standards Organization (Z39.48–1984).

10  9  8  7  6  5  4  3  2  1

# CONTENTS

# PREFACE

A raging bear; the figure of Time; a statue that turns out to be a living woman—these are features that make The Winter's Tale an unusual, even weird, drama. The play appealed well enough to Shakespeare's audience, with its taste for romantic adventure and tragedy that segues into comedy. And because our postmodern age appreciates sudden dislocations, dream-like strangeness, and the mythic dimension of dramatic literature, the play has come into its own again in the study and the theater, along with Shakespeare's other Late Plays that culminate in The Tempest. As the chapters that follow indicate, The Winter's Tale is a rewarding play on many levels. Chapter 1 discusses the transmission of the script in the First Folio and the play's most significant textual crux. Chapter 2 explores the cultural contexts of this drama—how it relates to the political climate under King James I and to social and agrarian developments in the early seventeenth century—and examines other texts that may have played a role in its genesis. The third chapter concentrates on the play's form and structure as it contributes to the genres of romance, pastoral, and tragicomedy evolving in Shakespeare's time. The powerful style of The Winter's Tale and its creation of dramatic characters is the subject of chapter 4, leading into a consideration of the play's key themes in chapter 5: how dangerous passion may be offset by faith in the loved one; the meaning of "honor"; the credibility of an "old tale"; and ways in which art, operating within the magic of theater, can illuminate the nature of life. Chapter 6 concentrates on critical approaches over the centuries that have opened windows on the play as they simultaneously reflect the biases of their own age. The varied stage history of The Winter's Tale and the videotape of the BBC's televised version (1980) are analyzed in detail in chapter 7.

All quotations from The Winter's Tale are taken from Frank Kermode (ed.), The Signet Classic Shakespeare (New York and London: Penguin, 1963; 1998). Quotations from Shakespeare's other plays are from G. Blakemore Evans (ed.), The Riverside Shakespeare (Boston: Houghton Mifflin, 1976; 1997).

Friends have helped to keep my enthusiasm for The Winter's Tale high. My thanks go to Nancy Mann, at the University of Colorado, Boulder, for her invaluable editing of the middle chapters; to Reg Saner for offering books and continued interest in the project; and especially to Arthur Tobias, whose analysis of the text and dedication to the highest standards of critical writing have proved an inspiration.

# ABBREVIATIONS OF CITED WORKS

| | |
|---|---|
| AMIAA | American Imago |
| BSUF | Ball State University Forum |
| BucknellRev | Bucknell Review |
| CompD | Comparative Drama |
| CompLitStud | Comparative Literature Studies |
| EIC | Essays in Criticism |
| ELH | English Literary History |
| ELR | English Literary Renaissance |
| ES | English Studies |
| E&S | Essays and Studies |
| HLQ | Huntingdon Library Quarterly |
| MLQ | Modern Language Quarterly |
| MLR | Modern Language Review |
| N&Q | Notes and Queries |
| PLLL | Papers in Language and Literature |
| PMLA | Publications of the Modern Language Association |
| PQ | Philological Quarterly |
| RenD | Renaissance Drama |
| Ren&R | Renaissance and Reformation |
| REL | Review of English Literature |
| RES | Review of English Studies |
| SEL | Studies in English Literature |
| SeR | Sewanee Review |
| SFNL | Shakespeare on Film Newsletter |

| | |
|---|---|
| ShakS | Shakespeare Studies |
| ShN | Shakespeare Newsletter |
| ShS | Shakespeare Survey |
| SQ | Shakespeare Quarterly |
| SSAB | Shakespeare Association Bulletin |
| SSEng | Sydney Studies in English |
| TexP | Textual Practice |
| TLS | Times Literary Supplement |
| Ucrow | Upstart Crow |
| UTQ | University of Texas Quarterly |
| WS | Women's Studies |

# 1

## *TEXTUAL HISTORY*

*The Winter's Tale* was listed in the Stationer's Register on November 8, 1623. Along with 15 other plays, it was licensed for inclusion in the First Folio of 1623—the edition of 36 of Shakespeare's plays that the playwright's colleagues, Heminge and Condell, had collected for publication six years after Shakespeare's death. Since the play was printed only in folio form, subsequent editors do not have to grapple with variants from quartos, those versions of the playtexts (where sheets of paper were folded twice, not once, as in the larger Folio) that were published while the play was still current in the theater.

In the Folio, *The Winter's Tale* is placed at the end of the section on the Comedies, after *Twelfth Night*. The anomalous blank verso page between the two plays indicates that there was a delay in obtaining the script of *The Winter's Tale;* apparently it was added after some of the history plays had been printed. Scholars agree that a copy of the play was prepared by Ralph Crane, a scrivener who worked quite closely with Shakespeare's company, the King's Men, and who provided transcripts for four other comedies for the First Folio: *The Tempest, Two Gentlemen of Verona, The Merry Wives of Windsor,* and *Measure for Measure*.[1] As is usual with Crane's transcripts, *The Winter's Tale* is divided into acts and scenes. Crane was most likely working from Shakespeare's "foul papers" (his final handwritten version of the play) and not from the promptbook used in the playhouse. Records from the Revels Office, copied by Edmund Malone and now lost, indicate that the "olde playe called *Winters Tale*" had to be relicensed on August 19 of 1623 because the original promptbook, which had been "allowed" by both George Buck and Henry Herbert, had gone "missinge."[2] Quite possibly Crane, using Shakespeare's foul papers or a "clean copy"[3] of the manuscript, replaced this missing promptbook and prepared a copy for the Folio.[4] The other theory, based on the assumption that the Folio's printing of *The Winter's Tale* was completed by December 1622,[5] is that the promptbook was "missinge" because it was being copied by Crane.[6]

Ralph Crane's work is generally acknowledged to be "clear and accurate."[7] Subsequent editors have had to make very few emendations, such as "hobbyhorse" to replace the nonsensical "holy-horse" (1.2.276) where a handwritten "b" might have been read as "l," and "kiln-hole" (4.4.246) to replace the phonetic spelling "kill-hole." Other typographical errors presumably were made by Compositors A (whose work was shared by more than one man), B, and apprentice E, all responsible for setting up the type in Isaac Jaggard's printing house. But despite *The Winter's Tale* being "one of the cleanest of Shakespeare's texts,"[8] we should not be overconfident that the play as we have it is entirely Shakespeare's script. Obscurities may have been smoothed out and words and punctuation added, since, as T. H. Howard-Hill comments, Crane was not "reluctant to interfere with his text"[9] or resort to intelligent guesswork.

One of Crane's trademarks was the "massed"[10] stage entry; that is, he sometimes lists all of a scene's characters as entering at the beginning of that scene even if they do not actually make their entrances until later. Six of the eight massed heading scenes fall under this category. In act 2, scene 1, for instance, although Leontes, Antigonus, and the Lords do not come onstage to disrupt the playful encounter of "Hermione, Mamillius, [and] Ladies" until line 32, they are grouped with them under "Enter" at the top of the scene. The heading to act 3, scene 4, which reads "Enter Antigonus, a Mariner, Babe, Sheepe-heard, and Clowne," jumbles together the three characters from Sicily with the two Bohemians (the Old Shepherd and his son). In actuality, of course, the last two make their entrances only after Antigonus has left the stage prompted by the Folio's notorious stage direction "Exit pursued by a Beare." Act 4, scene 4 lists Autolycus among the other named characters who troop in at the beginning of the sheep-shearing scene but then more properly provides "Enter Autolicus singing" at line 220. When all the Sicilian courtiers gather together for the finale (5.3), the opening stage direction includes "Enter ... Hermione (like a statue)." This sets a reader wondering whether, to avoid destroying theatrical surprise, the "statue" was carried in, pushed in on a dais, or concealed behind a curtain in the "discovery space" between the two main doors.

A few of the massed entries do offer scope for different interpretations by a director. Alan C. Dessen makes a case for not automatically assuming that Leontes comes on stage alone in act 2, scene 3. If the "Lords" enter at the same time that he does (in accordance with the scene's heading), this would indicate that the king's opening "Nor day, nor night no rest" speech is not a soliloquy but an aside that underscores his solipsism and obliviousness to the people around him.[11] And if Dion and Cleomenes are "in the Court from the outset"[12] of the trial scene (3.2), rather than entering with their oracular message at line 121, their presence throughout the scene could add to the theatrical suspense.[13]

As well as usually emending the entrances and exits of characters, later editors have felt the need to add stage directions to the sparse Folio ones. Yet often Shakespeare's script itself serves as a guide to the characters' movements. In act 5, scene 3, for instance, Paulina stage-manages the revelation that the statue is actually Hermione with these words, as punctuated in the Folio:

> Music; awake her: strike:
> 'Tis time: descend: be stone no more: approach (98–99)

Paulina's first command is addressed to the musicians while her second line is obviously spoken to Hermione. Yet editors usually add to the lines the pointers "Music" and "To Hermione," and all editions insert "Hermione descends" (*Signet* reads "Hermione comes down") three and a half lines later at "You perceive she stirs." In act 4, scene 2 we can deduce that Autolycus picks the Clown's pocket somewhere during lines 76–77: "Softly, dear sir; good sir, softly; you ha' done me a charitable office." Nevertheless, H. H. Furness in the *New Variorum* edition (1898) is full of praise for Edward Capell's addition of the direction "Picks his pocket" after "dear sir,"[14] which subsequently appears there in *Arden 1*, in the *Oxford Shakespeare* after "good sir, softly," and in *Signet* at the end of the line. At the opening of act 4, scene 4, there is no need for a stage direction that Florizel enters disguised, for Perdita soon informs us that he has "obscured" himself with a "swain's wearing" (8–9). Later we deduce that these shepherd's garments must still look fairly costly, since Autolycus is easily able to impersonate a courtier after exchanging clothes with the prince (651).[15]

The Folio's act 4, scene 4, the long sheep-shearing scene in Bohemia, contains only eight stage directions covering songs, dances, two entrances, and two exits. It has therefore proved a ready candidate for additional directions. Because several different groups of characters interact on stage, editors now add pointers to clarify who is addressing whom. To Perdita's catalogue of flowers, *Signet* adds "To Florizel" before "Now, my fair'st friend" (112) and "to Shepherdesses" before "and yours, and yours, / That wear upon your virgin branches yet / Your maidenheads growing" (114–

16). There is some confusion over who remains on stage for the "dance of twelve satyrs" after line 346. The Clown, revealing that his father is in serious conversation ("sad talk") with the disguised Polixenes and Camillo, presumably leaves with Mopsa and Dorcas, indicated by "follow me, girls" (320), to buy knickknacks from Autolycus. The peddler himself exits after his short "Will you buy any tape?" song (327). No entrance or exit is provided for the Servant who announces the "carters" and others who will dance the part of satyrs, but when Polixenes expresses interest, the show goes on.[16] Neil Freeman wonders if some of the festival guests stayed to watch; if so, "how many witnessed … the final angry exchange" between the king and prince (421–445)?[17] Although we cannot be certain, it seems likely that by the time Polixenes pronounces his "divorce" from his son at line 421, the stage has cleared of everyone but Polixenes, Camillo, the Old Shepherd, and the young lovers, Florizel and Perdita.

Judged by the end results, Crane's scripts for the printer were always carefully prepared. With its predilection for parentheses, apostrophes, colons, and hyphens (as in the anomolous compounds "Wat'ry-star" and "good-deed" [1.2.1,42], "Virgin-branches" and "Whitson-pastorals" [4.4.115,134]), *The Winter's Tale* is the "most heavily punctuated"[18] of the five comedies that Crane prepared for the First Folio. None of Crane's orthographic idiosyncracies cause problems for later editors. More to the point are early seventeenth-century conventions of punctuation that might at first confuse a modern reader. Nouns are usually, though not always, capitalized in the Folio; a modern editor's choice to retain some of these capitals can make a subtle difference in how we interpret certain words in the text. Many current editions of the play (*Arden 1, Signet,* and the *New Penguin,* though not the *Oxford*) leave "grace" capitalized in Hermione's response to Leontes's reminder of how she first accepted him: " 'Tis Grace indeed" (1.2.105). Wilbur Sanders, though, chides these editors for allowing the word to enjoy a "specious prominence—wearing a halo, as it were,"[19] arguing that "grace" here connotes as much a natural as a divine quality. Modern editors must decide whether it makes sense to preserve some of the capitals or, in the interests of consistency, to eliminate them all.

The colon and semicolon, often used interchangeably in playtexts of Shakespeare's time, mark both a "thinking and a speaking pause,"[20] as in the line already quoted, "Music; awake her: strike" (5.3.98). A question mark can indicate either the end of a question or serve as an exclamation point. Thus in act 1, scene 2, the Folio reads

> How sometimes Nature will betray it's folly?
> It's tendernesse? And make it selfe a Pastime
> To harder bosoms? (1.2.151–53)

Modern editors, as in the *Signet,* usually transcribe Leontes's speech as one long exclamation:

> How sometimes Nature will betray its folly,
> Its tenderness, and make itself a pastime
> To harder bosoms!

Understanding these conventions can make a difference to how we interpret the notorious speech Leontes delivers on "Affection" when he speculates on Hermione's behavior toward Polixenes. Called the "obscurest passage in Shakespeare,"[21] this speech has baffled readers, partly because of the way it is punctuated in the original but mainly because of its syntactic and semantic ambiguities. This is how it reads in the First Folio:

> Can thy Dam, may't be
> Affection? thy Intention stabs the Center.
> Thou do'st make possible things not so held,
> Communicat'st with Dreames (how can this be?)
> With what's unreall: thou coactive art,
> And fellow'st nothing. Then 'tis very credent,
> Thou may'st co-joyne with something, and thou do'st,
> (And that beyond Commission) and I find it,
> (And that to the infection of my Braines,
> And hardning of my Browes.) (1.2.137–46)

Most modern editions (*Arden 1, Signet,* and the *Oxford*) follow George Steevens (1773) in substituting an exclamation point for a question mark after "Affection." They also (with the exception of the *Oxford*) adopt the punctuation of Thomas Hanmer (1744) and add a question mark after "may't be?" The reading of *Signet* is thus

> Can thy dam, may't be?
> Affection! Thy intention stabs the center.

Whereas the Folio punctuation clearly links "affection" to Mamillius's "dam" (his mother, Hermione), the new version leaves the first line as an open question (can it be that your mother is committing adultery?) and makes "Affection" the vocative subject of "thy intention."[22] Commentators agree that "affection" denotes not our modern sense of warm fondness but instead strong passion. Often it meant lust or desire (*OED,* 3), as in the Prologue to act 2 of *Romeo and Juliet,* which tells us that "old desire doth in his death-bed lie, / And young affection gapes to be his heir" (1–2). If we assume that Leontes is contemplating what he takes to be Hermione's lust for Polixenes, and "intention" means significance or purpose,[23] then his second line can roughly be paraphrased (following the *Oxford* edition) as "the purposes of Hermione's lust cut to his heart."[24] Lust enables what had been "thought impossible, creating an imaginary world of wish-fulfilment in dreams."[25] "Center" could mean not only the individual's heart or soul but also the center of the world or universe, as when Leontes later declares that if his conviction is groundless, "The center is not big enough to bear / A schoolboy's top" (2.1.102–3). This extra layer of meaning does not, of course, change the import of the speech—that Leontes, and by extension the whole world, is wounded to the core by Hermione's sexual betrayal.

If we assume that the colon after "unreal" marks a significant break in the Folio version, then "With what's unreal" stands in apposition to "dreams" in the preceding line. But virtually all editors[26] remove the colon so that the lines read

> With what's unreal thou coactive art,
> And fellow'st nothing. Then 'tis very credent
> Thou may'st co-join with something, and thou dost …

Taking "coactive" to mean "acting in concert" (*OED*, 2, though rare), with "thou" referring back to Hermione's lustful "affection," we find Leontes assuming that Hermione may easily move from the "unreal" imaginary realm to finding an actual object—the "something" that is Polixenes—on which to fix her desire. "And thou dost" signifies Leontes deciding that this unlawful liaison ("beyond commission") is already taking place. Although there is no clear referent to "it" in "and I find it" (144), Leontes could be saying that the scenario he has just envisaged—Hermione moving from a fantasy of lust to its actual consummation—is what is maddening him (infecting his "brains"). It is also turning him into a cuckold—a husband who has sprouted invisible horns on his forehead (a "hardening" of the "brows") as a sign of his wife's infidelity.

What, though, if "Affection" refers not to Hermione's lust but to Leontes's passion of jealousy?[27] This is Frank Kermode's interpretation (*Signet* edition), so that he glosses the second line as "Passion! Your desire for fulfilment can pierce to the heart of things."[28] In what follows, Leontes is speculating on his *own* emotional upheaval. He makes the leap from how strong emotions often feed on illusion ("dreams," "what's unreal," and "nothing"), difficult as that may be to apprehend ("how can this be?"), to the way that passion can collaborate ("co-join") with what really exists. By now he is convinced that his intense feelings, as evidenced by his mental turmoil and cuckold's horns, have led him to discover the "something" that is true. Critics have not been slow to point out the lack of logic in Leontes's shift from acknowledging the dreamlike basis of his passion to accepting it as grounded in fact; but this may be the point. Allowing "indeterminacy" to become "certainty,"[29] Leontes has convinced himself that his imaginings about his wife's promiscuity point to the truth. His "infection of the brain ... has fitted the fantasy to the present instance"[30] rather than there being any objective cause for the effects of jealousy that he feels.

Which reading of "Affection" is more probable, or can they both be held in balance by the reader? On the face of it, the first reading (favored by *Arden 1* and the *New Penguin*), where Leontes is speculating on the progression of Hermione's lust, fits better with the Folio's run-on line "can thy Dam, may't be / Affection?" which associates Hermione firmly with the passion or "affection." It also jibes with "and thou dost" and "beyond commission"—Leontes's conviction that his wife has embarked on an illicit relationship with Polixenes. Stephen Orgel, editor of the *Oxford* edition, keeps both options alive, glossing "Thou dost make possible things not so held, / Communicat'st with dreams" as either that Hermione's lust "facilitates what had been thought impossible" or (if Leontes is pondering the sequence of his own emotions) "I can now believe things I had thought impossible, I am in touch with the world of fantasies and desires."[31] Orgel thinks that the speech may have been designed to convey "intensity, vagueness and obscurity"[32] even to its original audience. The blurring of referents belonging to "thou" and "it" is also appropriate, since "in talking about Hermione" Leontes is "also talking about himself."[33]

David Ward defends the second reading, but with a somewhat different analysis of the lines. He argues that Leontes is not justifying his jealous imaginings as much as "trying to understand the exaggerated and confounding power"[34] that his emotions have over him.[35] Ward bases this interpretation on the seventeenth-century meaning of affections as "involuntary"[36] manifestations of the appetite (unable to discriminate between the possible and the impossible) and on "intention" in its quasi-medical meaning of "intensification."[37] On this reading, Leontes is discussing how his uncontrollable emotions are intensifying to the point of attacking the very center of his being ("thy intention stabs the center"). Ward also takes "coactive" to mean "coercive" (*OED*, 1). Following the Folio's punctuation, which offers "thou coactive art / And fellow'st nothing," Ward finds Leontes expressing how he feels coerced or pushed into consorting with what doesn't exist. Instead of rushing headlong into jealous conviction, Leontes is "standing back from the disease, trying to assess it for what it is."[38] Unfortunately the king's remission, indicated by his asking "What cheer? How is't with you, best brother?" shortly afterward (a question given to him in the Folio text, though assigned to Polixenes by several editors)[39] is only temporary.

Carol Thomas Neely offers a compromise between the two readings, finding that the first half of the passage is more likely to be focusing on Leontes's own jealous "affection" while the second half, from "Then 'tis very credent," is "predominantly 'about' Hermione's and Polixenes's lust."[40] "And thou dost" could refer specifically to Hermione herself and her committing of adultery. But Neely notes that it is the third strand in the speech—the "ugly, free-floating image of intercourse"[41] suggested by Leontes's choice of the words "stab, "fellow'st," "hardening," "communicat'st," "coactive," and "co-join"[42]—that really drives his passionate, contorted speech and accounts for much of its incoherence.

## NOTES

1. See T. H. Howard-Hill, *Ralph Crane and Some Shakespeare First Folio Comedies* (Charlottesville: University Press of Virginia, 1972).

2. See J.H.P. Pafford (ed.), William Shakespeare, *The Winter's Tale,* The Arden Shakespeare (London: Methuen, 1963), p. xvi.

3. Ernest Schanzer (ed.), *The Winter's Tale* (Penguin Books: London and New York, 1986), p. 236.

4. This is T. H. Howard-Hill's theory, outlined in "Knight, Crane, and the Copy for the Folio *Winter's Tale,*" *N&Q* 211 (April 1966): 139–40.

5. See Charlton Hinman, *The Printing and Proof-Reading of the First Folio of Shakespeare,* vol. 2 (Oxford: Clarendon, 1963), p. 522.

6. See Stanley Wells, in Stanley Wells and Gary Taylor (eds.), *William Shakespeare: A Textual Companion* (Oxford: Clarendon, 1987), p. 601.

7. Pafford (ed.), *The Winter's Tale,* p. xix.

8. Frank Kermode (ed.), William Shakespeare, *The Winter's Tale,* The Signet Classic Shakespeare (New York and London: Penguin, 1963; 1998), p. 157.

9. Howard-Hill, *Ralph Crane,* p. 133.

10. Ibid., p. 129.

11. Alan C. Dessen, *Rescripting Shakespeare: The Text, the Director, and Modern Productions* (Cambridge: Cambridge University Press, 2002), pp. 226–27.

12. Pafford (ed.), *The Winter's Tale,* speculates on this possibility but discards it (60).

13. Dessen, *Rescripting Shakespeare,* p. 229.

14. H. H. Furness (ed.), William Shakespeare, *The Winter's Tale* (Philadelphia: J. B. Lippincott, 1898), p. xii.

15. This apparent anomaly bothered David Garrick to the point that in his 1756 production he cut the exchange of outfits and added a passage in which Autolycus explains how his courtly new clothes have been stolen from a "silken

gamester." Noted by Dennis Bartholomeusz, The Winter's Tale *in Performance in England and America, 1611–1976* (Cambridge: Cambridge University Press, 1982), p. 228.

16. Stanley Wells, in Stanley Wells and Gary Taylor (eds.), *William Shakespeare: A Textual Companion* (Oxford: Oxford University Press, 1987), argues that the passage introducing the dance of the satyrs may be a later interpolation, as lines 328–46 could be omitted "without disturbing the dialogue" (p. 601). In fact Polixenes's line to the Old Shepherd, "O father, you'll know more of that hereafter" (347), seems to conclude their "sad talk" mentioned by the Clown (317). Polixenes also shows no evidence of having witnessed the dance, even though he expresses a desire to do so at lines 338–39.

17. Neil Freeman (ed.), William Shakespeare, *The Winter's Tale,* Applause First Folio Editions (New York: Applause Books, 1998), p. li.

18. Howard-Hill, *Ralph Crane,* p. 83.

19. Wilbur Sanders, *The Winter's Tale,* Twayne's New Critical Introductions to Shakespeare (Boston: Twayne Publishers, 1987), p. 37.

20. Freeman (ed.), *The Winter's Tale,* Applause First Folio Editions, p. xxi.

21. Mark Van Doren, *Shakespeare* (New York: Henry Holt, 1939), p. 316.

22. This comes across most clearly in Schanzer (ed.), *The Winter's Tale,* New Penguin Shakespeare, which uses a comma and not an exclamation mark to read "Affection, thy intention stabs the center" (59).

23. Jonathan Smith, "The Language of Leontes," *SQ* 19 (1968): 317–27, points out that this is the only instance of "intention" used with this meaning in Shakespeare (318).

24. Orgel (ed.), *The Winter's Tale,* p. 102.

25. This is the paraphrase in Schanzer (ed.), *The Winter's Tale,* New Penguin Shakespeare, p. 166.

26. One exception is John F. Andrews, William Shakespeare, *The Winter's Tale,* The Everyman Shakespeare (London: Dent, 1995). Committed to preserving the Folio punctuation wherever possible, he nevertheless comes up with a similar gloss for the lines to that of most other editors: "You require a co-agent to act, and have no fellow (equal or partner). Therefore it is credible that you would seek a collaborator" (20).

27. Edmund Malone (1790) extends the meaning of "affection to "imagination," or "the disposition of the mind when strongly *affected* or possessed by a particular idea." See Furness (ed.), *The Winter's Tale,* New Variorum, p. 28.

28. Kermode (ed.), *The Winter's Tale,* p. 11.

29. Carol Thomas Neely, "*The Winter's Tale:* The Triumph of Speech," *SEL* 15, no. 2 (Spring 1975): 321–38, 325.

30. Harold C. Goddard, *The Meaning of Shakespeare,* vol. 2 (Chicago and London: University of Chicago Press, 1951), p. 265.

31. Orgel (ed.), *The Winter's Tale,* p. 102.

32. Ibid., p. 12.

33. Ibid., p. 102.

34. David Ward, "Affection, Intention, and Dreams in *The Winter's Tale*," *MLR* 82 (1987): 545–54, 552.

35. Hallett Smith, "Leontes' *Affectio*," *SQ* 14 (1963): 163–66, argues for reading "affection" as "affectio," glossed in Cooper's *Thesaurus* (1582) as "trouble of minde" (163); like Ward, Smith thinks that Leontes is addressing his "sudden perturbation of mind" (164). Laurence Wright, "When Does the Tragi-Comic Disruption Start?: *The Winter's Tale* and Leontes' Affection," *ES* 70, no. 3 (1989): 225–32, also draws on this meaning of affection as "trouble of mind" to argue that at first Leontes is "acknowledging that his overwrought state may be largely the product of an imagination untempered by reality." But at "Then 'tis very credent," Leontes convinces himself that his passion has a basis in reality, and the "tragi-comic disruption" begins (231).

36. Ward, "Affection, Intention and Dreams," p. 546.

37. Pafford (ed.), *The Winter's Tale,* Arden 1, p. 166, and Schanzer (ed.), *The Winter's Tale,* New Penguin Shakespeare, p. 166, also gloss "intention" as "intensity," though without the medical connotations. Simon Reynolds, "Pregnancy and Imagination in *The Winter's Tale* and Heliodorus's *Aithiopika, ES* 84, no. 5 (2003): 433–47, draws on the Scholastic sense of "intention" as a "mental image … coloured by the emotions" (442).

38. Ward, "Affection, Intention, and Dreams," p. 553.

39. This is the case in the *Arden 1* and *New Penguin* editions.

40. Neely, "*The Winter's Tale:* The Triumph of Speech," p. 327.

41. Ibid., p. 325.

42. Smith, "The Language of Leontes," points out these three latinate words appear here for the only time in Shakespeare's works (318).

# 2

## CONTEXTS AND SOURCES

### DATE OF THE PLAY

Although *The Winter's Tale* was not published until its inclusion in the 1623 Folio, an eyewitness account of its performance helps to date the play more precisely. Simon Forman, "notorious quack doctor and astrologer,"[1] writes about seeing the play at the Globe on May 15, 1611, which means that it was established in the repertoire of the King's Men by the first part of that year. Another clue that places it within that time frame comes in the sheep-shearing scene. There the Servant announces a dance of twelve "saltiers" (satyrs), three of whom claim to have "danced before the king" (4.4.331,341). This may well allude to the dance of satyrs in Ben Jonson's masque *Oberon,* which was performed at court for King James on New Year's Day, 1611.[2]

Forman's account covers much of the plot of *The Winter's Tale*. He notes how "Leontes the King of Sicilia was overcome with jealousy of his wife with the King of Bohemia" and how the Bohemian king escaped. The "lost" child specified in the oracle was "laid in a forest"—no sea coast is mentioned—and "brought up by a shepherd." When she was 16, the prince of Bohemia married her and, thanks to the shepherd's evidence, she was "known to be Leontes' daughter" after the couple fled to Sicilia. Forman also devotes a paragraph to the tricks of the "rogue" (Autolycus), dressed in rags like a "colt-pixie" (hobgoblin), and concludes with a warning not to trust "feigned beggars or fawning fellows."[3] Surprisingly he does not mention the theatrically stunning denouement, the statue scene. Still, it is hard to believe that Shakespeare added this key element later.

We know that *The Winter's Tale* was performed on November 5, 1611, probably at the Banqueting House in Whitehall, and again somewhere between December 1612 and February 1613, during the celebrations before Princess Elizabeth married Frederick the Elector Palatine. The play appears to have become a court favorite, with performances also noted in 1618 and 1624. It remained popular at the court of Charles I; its last recorded performance there was in 1634.[4]

Most likely Shakespeare was working on the play in 1610, the period during which he was composing his tragicomic romances. Although the editors of the Oxford Shakespeare date the play in 1609–10, before *Cymbeline,* most scholars agree that it was written after both *Pericles* (1608–09) and *Cymbeline* (1609–10). Certainly it was produced before Shakespeare's final romance, *The Tempest* (1611). In its frank discussion of the relationship between art and nature (4.4.86–103), *The Winter's Tale* echoes some of the concerns in *Antony and Cleopatra* (1607–08), where the Queen of Egypt seems to "outwork" both art and nature (2.2.201). The later play also intensifies the tragicomic mood of "wonder" generated at Cleopatra's death—a mood that separates the Roman tragedy, like Shakespeare's tragicomedies, from the starker endings of the three major tragedies, *Othello, King Lear,* and *Macbeth.*

## SOCIAL CONTEXTS

### Leontes and King James

By 1610, James I's honeymoon with his country was over. High hopes that he would prove a strong Augustus figure, confidently leading the country out of the uncertain years at the end of Elizabeth's reign, had foundered. James's cherished proposal for union between the countries of England and Scotland, discussed most fully in 1606–07, remained unratified.[5] Instead King and Parliament were anxiously debating several matters, including the king's revenue, that touched on Parliament's role in governing the country versus royal prerogative; but by late 1610 negotiations for the "Great Contract," which would have guaranteed James an annual revenue of 200,000 pounds in return for his granting more privileges to the House of Commons, had broken down. In both his treatises on kingship, *The Trew Law of Free Monarchies* (1598) and *Basilikon Doron* (1599), James had virtually identified kings with gods; it was therefore not surprising that again he reminded Parliament, on March 21, 1609, that "even by GOD himselfe" kings "are called Gods."[6] Two months later he sternly warned the Commons that they "should not go to the root and dispute [his] prerogative."[7] Although he had argued for the kind of constitutional monarchy in which the king's power was limited by the laws of the land,[8] he made it clear that monarchs themselves would establish the laws by which they were then controlled. This circularity could, of course, be the means to justify an absolute monarchy, even tyranny. No wonder that in May 1610, James's contemporary John Chamberlain wrote of his concern at seeing the "regall prerogative strained so high and made so transcendent in every way."[9]

All this is relevant to *The Winter's Tale,* where Leontes, overriding public opinion, asserts his right to act exclusively on his own will. As Bill Overton comments, "the play takes absolute power and its abuse seriously";[10] determined to impose his solipsistic vision on his councillors, Leontes temporarily acts the part of tyrant.[11] The courtiers in act 2 warn their king not to be senselessly autocratic, while Antigonus exorts him to be certain before he condemns Hermione, "lest your justice / Prove violence" (2.1.127–28). But when Leontes insists on his prerogative to direct affairs that are "properly" his own (170), he sounds disconcertingly like James telling Parliament not to meddle:

> Why, what need we
> Commune with you on this, but rather follow
> Our forceful instigation? Our prerogative
> Calls not your counsels, but our natural goodness
> Imparts this. (161–65)

The frank Paulina is the first to chide Leontes for "tyrannous passion" (2.3.27), even though he defends himself against the charge on the grounds that he has not instantly ordered her execution for defying him: "Were I a tyrant, / Where were her life?" (120–21). Again he is sensitive to this label when he defensively opens the sessions at Hermione's trial with "Let us be cleared / Of being tyrannous, since we so openly / Proceed in justice" (3.2.4–6). Hermione herself trusts that "Tyranny" will "Tremble at Patience" (30–31) and reminds the court that she would suffer "rigor, and not law" (112) were she to be sentenced on conjecture alone. But so total is Leontes's belief in the validity of his own judgment that he presumes to override the words of Apollo's oracle—a proclamation that, in a significant change from Shakespeare's source *Pandosto,* describes Leontes as a "jealous tyrant" (3.2.131) and not simply as "treacherous." Horrifyingly autocratic, Leontes insists that "The sessions shall proceed" despite the divine proclamation of the queen's innocence (138). After the deathlike swoon of the queen, Paulina is more outspoken in branding the king a tyrant—"What studied torments, tyrant, hast for me?" (173)—as part of her mission of making Leontes acknowledge the terrible consequences of his "weak-hinged fancy" (2.3.117).

If Leontes appears to act out an extreme version of James I's beliefs on the divine rights of kings, we may wonder how daring this presentation of monarchy seemed to Shakespeare's contemporaries. Yet *The Winter's Tale* was well-received by James. The fact that it was performed at court on November 5, 1611, the sixth anniversary of the Gunpowder Plot—a date on which to celebrate the apparently miraculous escape of king and Parliament from death by explosion—suggests that it was not perceived as a critique of royal authority. Having a high opinion of the sacredness of his kingship, James may have failed to see much connection between himself and the blustering Leontes. In act 2 especially, where the lords ignore four of the king's demands to "push" Paulina "out" (2.3.72), the Sicilian king becomes almost absurd, a far from terrifying image of authority. More likely James took the irrational behavior of Leontes as an object lesson in how *not* to abuse royal prerogative, since he was careful to distinguish true kings from tyrants when he told Parliament, on March 21, 1609, that "a King governing in a setled Kingdome, leaves to be a King, and degenerates into a Tyrant, assoone as he leaves off to rule according to his Lawes."[12]

In the first half of the drama the king's paranoia all but destroys his own marriage; Simon Shepherd notes an oblique parallel with James's "harshness and arbitrariness" in throwing his cousin Arabella Stuart into prison in 1610 for daring to defy his royal edict by marrying William Seymour.[13] But by the end of the play the patriarchal tyrant Leontes is a reformed character. No longer blindly asserting his absolute will, Leontes lauds Paulina as "good" and "true" (5.1.49,81) and listens to the advice that she and other courtiers give him on the issue of succession.[14] Finally Leontes turns into a reconciler when he promotes the wedding of Florizel and Perdita. Within the romance convention of a providential ending sealed by marriage, all of Leontes's previous faults as ruler—his tyrannous behavior in acting unilaterally and ignoring all "counsels" (2.1.164)—have evaporated.

Early audiences, at the Blackfriars and Globe Theatres as well as at court, might also have seen in the play a confirmation of the stability of the royal family, a "process of reconciliation"[15] following disruption. From his first speech to the House of Lords in 1604 James had promoted himself as "Husband" to his new country as well as comparing kings to "Fathers of families"[16]—a reminder to his audience that, unlike the unmarried Queen Elizabeth I, he had already produced two sons and a daughter by the time he took over the throne in 1603. We need not accept Glynne Wickham's theory that *The Winter's Tale* was produced for a special occasion, the investiture of Prince Henry as Prince of Wales,[17] in order to observe the importance of royal succession in the play. In an eerie foreshadowing of the untimely death of Prince Henry, James's much-admired heir, Leontes's son, Mamillius, "a gentleman of the greatest promise" (1.1.36–37), sickens and dies quickly in reaction to his mother's humiliation. This leaves only Perdita as the true successor to the throne. What most prevents Leontes from moving forward to solidify his kingdom after 16 years is the oracle's decree that no heir will be found until this lost daughter, cruelly rejected as a "bastard" (2.3.72), returns.[18] On one level *The Winter's Tale* opens with a depiction of what Catherine Belsey calls a "loving nuclear family";[19] a heavily pregnant queen is about to give birth to a daughter, and the couple's son Mamillius, obviously adored by both parents, dies of grief when his father inexplicably rejects his mother. Yet the family turns out not to be nuclear but dynastic, since the future of Sicily depends on the one remaining royal heir, Perdita, being found.

The question of royal inheritance is raised urgently in Bohemia too. King Polixenes vows to disown his son, Florizel, "bar" him from "succession" (4.4.433) if he dares to marry a shepherdess so far beneath him in rank. Stephen Orgel points out the importance of royalty marrying royalty in the early modern period because such marriages were an "essential diplomatic instrument" that often had "nothing to do with romance."[20] Around the time the play was written James was busy negotiating such matches for his children. Celebrating a match between Catholic Sicily and Protestant Bohemia, *The Winter's Tale* may touch on James's wish to marry Prince Henry to a Catholic princess, part of his plan to reunite peacefully "moderate Protestants and moderate Catholics in Europe."[21] Such a match would have counterbalanced the very Protestant marriage in 1613 of James's daughter, Elizabeth, to Prince Frederick, who later became King of Bohemia; Shakespeare's romance was performed as part of their prenuptial celebrations.

From a traditional royal perspective, it is surprising that Leontes, though chastened after 16 years, is prepared to promote a match between a prince (Florizel) and a presumed commoner (Perdita). The resolution of the romance plot, however, makes this egalitarian gesture a nonissue, for once Perdita is revealed to be the lost child of Leontes and Hermione, the dynasties of Sicily and Bohemia can happily be united through a decorous marriage. Again, conservative courtly values and royal genealogy appear to triumph at the end of this tragicomedy. Any fear of upsetting the status quo is defused by the ending, where not only has the tyrant been thoroughly humbled, but Sicily's royal succession, despite the permanent loss of the promising young prince Mamillius, is securely established.

## Bohemia and England

At first the countryside in Bohemia might seem to represent, if not the golden world of pastoral, at the very least an unmaterialistic and stable community, a contrast to the volatility and "diseased opinion" (1.2.297)

that Leontes has inflicted on the court of Sicily. The unnamed Old Shepherd is quickly established as a sensible and generous man. He is compassionate enough to rescue the baby he finds by chance even before he
discovers, as his son the Clown points out, that he's a "made old man"
because of the gold and jewels accompanying the child (3.3.119). Still, as
Autolycus puts it in one of his songs, "money's a meddler" (4.4.326); it
transforms everything. After the 16-year break we discover that the unexpected gift of gold has made the Old Shepherd wealthy to the point that
he is now "a man … that from very nothing, and beyond the imagination
of his neighbors, is grown into an unspeakable estate" (4.2.40–43). What
is partially effaced in the text of *The Winter's Tale* is more fully explained
in Robert Greene's *Pandosto*. There the narrator tells us that the princess's
foster father "left keeping of other men's sheep and, with the money he
found in the purse, he bought him the lease of a pretty farm and got a
small flock of sheep."[22] Later this shepherd adds to his land purchases.
Presumably Shakespeare's Old Shepherd has also bought up land ("estate") to increase his flock, as no less than "fifteen hundred" of his sheep
have been shorn for the festival (4.3.34), with wool totaling more than 140
pounds in value. We also learn that he keeps servants (4.4.181). Certainly
he can afford to host a lavish feast; his son is about to buy rice and spices
when he encounters Autolycus. Nor does the Shepherd seem totally averse
to climbing higher up the social ladder when he urges Perdita to bid welcome to the disguised (but presumably courtly in demeanor) Polixenes
and Camillo, "for it is / A way to make us better friends, more known"
(4.4.65–66).

The pastoral interludes, then, comment obliquely on the money to be
made from sheep-farming at a time when the wool trade was flourishing
in England. More specifically, they form part of the discourse on what had
become a pressing social topic by the sixteenth century and beyond—the
enclosing of common land, previously used for subsistence farming, in
order to pasture huge flocks of sheep. By this process, landlords grew rich
while the peasantry (land tenants) were often deprived of their living. In
*Utopia* (1516), Thomas More takes to task "greedy" landowners who may
enclose thousands of acres, forcing the tenants to "move out"; it is almost
as though sheep, once so "pliant," are now devouring men.[23]

Studies of agrarian change in the sixteenth and early seventeenth century show that large landowners were not the sole beneficiaries of the enclosure movement. The shepherds in *The Winter's Tale* are equivalent to
the small group of "free-tenant" peasants who also became "rich" by ac-
cumulating more land.[24] As such they can be seen as entrepreneurs, part of
the new trend toward the "ethos of accumulation" and the "social mobility

typical of a market economy."[25] But do the Old Shepherd and his family represent what Barbara Mowat calls the "wealthy, covetous men" who dispossess the peasantry by buying up "land for pasturage"?[26] The play suggests otherwise. These sheep-farmers have been "lucky" in benefiting from what seems to be "fairy gold" (3.3.122–24); yet there is no sense that they have disadvantaged their neighbors. On the evidence of the sheep-shearing festival they have been generous to others, converting wealth into "good deeds," as the Old Shepherd promised on first finding the baby (137–38).

Economically the shepherds have now joined the yeoman class, upwardly mobile but excluded from the gentry, at least until they arrive at the Sicilian court. This they reach not by design but by accident. Rather than being social climbers ambitious to join the aristocracy, they are hardworking men who have come to the palace to free themselves from any charge of conspiring to help marry a supposed commoner, the Shepherd's adopted daughter, to a prince. Jacobean comedies and tragedies alike satirize upstarts who sell their lands for ready cash or to buy titles at court; *The Revenger's Tragedy* is particularly scathing about the "farmers' sons," the rising yeoman who "agreed and met again / To wash their hands [sell off their land] and come up gentlemen" (2.1.220–21).[27] Without any such intention, the shepherds in *The Winter's Tale* again find themselves simply blessed by good fortune. Although the Clown may be something of an *arriviste,* absurdly proud of suddenly becoming (like many of King James's Scottish followers)[28] a "gentleman born before [his] father," the Old Shepherd behaves more sensibly. Like an ancient "conduit" or channel between court and country (5.2.59), he remains relatively detached from the glamour of such giddy promotion.

If these rustics are, as C.L. Barber contends, "absorbed into the gentry" by the end of the play, it may reflect less the generalized pastoral "hope for a regenerated England through a reunion of court and cottage"[29] than what Richard Wilson, focusing more sharply on paternalistic ways of controlling the country populace in the early seventeenth century, calls "the Stuart campaign to reunify agrarian society under aristocratic leadership."[30] Certainly Tudor and Stuart governments feared the destabilizing effects of enclosures—not only the depopulation of villages but also the commoners' violent opposition to engrossing landlords, as happened in the Midlands riots of 1607. Purportedly on the side of the dispossessed and concerned to quell social unrest, the ruling class nevertheless realized that some entire communities, and not just rich landowners and farmers, were benefiting from a more economical use of the land. It was ultimately in the government's interest, then, to control and supervise land development rather than to stop it.[31] In accordance with this pattern, the well-to-do sheep farmers at the end of *The Winter's Tale* are not brought to heel but are accommodated under the royal umbrella.

Still, the play leaves us wondering whether these countryfolk are truly appropriated by aristocratic society. There is no evidence that the Old Shepherd plans to stay at court indefinitely, hobnobbing with the likes of Cleomenes and Dion. The Clown, flaunting his new "gentleman" status, is eager to join the royal party when "the kings and princes, our kindred, are going to see the Queen's picture" (5.2.183–85). But no stage direction indicates that the commoners actually enter the final scene to participate in court mysteries. Some commentators have interpreted their exclusion as a means to "replicate seventeenth-century notions of hierarchy";[32] despite his penchant for selling knighthoods, this decorous maintaining of boundaries might have pleased King James. In a less elitist way, it could also suggest that the upwardly mobile are able to retain their independence. To be an outsider is to remain free of the "fantastical" affectation of court that puts a person (thanks to the Clown's malapropism) in a "preposterous" rather than a merely prosperous state (5.2.156–57).

### Autolycus, Rogue and Entrepreneur

Autolycus, comic trickster and entrepreneur, is even more difficult to assign to a particular level of society; but his roles in the play draw on several social contexts that would be familiar to audiences in the early seventeenth century. He reflects two areas in particular. The vagabond "rogue," for all his freedom from consequences, can be seen as a drain on the commonwealth, picking pockets and preying on honest country folk. In his other profession, Autolycus is an enterprising peddler of knickknacks and ballads, a social climber who aspires to return to the high life at court.

In act 4, scene 3, Autolycus quickly establishes himself as an opportunist who makes his living off the "silly cheat," or petty stealing from the unsuspecting (28). This is his main source of "revenue" and he is good at it; he boasts after the sheep-shearing feast that he "picked and cut" most of the "festival purses" when the country folk were distracted by the singing of the Clown (4.4.619). His first ruse is pretending to be "robbed" and "beaten" (4.3.62) so that he can steal the Clown's purse when this good Samaritan comes to his rescue. Indeed Autolycus's cozening of the rustic so impressed Simon Forman when he saw the play at the Globe that he drew from it the moral "Beware of trusting feigned beggars." Like Forman, Shakespeare's audience would have aligned Autolycus not only with the city "prig" (thief) but with the category of "rogue" or the counterfeit, "sturdy" beggar denounced as a scourge of the Elizabethan and Jacobean countryside; that is, one of the unemployed or homeless who pretended to be sick or injured and made a living by begging or stealing. A statute of 1572, followed by later ones, was designed to deal with such "Rogues, Vagabonds, or Sturdy Beggars,"[33] distinguishing these imposters from the truly needy that parishes were enjoined to help.

Such rootless, "masterless men"[34] were feared by the British authorities as potential troublemakers in the kingdom. Were they dangerous predators or hapless social outcasts? In fact some of the vagabonds roaming the countryside were viewed as victims of the enclosure movement. In *Utopia,* Thomas More's character pities displaced villagers who are forced to wander around the countryside and become "tramps and beggars." When he speculates that once their stock is used up, "what can they do but steal?"[35] More's words point to figures such as Autolycus, who wittily defends his "traffic" in "sheets" (4.3.23) or anything else that may be hanging out on hedges to dry. Yet Autolycus surely is not one of the indigents whose livelihood has been taken away by the enclosure of common land. Before his current way of life he was employed by Prince Florizel. "Whipped" out of the Bohemian court for dishonesty, he appears to be a victim only of his own "vices" (95). Ironically he is now actually benefiting from the "end product" of the enclosure movement[36]—a sheep-shearing festival that celebrates the commodity of wool—in order to make his own small fortune.

Autolycus, then, is more the self-made man than a victim with whom the audience might empathize. Nor is he socially subversive in the deepest sense.[37] His carnivalesque spirit and lack of respect for others' property may be disruptive, but he is no Jack Cade (from *Henry VI,* Part 2) wanting to overthrow the ruling class. Apparently he regrets his social decline from sheriff's officer to entertainer to wandering rogue (4.3.96–101), a profession just one notch below that of a tinker's but more likely to get him thrown in the stocks (19–22). When Camillo approaches him he shows a craven respect for authority, claiming to be simply a "poor fellow" (4.4.634). He would like nothing more, it seems, than to return to court and wear the "three pile" velvet of his former life.

His second main role, as entrepreneurial peddler, is a stepping stone toward that goal. He hawks wares that actually ape the aristocratic lifestyle—"Masks for faces," "golden quoifs," and the "new'st, and fin'st" commodities for beautifying women (4.4.223, 226, 325)—and he traffics in a second kind of "sheets," selling broadside ballads at a profit. Urging the rustic consumers to "come, come buy, come buy" (230), he becomes what Michael D. Bristol calls a "versatile economic opportunist,"[38] taking

his chances in the emerging market economy. Like the shepherds who
have gone up in the world, Autolycus is helped by unexpected "boot[y]"—
both the gold that Camillo gives him as a reward for trading clothes with
Florizel and the rich garments themselves (680). These clothes allow him
to metamorphose into a "fantastical" courtier, able to dupe the shepherds
into giving him still more gold if he will plead their case to the king. Thus
Shakespeare turns the interlude into pastoral satire on the superficiality of
the court, where clothes do indeed make the man. Simon Forman, it should
be noted, also associated Autolycus with "fawning fellows," a phrase that
suggests not only beggars but affected courtiers.

The ease with which Autolycus transforms himself again underscores
his aspiration to return to the court. This chameleon hopes to win "advancement" from Florizel for bringing the rustics on board the prince's
ship (4.4.843) and then "preferment" at the Sicilian palace (5.2.122). In a
comic reversal of fortune, though, he discovers that the Clown to whom
he felt so condescendingly superior in Bohemia, since "Nature might have
made" him simple too (4.4.751), has suddenly been made a "gentleman
born" (5.2.136) in Sicily.

Ironically Autolycus now depends on the very shepherds he once
fleeced to be his patrons and "good masters" (185–86). And so this temporarily masterless man, the consummate ripoff artist, appears set once again
to serve at court. Interpreted this way, the final destination of Autolycus,
who represents a "composite of Jacobean anxieties about the sources of
social instability,"[39] validates the pattern that new historians find in many
texts of the time: with his roguery defused, any threat of subversion or
unruly enterprise is finally contained within the ruling hegemony.[40] Yet
can we be so sure? When Autolycus promises the Clown that he will be
"a tall fellow of [his] hands" (175), his primary meaning is that he will
demonstrate courage. Underlying this, though, is a suggestion that he will
continue in his old profession as thief, using his hands, or what Hamlet
calls "pickers and stealers" (*Hamlet,* 3.2.336), to filch from pockets. This
incorrigible rogue, master of many disguises, will be hard pressed to fit
into a rigidly hierarchical society. The fact that Autolycus is absent from
the final scene at court, as are the rustics, cuts two ways. As Ronald W.
Cooley suggests, it could indicate not a reclaiming of "his proper subordi-
nate position" but a "return to a dangerous marginality."[41]

## PRIMARY SOURCE: *PANDOSTO*

The primary source of *The Winter's Tale* is *Pandosto,* by Robert Greene.
This prose romance, first published in 1588, remained so popular that it

went through four editions during Shakespeare's lifetime and two dozen reprints after 1700.[42] Shakespeare may well have kept *Pandosto* "at his elbow"[43] while he composed *The Winter's Tale,* since he lifts some phrases verbatim. Apparently he used one of the first three editions, as the words of the oracle (3.2.132–33) repeat Greene's original "the king shall live without an heir," whereas in the fourth edition of *Pandosto* (1607) the word "live" is changed to "die."[44] By studying what Shakespeare keeps from this source, what he modifies, and what he changes completely, we can understand more about how the playwright transmutes a fairly conventional pastoral romance[45] into compelling drama. Turning prose narrative into dramatic form calls for immediacy of events and a quickened pulse of emotion as characters react to one another. Shakespeare seems to revel in the challenges of showing rather than simply telling the "old tale." In the interests of a more economical plot he cuts or adds characters, as well as deepening the main protagonists of *Pandosto.* Above all, Shakespeare makes changes that shift the story away from Greene's romantic melodrama and toward the more satisfying resolution of tragicomedy.

What readers of the two pieces first notice is the reversal of locations: *Pandosto* begins in Bohemia and switches to Sicily, whereas Shakespeare more appropriately sets his pastoral scenes and romantic adventures in Bohemia,[46] leaving Sicily as the birthplace of Perdita.[47] The second, more major change is what happens to the king and queen by the end of the play. Hearing news of her son, Garinter's death, Greene's Bellaria (who becomes Shakespeare's Hermione) "fell down presently dead,"[48] and there is no reanimation after 16 years.[49] King Pandosto (Leontes in *The Winter's Tale*) goes through some changes but no real mellowing; overcome by remorse, he commits suicide at the end of the story. Shakespeare's changes here are essential in molding a denouement that stresses reunion. Other reshapings of Greene's tale serve to make the plot of *The Winter's Tale* tighter and more convincing. Especially in the second half of *Pandosto,* Greene frequently interrupts his narrative with passages in which characters mull over their dilemmas by way of "formulaic"[50] propositions carefully constructed through balance and antithesis. The playwright cuts most of this dialectical "self-communing"[51] and instead conveys conflict through characters' dialogue and interactions with one another. If he does briefly use Greene's debate technique, as when Camillo (Franion in *Pandosto*) wonders whether he should go ahead and poison the king's rival, it is much less elaborate; Franion's stylized rehearsal of possibilities, culminating in "There is nothing sweeter than promotion, nor lighter than report,"[52] is honed into Camillo's terse "To do this deed, / Promotion follows" (1.2.357–58).

In *Pandosto,* Greene can afford to use a larger time frame in getting his narrative started. The king's jealousy germinates over a "long time," and although the narrator terms it "causeless," he provides a few details that might give a husband cause for concern. The "secret uniting" of "affections" between Bellaria and Egistus may be "honest familiarity," but it does not preclude the queen's frequent visits to Egistus's "bedchamber to see that nothing should be amiss to mislike him."[53] Leontes's explosion into jealousy near the beginning of *The Winter's Tale* appears unmotivated and paranoid by comparison. And whereas Greene's Bellaria does not discover that she is "quick with child"[54] until she is sent to prison, Hermione's very visible pregnancy fuels the jealous fantasies of the king. Heightening the drama, it is Leontes and not a guard who confronts Hermione to accuse her of being "big" with Polixenes's child (2.1.61) and rush her off to prison. While it takes Egistus six days to leave the country, which he does by a "postern gate,"[55] Camillo immediately smuggles Polixenes and his men out "at several posterns" (1.2.439).

King Pandosto convenes a public assembly to accuse the queen of adultery before her case goes to trial.[56] Shakespeare conflates the two episodes, assembly and trial, into one climactic "session" where Hermione takes center stage. He works into the queen's dignified speeches strong points of argument that are separated by several pages in Greene's narrative: Bellaria's discussion of her unstained, "virtuous life"[57] informs Hermione's keener sense of wrong in the lines "my past life / Hath been as continent, as chaste, as true / As I am now unhappy" (3.2.32–34); Bellaria's confidence that "divine powers be privy to human actions—as no doubt they are" is closely echoed in Hermione's "if powers divine / Behold our human actions—as they do" (27–28); and the parallelism in Bellaria's carefully articulated "That I loved Egistus I cannot deny; that I honoured him I shame not to confess" transforms into the more spontaneous, urgent rhythms of Hermione's

> I do confess
> I loved him, as in honor he required;
> With such a kind of love, as might become
> A lady like me. (61–64)

As does Bellaria, Hermione protests that if she is condemned without further "proof" it is "rigor, not law" (112). Her final words at trial repeat Bellaria's "I refer myself to the divine oracle"[58] but intensify them with "Apollo be my judge!" (113–14).

The audience of *The Winter's Tale,* on stage and off, wait in suspense for the public pronouncement of this oracle. Readers of Greene's tale already know the outcome, however, since the narrator, using words that Shakespeare follows closely, reveals what is written on the sacred scroll before the embassy returns to court: "Bellaria is chaste; Egistus blameless; Franion a true subject; Pandosto treacherous; his babe an innocent."[59] It is true that in Shakespeare's playtext the "gracious ... issue" is partly prepared for by the awestruck report of Cleomenes and Dion on the "ear-deaf'ning voice o' the oracle" after the sacrifice to the god (3.1.22, 9);[60] nevertheless, the dramatic tension in the trial scene remains high. Hearing the oracle, Pandosto is immediately "ashamed of his rash folly."[61] In contrast, the jealousy of Leontes is so deep-rooted that he denies the oracle until the news of his son's death shocks him back to reality. Leontes's final resolve "Once a day I'll visit / The chapel where they lie" (3.2.236–37) echoes Pandosto's habit of "once a day repair[ing] to the tomb."[62]

In shifting from the narrated story of Pandosto to the fortunes of his lost daughter Fawnia, Greene can easily skip over the intervening years. He describes in some detail how the shepherd Porrus finds the child and takes her home, where his wife Mopsa at first angrily refuses to take in the "bastard brat."[63] In a "short time" the child Fawnia begins to speak; when she is "about seven years" old Porrus purchases his own land and sheep; and by the "age of sixteen years" Fawnia is amazing all the "rich farmers' sons"[64] with her beauty and wit. Instead Shakespeare, apologizing for the "crime" of breaking the dramatic illusion, employs the archaic device of Time—a choric figure who must "use" his imaginary "wings" to flit over the missing years (4.1.4).

In *Pandosto* Greene spins out the courtship of Fawnia by Prince Dorastus through the hesitations and lengthy soul-searchings of both lovers. So detailed is this part of the story that after 1635 Greene's novella became known simply as *The Pleasant History of Dorastus and Fawnia.*[65] Recalling, as does Florizel (4.4.25–30), that Apollo became a swain and Jupiter a bull,[66] Dorastus must disguise himself as a shepherd to be closer to his love. More economically, Shakespeare begins the sheep-shearing scene with Florizel and Perdita already committed to one another, ready to affirm their love publicly until Polixenes tries to break off their betrothal. In *Pandosto* there is no showdown between Dorastus and King Egistus, which gives the prince more time to prepare for his escape with Fawnia; when the king discovers that Dorastus is gone, his fear that his son has been "devoured" by "some wild beasts"[67] may have sparked Shakespeare's idea for how Antigonus meets his violent end. Unlike Polixenes, who pursues the lovers to Sicily, King Egistus never travels to Bohemia. He communicates with Pandosto by embassy when he discovers his son's whereabouts, and later he entertains the wedding party back in Sicily.

Greene's story becomes increasingly melodramatic once the lovers arrive at Pandosto's court. "Tickled with the beauty"[68] of Fawnia, the king attempts to seduce her after throwing Dorastus in prison. But as soon as he receives a request from King Egistus that Dorastus be released and Fawnia executed, Pandosto surprisingly agrees. What was lust turns rapidly to contempt, until Porrus gives the king some clue as to Fawnia's true parentage. At that point, with all the panache of a Victorian melodrama, Pandosto "leapt from his seat and kissed Fawnia, wetting her tender cheeks with his tears, and crying, "My daughter Fawnia, ah sweet Fawnia, I am thy father, Fawnia!"[69] These abrupt transitions from desire to hate to paternal love spice up the narrative but damage psychological credibility, as never happens in *The Winter's Tale*. There Leontes's brief attraction to Florizel's "precious mistress" is quickly absorbed into thoughts of Hermione before it becomes full-blown incestuous desire (5.1.223–25). Shakespeare also avoids staging the potential mawkishness of the father-daughter reunion. He chooses instead to have three unnamed gentlemen narrate, in the language of paradox that seems to parody *Pandosto*'s euphuistic style, the "wonder" of an encounter in "there was speech in their dumbness, language in their very gesture" (5.2.14–15).

As well as cutting and transforming elements of the original to enhance the dramatic logic of his own "tale," Shakespeare adds several characters who play essential roles in the action. As noted, the part of the cup-bearer Franion is given to Camillo, who serves as counselor to both kings and can therefore be instrumental in transporting Polixenes back to Sicily. Autolycus, the rogue who infiltrates the pastoral world, is entirely Shakespeare's creation. Whereas in *Pandosto* Florizel's servant Capnio is introduced solely for the purpose of luring Fawnia's foster father Porrus away from the king and onto the prince's ship, Autolycus, already fully established as an opportunistic character, is the logical choice to bring the shepherds aboard Florizel's vessel. Shakespeare also invents Antigonus who, true to his name, at first opposes King Leontes before agreeing to cast out the baby Perdita. Antigonus's wife, Paulina, whose name may connect her with the moral authority and spiritual leadership of St. Paul in the New Testament, has no direct counterpart in *Pandosto,* though she may be tenuously linked with Porrus's shrewish wife. Mopsa takes up a cudgel against her husband when he brings home a baby, while Leontes taunts Paulina as a termagant who "late hath beat her husband" (2.3.90).

The names that Shakespeare gives to his characters, some taken from Plutarch,[70] are a mixture of Roman and Greek, as befits a play set in a classical world in which Apollo's oracle foretells the outcome. The lost child is appropriately called Perdita. Leontes (the names Leonatus and Leontidas appear in Plutarch)[71] may recall the unjust ruler of Proverbs 28.15, termed both a "roaring lion" and a "raging bear." In classical contexts Hermione (wife of Cadmus) was sometimes confused with Harmonia, the balanced daughter of Mars and Venus.[72] Her name, more evocative than simply the beauty denoted by Bellaria, means "pillarlike,"[73] prefiguring her strength and steadfastness; in fact Hermione is a male character in Plutarch and in *The Rare Triumphs of Love and Fortune* (c.1581). She is also associated with Demeter or Ceres, the mother of Persephone/ Prosperpine. The name Florizel (a counterpart to Flora, the Roman goddess that Perdita resembles at the sheep-shearing) is probably indebted to Florisel, a lover who also disguises himself as a shepherd in book 9 of F. De Silva's *Amadis de Gaule*.[74]

Just as these names call up a wider range of relevant associations than do their equivalents in *Pandosto,* so Shakespeare deepens and refines the key characters of *The Winter's Tale*. Even the unnamed Old Shepherd, kind and wise, is cut from finer cloth than Greene's Porrus, who makes a mercenary decision to adopt the child when "the covetousness of the coin overcame him."[75] Unlike Leontes, Pandosto remains emotionally unstable throughout the story. Whereas Leontes's jealousy is fast-moving and all-consuming while it lasts (he never wavers in his conviction that Hermione is false), we are told that Pandosto's "sore" was "half-healed"[76] until he began to suspect that Bellaria was pregnant with Egistus's child. Years later this middle-aged king cannot suppress his "unfit fancies" for Fawnia until he wants to be reconciled with Egistus and agrees to execute her. The change from reviling Fawnia as "distainful vassal"[77] to falling about her neck in joy when he discovers she is his long-lost daughter makes Pandosto appear absurdly erratic. Curiously he commits suicide only after the wedding celebrations, overcome by remorse at causing the death of Bellaria and briefly desiring his own daughter. In this way Pandosto's character reflects the arbitrary shifts of a plot that Greene has decided must take a "tragical" turn at the end.[78]

Bellaria fares somewhat better in Greene's story, emerging more consistently as an admirable character. Her strong assertions of innocence (she "waxed bold")[79] impressed Shakespeare sufficiently for him to weave them into Hermione's dignified defense at her trial. Yet the private complaints that Greene gives to Bellaria tend, as do many of the internal debates, to make the character appear somewhat self-pitying; laments such as "alas, poor soul, how canst thou but sorrow" alternate with her firm resolve that her husband "shall never discredit [her] virtues." Unlike Hermione, who is not "prone to weeping" (2.1.108), the imprisoned Bellaria is given to "wringing her hands, and gushing forth streams of tears."[80]

Prince Dorastus is by no means as idealistic in love as is Florizel. While *The Winter's Tale* introduces us to a prince who is totally devoted to his shepherdess (he cannot be "anything" without her, and imagines the destruction of the whole world if he ever violates his faith [4.4.44, 480–83]), Dorastus at first hopes that his attraction to Fawnia is simply lust. Cross-examining himself, he is full of self-recrimination for disregarding his high "birth" and "dignities," and he blames the baseness of mind that would be attracted to a "country slut."[81] Love wins the day, however, and he commits himself to Fawnia, vowing, in a paler version of Florizel's enthusiasm, that "neither distance, time, nor adverse fortune" will "diminish his affections."[82]

Fawnia, we are told, possesses "singular beauty and excellent wit,"[83] shaming "all the courtly dames"[84] even when she is dressed in country attire, and speaking the same carefully crafted language as the other high-born characters. At first the practical Fawnia feels constrained by her "poor" estate not to "gaze" at the "sun."[85] But whereas Perdita, sensitive to rank, feels acutely that marrying a prince may be impossible—to her "the difference forges dread" (4.4.17)—Fawnia is not above wishing to better her position. After a promise of marriage from Dorastus she rejoices, hoping "in time to be advanced from the daughter of a poor farmer to be the wife of a rich king."[86] Her chastity comes first, of course; when Pandosto tries to seduce her she makes it clear that she would rather be a "beggar" than live as the king's wealthy concubine.[87]

Despite *Pandosto*'s subtitle, "the Triumph of Time," Fawnia's hope that "time" will produce the desired outcome for her is one of the few such references in the story. More typical is Fawnia's observation that "Fortune had favored her so as to reward her with the love of a prince."[88] When the characters in this story analyze their situations dialectically, they often touch on the doubleness of Fortune. Thus Bellaria ponders the future of her child by asking "shalt thou, sweet babe, be committed to Fortune when thou art already spited by Fortune?"[89] and Dorastus plays on the differing implications of the word when he resolves that "Fawnia shall be my fortune, in spite of Fortune."[90] Indeed all the characters seem to be thrown at the mercy of this fickle goddess who is mentioned close to 40 times in Greene's tale. The initial happiness of Pandosto and Bellaria proves short-lived because "envious" Fortune "turned her wheel and darkened" their prosperity.[91] After the death of Bellaria the courtiers interpret Pandosto's despair and attempted suicide as the "tragical discourse of Fortune";[92] yet "wanton"[93] Fortune smiles briefly again when she allows the storm-tossed, unsteered boat carrying Pandosto's infant to reach Sicilia. Creating love complications for Dorastus and Fawnia, Fortune again shows her "louring countenance"[94] until she relents with a "lucky gale of wind"[95] when they set sail and reach Bohemia. The bizarre twists of Greene's plot are thus driven not by a sense of purposeful design in which wrongs are eventually revealed and redressed but by the vagaries of a "mechanically capricious"[96] Fortune.

In *The Winter's Tale* the lovers also hope to surmount their difficulties through good fortune: Perdita prays "O Lady Fortune, / Stand you auspicious!" (4.4.51–52), while Florizel challenges Fortune as an enemy against whom he must "Tug for the time to come" (501). But it is not arbitrary Fortune but Providence that informs the play, working toward the fulfilment of Apollo's oracle through the natural course of time. Whereas *Pandosto* never refers specifically to Apollo's oracle after the death of Bellaria, act 5 of *The Winter's Tale* is full of reminders of the divine prophecy.[97] Paulina insists to Leontes that "the gods / Will have fulfilled their secret purposes" (5.2.80–81), while Hermione claims that she has "preserved" herself only to see the gracious "issue" of the oracle (5.3.126–28). It is on Paulina's cue that it is "time" to rejoin life (99) that the queen transforms from a statue; and indeed Time in his role of renewer as well as destroyer is much more prominent in *The Winter's Tale* than in *Pandosto*. Actually presented on stage as a character who "makes and unfolds error," Time is the perfect vehicle for ushering in the "joy" (following "terror") of a tragicomic outcome (4.1.1–2). Through the "perspective of naturally ripening time"[98] in *The Winter's Tale,* human beings may eventually heal their rifts.[99] No such happy resolution through time is developed in *Pandosto*. Although the union of Dorastus and Fawnia affirms the triumph of young love, Greene returns at the end of the story to what he promised at the beginning—"endless sorrow and misery"[100] for Pandosto. In order to "close up the comedy with a tragical stratagem,"[101] the narrative switches with awkward haste from a wedding celebration to the king's remorse and suicide.

## MINOR SOURCES AND ANALOGUES

In *Groatsworth of Wit*, published soon after his death in 1592, Robert Greene wrote scathingly about the newcomer playwright Shakespeare ("Shake-scene") as an "upstart Crow, beautified with our feathers."[102]

Little did he know what was in store by 1611. Not only did Shakespeare plunder wholesale from *Pandosto,* but he drew freely from Greene's pamphlets on the tricks of London thieves for his portrait of Autolycus. The *Second Part of Conny Catching* (1591–1592) outlines how a "foist" with a "nimble hand and great agility" tricks a "plaine Country farmer" by St. Paul's. In similar fashion to Autolycus, who fakes injury and cries out "Oh help me, help me" (4.3.53), Greene's thief appeals to the naive countryman with "Alas honest man, help me, I am not well" before he falls in a swoon. Of course when the "pore Farmer" rushes to help he promptly has his pockets picked.[103] The *Third Part of Conny Catching* demonstrates how the "singing of Ballets" (ballads) outside playhouses, in "open markets" and "other places of this Cittie, where is most resort,"[104] offers the perfect cover for cutting purses; likewise Autolycus, who sells ballads at the sheep-shearing feast, seizes the opportunity to cut most of the "festival purses" (4.4.619) while the crowd is spellbound by the Clown's singing (4.4.617–19).

Just as Shakespeare took much of his plot for *The Winter's Tale* from *Pandosto,* so Francis Sabie cribbed from Greene's novella in his poem *The Fisherman's Tale* and its continuation, *Flora's Tale* (1595). E.A.J. Honigmann, though, has pointed out the possible direct indebtedness of *The Winter's Tale* to Sabie's poem, which looks forward to the play title in its aim to "expell … the accustomed tediousnes of colde winters nightes."[105] In addition, the dream vision of Hermione, whose "eyes / Became two spouts" (3.3.24–25), may recall the "fountaines of … teares" in Sabie's *The Fisherman's Tale,* while in *Flora's Tale,* as in Shakespeare's play, only two messengers are sent to Apollo's temple as opposed to six in *Pandosto.*[106]

Earlier scholars speculated that Shakespeare found a precedent for his figure of Time in *The Thracian Wonder*—a pastoral play that draws on Greene's romance *Menaphon* (1589).[107] Time in *The Thracian Wonder* remains mute but holds an "hourglass" during the Chorus's speech at the end of act I. More recently, though, this play's date of composition has been narrowed down to 1611 or 1612, so the influence may run the other way.[108] Certainly Shakespeare drew on the convention of the "ravenous wilde Beare"[109] current in romance fiction of the time for the stage business in act 3, scene 3. Geoffrey Bullough points out that both Sidney's *Arcadia* (1590) and book 6 of Spenser's *The Faerie Queene* (1596) feature episodes in which a savage bear is killed by a heroic man.[110] A closer parallel to Shakespeare's stage bear, though, comes in the anonymous *Mucedorus.* This play, performed by Shakespeare's company for the king on Shrove Tuesday (February 3) of 1610, contains the stage direction "*Enter*

*Segasto runing and Amadine after him, being persued with a beare*" (1.3).
The Clown also comments, in scene 4, that he does not want "to go home
againe to be torne in peces with beares." As the comic character Mouse
"tumbles" over the bear in scene 2, we can assume that the animal in question was not the genuine article but a man wearing a bear costume or
"Beares Doublet."[111]

Especially for audiences attuned to Greene's tale, a statue that turns
out to be a real woman is a stunning theatrical coup at the end of *The
Winter's Tale*. Yet the statue coming to life was a well-established motif
in nondramatic texts of the time.[112] No English translation of F. De Silva's *Amadis de Gaule* before 1693 has been found, but Shakespeare may
have read it in the French version first published in 1577 and taken the
name Florisel from it. In book 9 of *Amadis* a magician creates likenesses
of Prince Anpilor and Princess Galathea (the actual characters are kept
hidden in prison) and then decapitates the statues to appease the jealous
king.[113] Even closer to *The Winter's Tale* is a scene from the anonymous
*The History of the Trial of Chivalry* (1605). There the scorned lover Ferdinand poses as a statue for Katharine, who believes he is dead. Her fervent
wish that "Life might descend into this sencelesse stone"[114] looks forward
to Paulina's "be stone no more … Dear life redeems you" (5.3.99,103).
Another possible analogue is Euripides's play *Alcestis,* translated late in
the sixteenth century by George Buchanan, in which Heracles brings the
veiled Alcestis back from the Underworld to her husband, Admetus.[115]

A more sensuous version of a beloved statue transforming into a woman
is the Pygmalion story from Ovid's *Metamorphoses*. Shakespeare could
have read this in book 10 of the original, or, on the evidence of several
verbal parallels, he most likely drew on Arthur Golding's verse translation of Ovid's poem published in 1567. After Pygmalion falls in love with
his own creation he prays to Venus for an identical wife. When he again
kisses his creation, the "Ivory wexed soft" (309);[116] Leontes, too, is determined to kiss the statue of Hermione. Golding's description of the gradual
animation of the statue, "In hir body streyght a warmenesse seemd too
spred" (306), is echoed in the wondering reaction of Leontes as he touches
Hermione: "O, she's warm!" (5.3.109). Pygmalion stands "amazde"
(312); Leontes is rapt in "wonder" (22).[117] In Golding's Ovid the "perfect"
maid "blusht" (318–19) to feel Pygmalion's kiss; *The Winter's Tale* prepares the audience for a similar "depetrification"[118] of the queen through
the description of the earlier father-daughter reunion, where "Who was
most marble there changed color" (5.2.96–97). A modernized version of
the story, set in Piedmont, appears in *Pettie's Petite Pallace of Pettie his
Pleasures,* reprinted in 1608.[119] John Marston's more prurient version, *The*

*Metamorphosis of Pygmalions Image* (1598), skirts around the "wanton sporting" of the lovers (stanza 35) after the stone changes to flesh. But in stanza 7 Marston adds the detail, not in Golding's Ovid, of how Pygmalion imagines "So sweet a breath"[120] issuing from the images's lips, just as Leontes thinks "an air comes" from the statue, even though no chisel could ever "cut breath" (5.3.78–79).

Shakespeare weaves into the statue scene another myth from book 10 of the *Metamorphoses*—Orpheus's loss of his wife, Euridyce, when he tries to bring her back from the Underworld. Paulina's warning to Leontes not to "shun" Hermione until she really dies, "for then / You kill her double," provides a fresh twist on Ovid's story. In the words of Golding's translation, Euridyce died a "second tyme" (64), because Orpheus loved her so much that he turned around, "desyrous" to "see her" (60) before the appointed time. Hence she "slipped backe" into Hades (61).[121] Conversely, Leontes must show his love for his wife—help to revive Hermione—by both gazing at her and moving toward her.

Ovid's *Metamorphoses,* a storehouse of classical fables, was ransacked for its treasures by Shakespeare and his contemporaries. The poem even furnished the playwright with a name for his wily Bohemian trickster. Book 11 recounts how the young girl Chione bears twins, one conceived by Mercury and the other by Apollo. The son of Mercury is Autolycus, described as a "wyly pye" (magpies are notorious for thievery) and "such a fellow as in theft and filching had no peere" (360–61).[122] More germane to the whole of *The Winter's Tale* is the myth of Proserpine. In book 5[123] Ovid provides a full account of how Proserpine, abducted by Dis, must spend six months of the year in his underworld kingdom, thus creating the season of winter before returning in the spring to bring fruitfulness to the earth. Perdita, welcomed by Leontes when she returns to Sicily (the birthplace of Proserpine) as "the spring to th' earth" (5.1.152), earlier addresses the goddess directly when she longs for the spring flowers that "frighted, thou let'st fall / From Dis's wagon!" (4.4.117–18). To the violets and lilies mentioned in Golding's Ovid (492), Perdita adds daffodils that "take the winds of March with beauty," primroses, oxlips, and yellow fritillaries—the "crown imperial" (118–26). Even though the sheep-shearing takes place in summer, Perdita magically creates the delicacy of the spring season through her catalogue of flowers.[124] When Florizel assures her that nature will crush the earth and "mar the seeds within" if ever he breaks faith with her (483), he echoes the action of Prosperpine's mother, Ceres, who, angry at Sicily because she lost her daughter there, "marrde the seede" (597) and made the earth barren.[125] Ceres also "stoode as starke as stone" (632)—a parallel with Hermione as a statue—when she first heard that her daughter was in the Underworld.

Golding's translation of Ovid's poem was almost certainly Shakespeare's immediate inspiration here, but the tale was often reworked in Renaissance contexts. Drawing from Ovid's account of the Four Ages in book 1 of *Metamorphoses,* Thomas Heywood dramatized the rape of Proserpine in *The Silver Age.* By the time Heywood's *The Golden Age* was registered at the Stationer's Office on October 14, 1611, his partner play *(The Silver Age)* had already "adventured the stage"; it must therefore have been performed not long before *The Winter's Tale.*[126]

In Shakespeare's day so much material was shared and recirculated, without concern for plagiarism, that it is often wise to consider the intertextuality of *The Winter's Tale* rather than what may have influenced it directly. Two overlaps in material that might have been conscious borrowings by Shakespeare or simply coincidental handling of the same well-rehearsed material come in the debate on art and nature in act 4 of the play. In *The Arte of English Poesie* (1589), George Puttenham covers the position of Polixenes on grafting ("Nature makes that mean" [4.4.90]) when he terms art an "ayde and coadiutor to nature … or peradventure a meane to supply her wants."[127] More specifically he describes how the gardener may fashion what "nature of her selfe woulde never have done," for the horticulturalist can "make the single gillifloure, or marigold, or daisie, double," as well as the "carnation."[128] It is striking that Perdita's distaste for hybrids, or anything that interferes with nature, also focuses on carnations and "streaked gillyvors" (82). While conceding Polixenes's point that "the art itself is Nature" (97), she still refuses "to set one slip" of "Nature's bastards" in her garden (100, 83); and in this she echoes Montaigne's essay "Of the Caniballes" (in Florio's 1603 translation of the *Essais*). Montaigne privileges nature above art when he argues that cannibals, often called barbaric, are actually like the "wilde" fruits that "nature of her selfe, and of her ordinarie progresse hath produced." It is hybrid fruits, which we "have altered by our artificall devices" and "bastardized," that should more properly be called "savage."[129]

## NOTES

1. J.H.P. Pafford (ed.), William Shakespeare, *The Winter's Tale,* The Arden Shakespeare (London: Methuen, 1963; 1966), p. xxi.

2. Stanley Wells, in Stanley Wells and Gary Taylor (eds.), *William Shakespeare: A Textual Companion* (Oxford: Oxford University Press, 1987), argues that the passage introducing the dance of the satyrs may be a later interpolation, as lines 328–46 could be omitted "without disturbing the dialogue" (p. 601).

3. Reprinted as Appendix A in Stephen Orgel (ed.), William Shakespeare, *The Winter's Tale,* The Oxford Shakespeare (Oxford: The Clarendon Press, 1996), p. 233.

4. Orgel (ed.), *The Winter's Tale,* p. 80.

5. In *"The Winter's Tale* and the Language of Union, 1604–1610," *ShakS* 21 (1993): 228–50, Donna B. Hamilton argues that discourse on this proposed union is reflected in Shakespeare's play. In treating the division and eventual reconciliation between Sicily and Bohemia, the play "evaluates the compromised and conflicted situation of King James" in his efforts to unite England and Scotland (238).

6. Charles Howard McIlwain (ed.), *The Political Works of James I, Reprinted from the Edition of 1616* (Cambridge, Mass.: Harvard University Press, 1918), p. 307.

7. Elizabeth Read Foster (ed.), *Proceedings in Parliament, 1610,* vol. 2 (New Haven and London: Yale University Press, 1966), p. 102.

8. Discussed in Paul Christianson, "Royal and Parliamentary Voices on the Ancient Constitution, c. 1604–1621," in *The Mental World of the Jacobean Court,* ed. Linda Levy Peck (Cambridge: Cambridge University Press, 1991), pp. 71–95. See also Constance Jordan, *Shakespeare's Monarchies: Ruler and Subject in the Romances* (Ithaca and London: Cornell University Press, 1997), pp. 14–33.

9. Norman McClure (ed.), *John Chamberlain, Letters,* vol. 1 (Philadelphia: The American Society, 1939), p. 301.

10. Bill Overton, The Winter's Tale: *The Critics Debate* (Atlantic Highlands, N.J.: Humanities Press International, Inc., 1989), p. 59.

11. Paul Siegel, "Leontes A Jealous Tyrant," *RES* 1 (1950): 302–7, points out that within Renaissance political theory, Camillo's defection from Leontes would be a legitimate "flight from tyranny" (304). Daryl W. Palmer, "Jacobean Muscovites: Winter, Tyranny, and Knowledge in *The Winter's Tale,*" *SQ* 46, no. 3 (1995): 323–39, finds Leontes's tyranny accentuated by oblique allusion to the cruelty of Ivan IV, the "Emperor of Russia" (330–31).

12. McIlwain (ed.), *The Political Works of James I,* p. 309.

13. Simon Shepherd, *Amazons and Warrior Women: Varieties of Feminism in Seventeenth Century Drama* (Brighton, U.K.: Harvester Press, 1981), p. 119.

14. In "'We need no more of your advice': Political Realism in *The Winter's Tale,*" *SEL* 31 (1991): 365–86, Stuart M. Kurland argues that the play is "deeply concerned with the question of advice-giving in a monarchy," especially in the context of the fall from favor of Salisbury, James's preeminent minister, that began in 1610 (372).

15. David M. Bergeron, *Shakespeare's Romances and the Royal Family* (Lawrence: University Press of Kansas, 1985), p. 4. Gary Schmidgall, *Shakespeare and the Courtly Aesthetic* (Berkeley, Los Angeles, London: University of California Press, 1981), also notes that courtly art, such as *The Winter's Tale,* offers the "promise of peaceful succession" (80). Leonard A. Tennenhouse, *Power on Display: The Politics of Shakespeare's Genres* (New York: Methuen, 1986), finds that the Romances "reinscribe the self-enclosed family within the kind of

argument James himself made on behalf of his particular style of patriarchal rule" (174).

16. McIlwain (ed.), *The Political Works of James I,* p. 307.

17. Glynne Wickham, "Shakespeare's Investiture Play: The Occasion and Subject of *The Winter's Tale,*" *TLS,* 18 December 1969, 1456.

18. In "'Good queen, my lord, good queen': Sexual Slander and the Trials of Female Authority in *The Winter's Tale,*" *RenD* 25 (1994): 89–118, M. Lindsay Kaplan and Katherine Eggert find in the play reminiscences of Henry VIII charging Anne Boleyn with adultery and bastardizing her daughter, the future Elizabeth I (96).

19. Catherine Belsey, *Shakespeare and the Loss of Eden: The Construction of Family Values in Early Modern England* (New Brunswick, N.J.: Rutgers University Press, 1999), p. 21.

20. Orgel (ed.), *The Winter's Tale,* p. 47.

21. James Ellison, "*The Winter's Tale* and the Religious Politics of Europe," in Alison Thorne (ed.), *Shakespeare's Romances,* New Casebooks (Basingstoke: Palgrave Macmillan, 2003), pp. 171–204, 175.

22. Orgel (ed.), *The Winter's Tale,* p. 251. Stanley Wells's edition of Robert Greene's *Pandosto* (1588) is included in the Oxford Shakespeare, as Appendix B, pp. 234–74. All subsequent page references to *Pandosto* are from this edition.

23. Thomas More, *Utopia,* trans. Paul Turner (Harmondsworth, Middlesex: Penguin Books Ltd., 1965), pp. 46–47.

24. See John E. Martin, *Feudalism to Capitalism: Peasant and Landlord in English Agrarian Development* (Atlantic Highlands, N.J.: Humanities Press, 1983), p. 129.

25. Michael D. Bristol, "In Search of the Bear: Spatiotemporal Form and the Heterogeneity of Economies in *The Winter's Tale,*" *SQ* 42 (1991): 145–67, 164.

26. Barbara Mowat, "Rogues, Shepherds, and the Counterfeit Distressed: Texts and Infracontexts of *The Winter's Tale, 4.3,*" *ShakS* 22 (1994): 58–76, 68. Maurice Hunt, "The Labor of *The Winter's Tale,*" in Maurice Hunt (ed.), The Winter's Tale*: Critical Essays* (New York and London: Garland Publishing, Inc., 1995), is also skeptical about the ethos of the Old Shepherd, commenting that he "easily gives up his quest for his two lost sheep when greed and gold displace them" (346).

27. R.A. Foakes (ed.), Cyril Tourneur, *The Revenger's Tragedy,* The Revels Plays (1966; Manchester: Manchester University Press, 1986).

28. James knighted over 300 suitors on his way down from Edinburgh to Scotland to claim the throne of England; see David Harris Willson, *King James VI and I* (1956; New York: Oxford University Press, 1967), p. 161.

29. Charles Barber, "*The Winter's Tale* and Jacobean Society," in Arnold Kettle (ed.), *Shakespeare in a Changing World* (New York: International Publishers Co., 1964), pp. 238, 251.

30. Richard P. Wilson, "*As You Like It* and the Enclosure Riots," in *Will Power: Essays on Shakespearean Authority* (Detroit: Wayne State University Press, 1993), p. 79.

31.   See William C. Carroll, "The Nursery of Beggary": Enclosure, Vagrancy, and Sedition in the Tudor-Stuart Period," in *Enclosure Acts: Sexuality, Property, and Culture in Early Modern England,* ed. Richard Burt and John Michael Archer (Ithaca and London: Cornell University Press, 1993), pp. 34–47, 37–39.

32.   Martin Orkin, "A Sad Tale's Best for South Africa?" *TexP* 11 (1997): 1–23, 9.

33.   See E. K. Chambers (ed.), *The Elizabethan Stage,* vol. 4 (Oxford: Clarendon Press, 1923), pp. 269–70, spelling modernized.

34.   In 1597 the Mayor of London complained to the Privy Council that theaters were common places for "maisterles men" to come together. In Chambers (ed.), *The Elizabethan Stage,* p. 321.

35.   More, *Utopia,* p. 47.

36.   William C. Carroll, *Fat King, Lean Beggar: Representations of Poverty in the Age of Shakespeare* (Ithaca and London: Cornell and London, 1996), p. 178.

37.   Nor is Autolycus one of the "conspiratorial underworld" that might join in urban riots, mentioned in Lee Beier, *Masterless Men: The Vagrancy Problem in England, 1560–1640* (London; New York: Methuen, 1985), p. 15.

38.   Bristol, "In Search of the Bear," p. 163.

39.   Ronald W. Cooley, "Speech Versus Spectacle: Autolycus, Class and Containment in *The Winter's Tale,*" *Ren&R* 21, no. 3 (1977): 5–21, 5.

40.   Richard Hillman, *Shakespearean Subversions: The Trickster and the Play Text* (London: Routledge, 1992), finds that he is "integrated, vices and all, into the new dispensation" (224).

41.   Cooley, "Speech Versus Spectacle," 18.

42.   Lori Humphrey Newcomb, *Reading Popular Romance in Early Modern England* (New York: Columbia University Press, 2002), p. 23. Newcomb defends *Pandosto* as popular literature that was "innovative and influential" (5), despite its being condemned by "elite" readers (2).

43.   Pafford (ed), *The Winter's Tale,* p. xxxi.

44.   Orgel (ed.), *The Winter's Tale,* p. 234.

45.   Stanley Wells, "Shakespeare and Romance," in John Russell Brown and Bernard Harris (eds.), *Later Shakespeare,* Stratford-upon-Avon Studies 8 (New York: St. Martin's Press, 1967), finds *Pandosto* a "crudely constructed … collection of cliches" (64).

46.   Geoffrey Bullough (ed.), *Narrative and Dramatic Sources of Shakespeare,* vol. 8 (London: Routledge, 1975), thinks that Sicily was more appropriate for "crimes of jealousy and revenge" (125).

47.   E.A.J. Honigmann, "Secondary Sources of *The Winter's Tale, PQ* 33 (1955): 27–38, was one of the first critics to note the parallel between Proserpina and Perdita and Ceres and Hermione, Queen of Sicily (34–35).

48.   Orgel (ed.), *The Winter's Tale,* p. 248.

49.   As suggested by Fitzroy Pyle, The Winter's Tale: *A Commentary on the Structure* (New York: Barnes and Noble, Inc., 1969), Bellaria's swoon in prison,

where "all thought she had been dead" may have sown the seed for Shakespeare's deception of the audience over Hermione's supposed death (55).

50. Inga-Stina Ewbank, "From Narrative to Dramatic Language: *The Winter's Tale* and Its Source," in Marvin and Ruth Thompson (eds.), *Shakespeare and the Sense of Performance* (London and Toronto: Associated University Presses, 1989), pp. 29–47, 38. Ewbank perceptively discusses these "inner debates, where the terms of a binary opposition are scrutinized and weighed against each other," as opposed to the "movement of mind in individual characters" that we find in Shakespeare's play (38).

51. Pyle, The Winter's Tale: *A Commentary on the Structure*, p. 161.

52. Orgel (ed.), *The Winter's Tale,* p. 238.

53. Ibid., p. 236.

54. Ibid., p. 242.

55. Ibid., p. 240.

56. At the assembly Bellaria kneels to ask that an embassy consult the oracle at Delphos; in *The Winter's Tale* it is not Hermione but the courtiers who kneel to Leontes to beg him to reconsider his position, while it is the king's decision to refer to the oracle (2.1.180–85).

57. Orgel (ed.), *The Winter's Tale,* p. 245.

58. Ibid., p. 247, for the last three citations.

59. Ibid., p. 246.

60. This whole scene is developed out of a few hints from Greene on the "loud voice" of the god and "great devotion" of the supplicants (Orgel [ed.], *The Winter's Tale,* p. 246). Following Greene, Shakespeare conflates Delos, the birthplace of Apollo, with Delphi, the site of the oracle, into Delphos.

61. Orgel (ed.), *The Winter's Tale,* p. 247.

62. Ibid., p. 249.

63. Ibid., p. 250.

64. Ibid., p. 251.

65. Newcomb, *Reading Popular Romance,* p. 132.

66. Orgel (ed.), *The Winter's Tale,* p. 260.

67. Ibid., p. 266.

68. Ibid., p. 268.

69. Ibid., p. 273.

70. Bullough (ed.), *Narrative and Dramatic Sources,* points to Camillus, Cleomenes, Dion, and Archidamus as names from Plutarch's *Lives* (124).

71. See Pafford (ed.), *The Winter's Tale,* p. 163. Pafford also finds connections between Leontes and the jealous Posthumous Leonatus in Shakespeare's *Cymbeline.*

72. Noted by Alastair Fowler, "Leontes' Contrition and the Repair of Nature," *E&S* 13 (1978): 36–64, 38.

73. See Charles Frey, *Shakespeare's Vast Romance: A Study of* The Winter's Tale (Columbia and London: University of Missouri Press, 1980), pp. 61–62.

74. See Bullough (ed.), *Narrative and Dramatic Sources,* pp. 225–28.

75. Orgel (ed.), *The Winter's Tale,* p. 250.
76. Ibid., p. 243.
77. Ibid., p. 272.
78. Ewbank, "From Narrative to Dramatic Language," comments on how Pandosto appears "a victim more of the decorum of genre than of conscience or moral retribution" (33).
79. Orgel (ed.), *The Winter's Tale,* p. 244.
80. Ibid., p. 242.
81. Ibid., p. 255.
82. Ibid., p. 261.
83. Ibid., p. 251.
84. Ibid., p. 257.
85. Ibid., p. 256.
86. Ibid., p. 262.
87. Ibid., p. 269.
88. Ibid., p. 262.
89. Ibid., p. 244.
90. Ibid., p. 255.
91. Ibid., p. 235.
92. Ibid., p. 248.
93. Ibid., p. 249.
94. Ibid., p. 252.
95. Ibid., p. 266.
96. Frey, *Shakespeare's Vast Romance,* p. 52.
97. In "The Apollo Mission in *The Winter's Tale,*" in Hunt (ed.), The Winter's Tale*: Critical Essays,* David M. Bergeron argues that Apollo, the god of "wisdom, healing, music, and prophecy" familiar from other Renaissance contexts, "permeates the spirit and outcome" of the play's final scene (378).
98. Inga-Stina Ewbank, "The Triumph of Time in *The Winter's Tale,*" *REL* 5 (1964): 83–100, 85. Ewbank analyzes in detail the change in pace from the "mad onrush" of Leontes's jealousy" (89) to the slower rhythms of regeneration in the second part of the play; thus Time is "intensely present as a controlling and shaping figure behind the dramatic structure and technique" (84).
99. Wells, "Shakespeare and Romance," comments on how in the play human relationships are felt to stand as "bulwarks against the forces of disaster" (70). John Lawlor, "*Pandosto* and the nature of Dramatic Romance," *PQ* 41 (1962): 96–113, also notes that the finale of *The Winter's Tale* fulfills the "human wish to triumph over time" (105).
100. Orgel (ed.), *The Winter's Tale,* p. 234.
101. Ibid., p. 274.
102. Reprinted as Appendix C.8 in G. Blakemore Evans (ed.), *The Riverside Shakespeare* (Boston and New York: Houghton Mifflin, 1997), p. 1959.
103. Reprinted in Bullough (ed.), *Narrative and Dramatic Sources,* pp. 214–15.

104. Ibid., p. 218.

105. Honigmann, "Secondary Sources of *The Winter's Tale*," p. 29.

106. Ibid., pp. 28, 29.

107. See Pafford (ed.), *The Winter's Tale*, p. xxxv.

108. See William Rowley and Thomas Heywood, *The Thracian Wonder*, ed. Michael Nolan (Salzburg, Austria: Institut für Anglistik und Amerikanistik, Universität Salzburg, 1997), pp. liv–lvii.

109. From Emmanuel Ford's story *Parismenos* (1609 edition); an excerpt is reprinted in Bullough (ed.), *Narrative and Dramatic Sources*, pp. 203–4.

110. Bullough (ed.), *Narrative and Dramatic Sources*, pp. 125–26.

111. Ibid., pp. 205–6.

112. See Leonard Barkan, "Living Sculptures": Ovid, Michelangelo, and *The Winter's Tale*," *ELH* 48 (1981): 639–67, 639. Ellison, "*The Winter's Tale* and Religious Politics," points out that moving statues were a feature of civic pageants, as in King James's entrance into London in 1604 (190), while Janette Dillon, *Theatre, Court and City, 1595–1610: Drama and Social Space in London* (Cambridge: Cambridge University Press, 2000), points out how *Britain's Burse*, celebrating the opening of London's New Exchange in 1609, featured the singing statue of Apollo (121–22). Frances A. Yates, *Shakespeare's Last Plays: A New Approach* (London: Routledge and Kegan Paul Ltd., 1975), finds in Paulina's revival of the statue a hint of the *Asclepius* of Hermes Trismegistus, a reference to "the religious magic through which ancient Egyptians were supposed to infuse life into the statues of their gods" (90).

113. Excerpted in Bullough (ed.), *Narrative and Dramatic Sources*, pp. 224–25.

114. Ibid., p. 231.

115. See Martin Mueller, "Hermione's Wrinkles, or, Ovid Transformed: An Essay on *The Winter's Tale*," *CompD* (1971): 226–39, 230–31.

116. W.H.D. Rouse (ed.), *Shakespeare's Ovid: Arthur Golding's Translation of* The Metamorphoses (London: Centaur Press, 1961), p. 207. All line references, given in parenthesis, are to this edition.

117. A. D. Nuttall, "*The Winter's Tale:* Ovid Transformed," in *Shakespeare's Ovid:* The Metamorphoses *in the Plays and Poems*, ed. A. B. Taylor (Cambridge: Cambridge University Press, 2000), notes how the "perverse erotic attachment" of Pygmalion to his statue is minimized in *The Winter's Tale* (p. 139). Barbara Roche Pico, "From 'Speechless Dialect' to 'Prosperous Art': Shakespeare's Recasting of the Pygmalion Image," *HLQ* 48, no. 3 (1985): 285–95, also argues that the "Pygmalion ritual" at the end of *The Winter's Tale* avoids the "idolatrous or unseemly" overtones it had acquired in other Renaissance contexts (292).

118. See Jonathan Bate, *Shakespeare and Ovid* (Oxford: Oxford University Press, 1993), p. 233.

119. Bullough, *Narrative and Dramatic Sources*, p. 134.

120. J. O. Halliwell (ed.), *The Works of John Marston*, vol. 3 (London: John Russell Smith, 1856), pp. 210, 204.

121.   These parallels are noted by Bate, *Shakespeare and Ovid,* p. 233, and Nuttall, *"The Winter's Tale:* Ovid Transformed," p. 142.

122.   Mary Ellen Lamb, "Ovid and *The Winter's Tale:* Conflicting Views toward Art," in *Shakespeare and Dramatic Tradition,* ed. W. R. Elton and William B. Long (London and Toronto: Associated University Presses, 1989), pp. 69–87, explores Autolycus as one of the "Ovidian artist-figures" who contrasts with the moral artist, Paulina (69).

123.   Rouse (ed.), *Shakespeare's Ovid,* pp. 111–16.

124.   Nuttall, *"The Winter's Tale:* Ovid Transformed," comments on the "presence" of spring created through these lines (136).

125.   Noted by Honigmann, "Secondary Sources of *The Winter's Tale,*" p. 37.

126.   Noted by Bate, *Shakespeare's Ovid,* p. 225.

127.   Gladys Doidge Willcock and Alice Walker (eds.), George Puttenham, *The Arte of English Poesie* (1589; Cambridge: Cambridge University Press, 1936), p. 303.

128.   Ibid., p. 304. This was first pointed out and discussed by Harold S. Wilson, "'Nature and Art' in *Winter's Tale* 4. 4. 86 ff.," *SSAB* 18 (1943): 114–20.

129.   Michel Eyquem de Montaigne, *Montaigne's Essays,* vol. 1, trans. John Florio (1603), intro., L. C. Harmer (London: Dent, 1965), ch. 30, p. 219.

# 3

## DRAMATIC FORM

In form and content, *The Winter's Tale* seems obsessed with doubling. It presents two European countries divided by an ocean; two kings ("twinned lambs" as boys, now perceived by Leontes as rivals) who both have young sons at the start of the play; and, until the final act, a binary structure,[1] the first part heading toward catastrophe, the second a pastoral romance. To offset this dividedness, however, the play's separate locales and actions are bound together by symmetries and mirrorings, while the progress of the younger generation—by act 4 the Bohemian prince Florizel has fallen in love with a shepherdess who turns out to be the lost Sicilian princess, Perdita—provides continuity between the plots. In act 5, when the two halves meet, we can apprehend *The Winter's Tale* as a triumphant tragicomedy rather than as a drama that moves in different directions but is suddenly wrenched into a happy ending.

### THE TWO SETTINGS: SICILY AND BOHEMIA

The drama opens in the court of Leontes and remains in Sicily through act 3, scene 2. The pivotal storm scene at the play's midpoint (3.3) transports the action to the coast of rural Bohemia where it stays, after Time's speech and a brief scene at the court of Polixenes, until the end of act 4. Act 5 circles back to Sicily, as do Polixenes, Camillo, and the adult Perdita; Prince Florizel, Autolycus, and the two shepherds arrive there for the first time.

Notoriously, Shakespeare has reversed the locations used in his source *Pandosto* (which begins in Bohemia while the lost princess Fawnia grows up in Sicily) to create a topographically impossible seacoast in Bohemia. This, something of an old joke for Shakespeare's contemporaries,[2] may be the playwright's nod and wink to the audience that he is creating a fantasy land where real-world laws need not apply. It also allows him to align Leontes's court more closely with the world of Mediterranean culture. Sicily's neighbor Italy, renowned for its advanced civilization, was infamous as well for passionate intrigues and machiavellian arts; in line with this Camillo suggests a "lingering dram" when Leontes proposes poisoning Polixenes (1.2.320). The connection with classical Greece is important because Apollo, though kept in the background, is the god whose oracle predicts the play's outcome. Act 3, scene 1, the only scene in Sicily that takes place outside the claustrophobic court, offers important reassurance of this divine guidance; returning from the god's shrine, Cleomenes and Dion are confident that the "issue" will be "gracious" (22). Another linking of Sicily to the Hellenic world comes in a parallel to the Oedipus fable. Like the infant prince Oedipus, whose destiny is also foretold by Apollo's oracle, the princess is abandoned in some "remote" place (2.3.174) rather than, as in *Pandosto,* placed on the ocean in a rudderless boat. Finally Sicily, not Bohemia, is the appropriate birthplace for Perdita. Longing for spring flowers, she likens herself to Proserpina, the goddess who also was born in fertile Sicily, the land to which Perdita returns to bring Leontes's long winter to an end.

The language of the play's opening scene establishes a tone of generalized courtly refinement in Sicily that is echoed and intensified in the ornate report of the royal reunions in act 5, scene 2. Yet ironically, it is the Bohemian ambassador Archidamus, with his "Verily" and his hope that royal visitors to Bohemia will remain "unintelligent of our insufficience," who tries to outdo the Sicilian courtier Camillo linguistically as the play starts (1.1.9–15). Then it is Bohemian Polixenes, politely trying to turn down the invitation to stay longer, who introduces this courtly register into the play's second scene. In contrast, the Sicilian royals often counterpoint formal language with earthy idiom. Down-to-earth Hermione teases Polixenes for adding that affected word "Verily" to his "I may not" (1.2.45–46). Her comparison of herself to a domestic animal, crammed with praise to make her "As fat as tame things" (92), extends into the homely images of "eggs," "kernel," and "squash" (130, 159–60) that Leontes associates with his son and, more crudely, into his image of an adulterous wife as a "pond" being fished by his next-door neighbor (195). In fact the Sicilian scenes where Leontes's fantasy becomes most virulent are domestic rather than royal in tone. His jealousy precipitates not a dynastic upheaval so much as a rift between husband and wife, in which the young son Mamillius suffers by being severed from his mother. As an "unroosted husband," the courtier Antigonus joins the domestic fray in act 2 by giving his wife Paulina "rein" to "run" in her slanging match with the king (2.3.73, 50). Not until the trial of Hermione in act 3, scene 2, with its gathering of "Lords" and "Officers" as well as "Ladies" attending on the queen, does the mode shift back to the ceremonial, when the queen offers her dignified defense to the assembled Sicilian court and the oracle of Apollo is solemnly declaimed.

As the play begins, Archidamus reminds Camillo of the "great difference betwixt our Bohemia and your Sicilia" (1.1.3–4). Initially the contrast holds. The first creature to emerge in Bohemia is an uncivilized bear, giving sudden life to Antigonus's allusion to wild animals ("wolves and bears") that he fancifully hopes will nurture the baby abandoned in a foreign land (2.3.185). Notwithstanding that the bear proceeds to kill Antigonus, the Bohemia of Part 2 is quickly established as sheep country, for almost immediately an Old Shepherd finds the abandoned baby while searching for two of his flock. This gives Bohemia the flavor of traditional pastoral, but also links it—together with Perdita's anachronistic reference to "Whitsun pastorals" (4.4.134) and the Clown's mention of a Puritan singing psalms (4.3.45)—to the England of the early seventeenth century,[3] where widespread grazing of sheep to accommodate an expanding wool trade led to further enclosure of arable land. In addition, the rogue Autolycus is a reminder of England's repeated efforts to contain rural vagrants and cony-catching thieves.

Following Time's fast-forwarding over 16 years and a short scene of exposition at the court of Bohemia, the action remains in the Bohemian countryside. The realism of this pastoral world is accentuated through what most interests Autolycus—the (very English) songs of the lark, thrush, and jay, a "quart of ale," and the "white sheet bleaching on the hedge" (4.3.5–10)—together with other concrete details of domestic country life, as when the down-to-earth Clown calculates the cost of "three pound of sugar, five pound of currants" for refreshments at the sheep-shearing festival (39). With "the peddler at the door" and the Clown scolding Mopsa and Dorcas for "tittle-tattling" beyond "milking time" (4.4.181, 245–47), there is rustic naturalism aplenty. But just as the outsiders Archidamus and Polixenes inject courtly manners into the Sicilian environment, so members of the Bohemian court (and the shepherdess who is really the princess of Sicily) alter the flavor of pastoral Bohemia. Florizel yearns to transform the sheep-shearing into a "meeting of the petty gods" at which Perdita, yoking the royal with the rural, can reign as the goddess Flora or "Queen" of the event (4.4). Having grown up in the country, Perdita gives texture to this pastoral world by recalling daffodils, primroses, and oxlips as well as distributing lavender, savory, and majoram. Yet the mention of late summer flowers, carnations, and gilyflowers prompts a sophisticated discussion with Polixenes about art and nature—a courtly conversation that offsets the Servant's homely description of the peddler's "Jump her, and thump her" ballads and of the "three swineherds that have made themselves all men of hair" to dance as satyrs (195–96, 329–30). Autolycus also spans both worlds. Although he now happily tumbles "in the hay" with his country whores, he once boasted velvet clothes at court (4.3.12–14). This Bohemian rogue, who touts "Perfume for a lady's chamber" and "Golden quoifs" (4.4.225–26), effortlessly metamorphoses back into a courtier at the end of the scene to try to scare the "rough, and hairy" shepherds (726).

Perdita's criticism of the King of Bohemia's highhandedness—"The selfsame sun that shines upon his court / Hides not his visage from our cottage" (448–49)—is thus an apt comment on how social distinctions are blurred in rural Bohemia. It is also a reminder of subtle ways in which the separate locales of Sicily and Bohemia are linked. Even though one is centered at court and the other in the countryside, the two worlds are not as sharply opposed as are, for instance, the intercut societies of abstemious Rome and opulent Egypt in *Antony and Cleopatra*. Though characterized in general by country common sense and seasonal rhythms, the Bohemian shepherds' world in *The Winter's Tale* is continually infiltrated by courtly sophistication and, in the case of Autolycus's brilliant parody of a courtier, more than a hint of aristocratic exploitation. Even the dances at the sheep-shearing festival may be perceived as an "amateur court masque" imported into a "country carnival."[4] In a similar crossover in Sicily, Leontes plays a tyrannical husband as well as an autocrat. There is no jolt, then, when all the important characters converge in Sicily in the final act and, temporarily at least, rural Bohemia is assimilated into the Sicilian court.

## PART 1: THE "SAD TALE" (ACT 1–ACT 3, SCENE 2)

Structurally, the first half of the play (act 1 through the end of act 3, scene 2) approximates to tragedy. The lives of both Hermione and Polixenes are immediately threatened once Leontes becomes acutely jealous in the play's second scene. Appalled by the king's murderous fantasies, the nobleman Antigonus feels sure that Leontes has been "abused" by some malicious plotter (2.1.141). But unlike Othello, Leontes needs no Iago to sow the seeds of suspicion that his wife is committing adultery with his friend; the evil lies in his own "diseased opinion" (1.2.297). As is the pattern in *Macbeth,* Leontes becomes his own villain: he asks Camillo to poison his boyhood friend, and when he discovers that Polixenes has escaped he not only imprisons Hermione but tyrannically vows to commit both her and her newborn baby to "the fire" (2.3.8).

Act 3 builds toward the climax of Hermione's trial. Because Leontes has prejudged the issue, we sense that none of Hermione's rational defense will dissolve his obsession; his conviction that the queen is "most disloyal" contradicts his promoting her trial as "just and open" (2.3.201–3), just as he later equates his "justice" with her "death" (3.2.88–89). When even Apollo's oracle proclaims Hermione's innocence, he hubristically declares, "There is no truth at all i' th' oracle" (136). The death of Prince Mamillius and the death-like swoon of the queen follow in quick response to this "profaneness" (151); and when Paulina comes back prepared to swear that Hermione is dead, the "foul issue" predicted by the courtiers (2.3.151) has apparently come to pass. In Aristotelian terms, this constitutes a tragic peripety (reversal) accompanied by anagnorisis (discovery), since by recognizing his hamartia (error) in falsely accusing Hermione, Leontes acknowledges his own "shame perpetual" (3.2.236). If Paulina is correct, the king has been sentenced to a life of "despair" for a crime that no amount of fasting and praying can induce the gods to forgive (208–12).

Yet the tragedy is strangely incomplete. And the audience, not simply because they have been in the theater for less than two hours, will sense that.[5] Not only does the oracle point to a possible future, suggesting that the action has reached a point of complication rather than resolution, but Leontes remains curiously calm, resigned too quickly to the loss of his wife and son. Whereas Othello roars with anguish when he discovers that he has killed his innocent wife, finding "No way but this, / Killing myself, to die upon a kiss" (*Othello,* 5.2.358–59), Leontes never considers suicide. As he plans a future of mourning—"tears … Shall be my recreation" (3.2.237–38)—his final word, a curious one to use about the penance of visiting graves, may suggest re-creation of another sort.

What is more, even at the height of his tyrannous behavior, there are moments when Leontes appears absurd rather than terrible in his passion.[6] Petty in his suspicions, carving out for himself the ignominious role of the betrayed husband, Leontes never attains the grandeur of the tragic figure Othello, who was "great of heart" before his fall from nobility (*Othello,* 5.2.361). While he attempts to terrorize the councillors who are trying to deflect his rage[7] by insisting they are "liars all " (2.3.144), and bullies them into compliance with "Have I done well?" (2.1.187), Leontes cannot silence the "audacious" Paulina (2.3.41). Haranguing his courtiers, he struts and frets about the stage like the "poor player" that Macbeth envisages near the end of that tragedy (*Macbeth,* 5.4.24).[8] Horrible threats of violence, such as dashing out the newborn's "bastard brains" (138), vie with domestic comedy as the king calls Paulina a "lewd-tongued" shrew whose henpecked husband cannot control her (170, 74, 158). This is a tyrant without absolute power, who switches erratically from insisting that his newborn daughter be "consumed with fire" to commanding that she be abandoned in some "desert place" (132, 174–76). Moreover the image of Leontes's jealousy as a "sickness" (1.2.385) makes its terrible consequences less the result of an act freely chosen by him than the nightmarish ravages of a disease, or the madness of "unsafe lunes" (2.2.29).

Perspectives on Leontes veer rapidly. On one hand he appears a destructive force, on the other absurdly deluded, possibly the victim of mental illness. Distanced in this way from the character, the audience cannot experience the pity and fear (for Leontes and his situation) that Aristotle found essential to produce the catharsis or emotional release of tragedy.

Leontes's sudden changes of direction—he admits "I am a feather for each wind that blows" (2.3.152)—are reflected, too, in how dramatic expectations shift within the first part of the play. The overall drive of the plot is toward catastrophe, but we would not glean that from the opening scene. Here there is no division of the kingdom prefiguring tragic conflict, as in *King Lear*. Instead two commentators are optimistic about the future of the long-term friendship between Leontes and Polixenes—"Sicilia cannot show himself overkind to Bohemia" (1.1.22–23)[9]—and full of praise for Mamillius, Sicilia's heir apparent. Camillo's belief that the kings' relationship "cannot choose but branch now" suggests not a split[10] but a growing fondness, a "rooted" affection that seems destined to extend, like a mature tree, into fresh branches (24–25). In the following scene we may register, especially in hindsight, some underlying tension in the references to lost "innocence" and adult "fault" (1.2.69, 85). There are hints of one-upmanship too. Apparently Leontes needs to prove just how hospitable he is by persuading, even coercing, his friend into staying another week. But his emotional outburst in the aside "Too hot, too hot!" (108), as he misinterprets his wife's gracious affection toward his friend as lust, surely comes as a shock.

Antigonus's wry prediction, after Hermione is packed off to prison, that the whole "business" will end in "laughter" (2.1.197–98) briefly introduces a lighthearted mood that cuts away from imminent catastrophe.[11] Yet by the end of the next scene this loyal servant is pushed into becoming an instrument of the king's tyranny, swearing to transport the newborn child to a remote region where she will almost certainly die; and his own violent demise makes his earlier optimistic prediction seem hollow, another case of the dramatist keeping the audience off-balance by confusing their expectations over what will happen. With a similar effect at the opening of act 3, Cleomenes and Dion, fresh from the "delicate" and "fertile" isle of Delos, are reassuringly confident that "Great Apollo" will "Turn all to th' best" (3.1.14–15). But such optimism fades to ashes in the rigged trial of the following scene, where Leontes repudiates the oracle. At the midpoint of the play, Leontes is left to lament not only his cruel abandonment of his baby daughter but what he believes to be the death of his wife as well as his son.

## SHIFTING EXPECTATIONS: "THINGS NEW-BORN" (ACT 3, SCENE 3–ACT 4, SCENE 4)

In act 4 the play seems to start over, 16 years later, as a pastoral comedy in Bohemia. The real division, though, comes before this. Preparing for a sudden change of direction and tone is the pivotal third scene of act 3, a "dramaturgical hinge"[12] where catastrophe takes on farcical overtones and the ultra-serious gives way to comic optimism. In a somber speech, Antigonus recounts how Hermione appeared to him in a dream. Although her apparition is contained in a report and is not an onstage ghost, Antigonus's conviction that "the spirits o' th' dead / May walk again" (3.3.38, 15–16) strengthens the illusion that the first half of the play has indeed concluded tragically with the death of Hermione.[13] But now we are in a strange world between realistic tragedy and romance, one in which the Mariner's observation on the threatening storm, that "the heavens" are "angry," is quickly followed by Antigonus's fervent acknowledgment of divine providence: "Their sacred wills be done!" (5–6).

No sooner has Antigonus placed down his bundle than, with dreamlike logic, the focus shifts suddenly to the "savage clamor" (55) that precedes the rude arrival of a hungry bear. The exit of Antigonus "pursued by a bear" combines the grim with the grotesque; and if we assume an actor dressed in a bear costume rather than a real animal lumbering across the stage, the moment approaches farce. In another pronounced shift of tone, a dreamlike dissolve into a fresh scenario, the Old Shepherd enters chatting about the follies of adolescents and grumbling that his sheep have been scared off by young hunters. Discovering the baby, he perceives her not as a tragic victim but as a "very pretty" though illegitimate "barne" (69–70). The Shepherd's son, bursting with news, provides yet another disorienting perspective on what he has just witnessed offstage. His graphic account of two amazing "sights" counterpoints a shipwreck, complete with sound

effects (the sea chafing, the men crying out), with the demise of Antigonus, who also "cried" for help even as he was destroyed by a loudly roaring bear (82, 95). Yet this report, which should generate horror (as does
the Messenger's account of Jocasta's offstage death in *Oedipus the King*),
does the reverse. Death is distanced by the Clown's colorful narrative,
where his lively image of the ship "swallowed" by the "yeast and froth" of
the ocean is juxtaposed with a wryly matter-of-fact reference to the bear
having already "half dined" on the "gentleman" (92, 105). And so "things
dying" transform into "things new born" (113), an optimism reinforced by
the promise of good fortune implied in the gold and valuables accompanying the baby.

After Time's choric speech introducing act 4, and a short scene establishing Polixenes's anxiety over his son's interest in a shepherdess,
"Enter Autolycus, singing." Immediately this enterprising rogue propels
the mood of the play into comedy. Contrasting with the monomania that
has turned the Sicilian court into a nightmare world, his "merry heart"
refreshingly finds reason for being simply in wandering (like the poetic
imagination) "here and there" (4.3.129, 17). Though a conman and a thief,
Autolycus is far removed from the dangerous villainy of Leontes;[14] as in
a dream, his actions appear to have no harmful consequences, since no
one ever complains about having been robbed. When the action moves
swiftly into the sheep-shearing scene, the focus is now on the exalted love
between Perdita, grown to "grace / Equal with wond'ring" as the adopted
daughter of the Shepherd (4.1.24–25), and Prince Florizel. Brushing aside
apparent class distinctions, the romantic prince exhorts his love to "Apprehend / Nothing but jollity" (4.4.24–25). Further shifting the tone away
from Leontes's diseased, death-oriented obsession with infidelity, Perdita
wishes to know Florizel not as a corpse but (playing on the sexual sense of
"to die") buried alive in her arms (130–32).

Still, just as the first portion of the play affords glimpses of comedy
within a tragic framework, so "we find the painful invading the comic
world" in Part 2.[15] In act 4, scene 2, Polixenes is sharply reminded of
Leontes's loss of his wife and children, who are "even now to be afresh lamented" (26). His own son, a truant from the court, makes him "unhappy"
(28). The role of Autolycus is refreshingly comic, but his antics inject some
realism into the rural community, reminding Shakespeare's audience of
thieves and confidence tricksters who trouble their own society. Though
the sheep-shearing scene overall is a celebration of love and youthful
vitality, it is not all sweetness and light. The darkest shadow falls when
Polixenes breaks up the young couple's betrothal, threatening to scratch
Perdita's face with briars; but Perdita has already felt some "dread" about

their prospects (4.4.17), and Camillo reminds us of what could happen if Florizel and Perdita abandon themselves to "unpathed waters, undreamed shores" (571). Autolycus, with his superbly detailed fantasy of how the young shepherd will be tortured to death because his father promoted an unsuitable match (4.4.790–98), helps to defuse the violence that Polixenes has unleashed. Yet it doesn't entirely cancel out the Shepherd's sense of devastation when he realizes that Florizel has deceived him ("You have undone a man of fourscore three") and his dignified wish to "die within this hour" (457, 465).

## DIVISION OR CONTINUITY?

As the above analysis has emphasized, neither of the play's two sections is truly unified in tone. Shifts in mood and perspective leaven the heaviness of Part 1 even as they temporarily darken Part 2. This is one of the ways in which Shakespeare fosters a tragicomic mood throughout and thus avoids any facile wrenching of the play's ending into comedy. Structural and verbal mirrorings[16] also serve to link the two halves of the play, so that spatially *The Winter's Tale* comes to resemble the two balancing halves of Time's hourglass.[17] Simultaneously the play offsets its discontinuities by creating the illusion of recurrence,[18] a predictable seasonal cycle in which spring will eventually lead to winter, winter give way to spring.

Right from the play's opening, where Camillo fancifully claims that in absence the two kings have "embraced … from the ends of opposed winds," we are conditioned to expect a bridging of "vast" distances between Sicilia and Bohemia (1.1.31–32). In fact the most obvious symmetrical patterning between the two halves of the action is the way that each king violently disrupts a healthy relationship. Leontes's public denunciation of Hermione as an adulteress (2.1.65–78) and his planned vengeance on Polixenes (1.2.316–18) are paralleled by Polixenes's own disruption of his son's engagement and his determination to "devise" a "cruel" death for Perdita if she ever receives the prince again (4.4.444). Other mirrorings, though less obvious, help to bind the two parts together. Camillo's opening conversation with the Bohemian ambassador Archidamus celebrates a royal friendship that ironically will shortly be severed; act 4, after Time's monologue, opens with a similar two-person scene, Camillo now discussing with Polixenes the budding love between the prince and Perdita that the king almost immediately attempts to destroy. At the end of act 1, Camillo transfers his loyal "service" from his old master Leontes to Polixenes, helping the king of Bohemia to escape back to his homeland

(1.2.441). In a semireversal of this pattern at the end of act 4, Camillo, who now wants to return to *his* homeland, switches to become the "preserver" of Florizel (4.4.590), temporarily saving him from the wrath of Polixenes by steering him in the direction of Sicily so that he can return there himself with the king. The "sad tale" that Mamillius ominously begins to tell his mother just before Leontes rushes her off to prison (2.1.25) finds a comic counterpart in the "merry" ballads that Autolycus peddles in Bohemia (4.4.288). When we first see Perdita she is taking on the "hostess-ship" of the feast (4.4.72), just as earlier her mother, Hermione, acted as "kind hostess" (1.2.60) to Polixenes.[19]

Patterns from Part 1 extend, too, into the play's final act. The choric opening of act 3, in which Cleomenes and Dion predict that "something rare" is bound to "rush to knowledge" when the oracle is opened (3.1.21), clearly anticipates the Gentlemen's recounting of royal reunions in act 5, scene 2. This report from Delphos seems out of keeping with the wintry tone of the trial scene that follows it. But it aptly foreshadows the later narrative report in which the keynote is "amazedness," "admiration," and "wonder" (5.2.5, 12, 17)—a mood that extends into the statue scene. The arresting tableau of Hermione standing motionless until commanded to move echoes the trial scene of act 3.[20] There the immobile queen is also the center of attention although she is far from silent, forced instead to defend herself while "standing / To prate and talk for life and honor" (3.2.39–40).

Sicily focuses on the sophisticated world of the court, while the Bohemia of act 4 is rural. Yet images of nature[21] forge links between these separate communities. In his very first words, Polixenes reminds his hosts that he has stayed in Sicily for "nine changes" of the moon, presenting time as seasonal cycles that a shepherd might "note" (1.2.1–2). A little later this king envisages his boyhood with Leontes in even more pastoral terms: "We were as twinned lambs, that did frisk i' the sun / And bleat the one at th' other" (67–68). Sure enough, the play's second half produces the more practical side of animal husbandry: the Old Shepherd tries to find two of his "best sheep" (3.3.65), and his son calculates how many pounds of wool translate into how much cash. Leontes's mistaken view of Hermione as a "flax-wench, that puts to / Before her troth-plight" (1.2.277–78) materializes in the Clown's Bohemian girlfriends, Mopsa and Dorcas. Feeling humiliated by what he takes to be a cheating wife, Leontes associates himself with animals—heifers, steers, and deer—that, like the cuckolded husband, wear horns. Moreover his anguish, as he watches Hermione hold up her "neb" (beak) to Polixenes (183), is as sharp as "thorns, nettles, tails of wasps" (330); Autolycus later invokes a "wasp's nest" as part of the gruesome punishment the young shepherd may face (4.4.792).

At the Sicilian court Paulina finds a different kind of solace in Nature. In act 2 she celebrates how the "law and process" of "great Nature," independent of Leontes's arbitrary decrees, has "freed" Perdita from her mother's womb (2.2.59–60). Observing how the daughter is a true copy of her father, Paulina also prays that the "good goddess Nature" may protect the child from any genetic predisposition toward jealousy (2.3.102–5). Thus the audience is prepared for the central discussion of "great creating Nature" between Polixenes and Perdita in act 4 and for the "art" of the statue to become nature—the actual Hermione—in the play's final scene. Even the presiding deity Apollo, whose island is described as "fertile" and blessed with "sweet" air (3.1.1–2), finds his way into Part 2. Appropriately the god resurfaces in Florizel's catalogue of divine metamorphoses, acting the same role of "humble swain" as the prince does in the sheep-shearing festival (4.4.30). Later Perdita recounts how early primroses die before they can encounter the virile sun god (124). Arriving in Sicily, Perdita herself is described by the Servant as "the most peerless piece of earth … / That e'er the sun shone bright on" (5.1.94–95). Such verbal echoes are not pointedly ironic, as becomes the case with words such as "bond" in the tragedy of *King Lear.* Instead repeated references work "at a deeper level of unconscious association"[22] to interrelate the two parts of *The Winter's Tale.*

The opening song of Autolycus reminds the audience of seasonal renewal—that the "red blood reigns in the winter's pale" (4.3.4). Whisking the audience from wintry Sicily to spring daffodils and the "summer songs" of Bohemian larks, it also promises that youthful Eros will surge ahead even while Leontes (whose presence is evoked in the line "a quart of ale is a dish for a king") endures his "sixteen winters" of sorrow (5.3.50). Perdita, a realist, is as aware of the "blasts of January" and "winds of March" as of the warmer Whitsun pastorals and the flowers of summer (4.4.111, 120). Her delicate image for the barely perceptible advent of autumn—a time just before the "death" of the summer and the "birth / Of trembling winter" (80–81)—points to the revolving of the seasons that informs both plots.[23] Part 1 begins in the brief "summer" of a mature relationship between the kings of Sicily and Bohemia (1.1.5), with a retrospective glance at the spring of their youth, and ends in the winter of destruction and apparent death. Part 2, despite its relatively "leisurely" rhythms compared to the "linear, impetuous"[24] momentum of Part 1, mimics this to some extent. Florizel and Perdita represent the regenerative springtime of love, for while in calendar terms it is summer in Bohemia,[25] Perdita appears like

"Flora, / Peering in April's front" (4.4.2–3) and catalogues the flowers of spring. Because act 5 begins in the prolonged winter of Leontes's discontent, the audience is conditioned to expect another seasonal change—the return of spring, heralded by the arrival of Perdita and Florizel in Sicily. Hermione's unforeseen resurrection means that late summer and autumn will also be revived. This variation on the usual pattern creates a marvelous sense, as in the masque of fertility in *The Tempest,* that "spring" may actually come "In the very end of harvest" (4.1.115).

## TIME AS BRIDGE AND CHORUS

At first the figure of Time may seem a crude device to excuse to the audience the "great gap" between Perdita's arrival in Bohemia as a baby and her entrance, 16 years later, as a young woman at the sheep-shearing festival. Yet, as Nevill Coghill notes, all the important narrative information—that Leontes continues penitent in Sicily, while in Bohemia Florizel has met the supposed shepherdess, Perdita—emerges from the conversation between Camillo and Polixenes in the following scene.[26] Rather than providing necessary exposition, Time's chorus articulates concepts integral to the play. His gnomic couplets offer a tragicomic perspective on how time is both destroyer and renewer,[27] working through revolutions akin to seasonal cycles. Time, whose purpose is to "try all" (4.1.1), will test the patience of Leontes, who now "shuts up himself" for16 years to face the destructiveness of his past (19). Meanwhile Time's "growing" (16) opens up the new world of Florizel and Perdita, revealing a love affair that flows more freely into the future.

Poised at "the turn of the tide of mood, from tragedy to comedy,"[28] Time's report mirrors the death-into-life dynamics of the preceding scene (3.3). There Time shows two faces, delivering both comic "joy" and tragic "terror," perhaps according to just deserts, perhaps randomly to "good" and "bad" alike (1–2). As part of his doubleness, Time embodies the "move still, still so" paradox that Florizel later expresses (4.4.142), for this choric figure defines himself as stable ("The same I am, ere ancient'st order was / Or what is now received" [10–11]) yet perpetually in motion. His wings are so "swift" that he is able to "slide / O'er sixteen years" (5–6), and he can "pace" with such "speed" (23) that one moment he is "leaving" Leontes, the next he is "In fair Bohemia" (17–21).

Time makes it clear that in this play his movement can be expedited only by the audience's imagination and good will. It is our "allowing" (15) that enables speedy transitions from location to location, just as we must graciously accept a bypassing of the 16 years during which Perdita is "grown in grace" (24). In fact this telescoping coincides with our "imaginative elasticity"[29] in response to duration. A "July's day" can feel short as a December one (1.2.169), whereas Leontes complains that his three months of laboriously courting Hermione seemed sour ("crabb'd") and lengthy (102), and Paulina reminds him that to expiate the crime of causing Hermione's death, "ten thousand years" of agonizing contrition may not prove long enough (3.2.209). Time contracts as we travel back in memory, so that Leontes can instantly "recoil / Twenty-three years" and be a boy again with Polixenes (1.2.154–55). Or it may be foreshortened, with Camillo anticipating how Leontes's "kindness" toward Florizel and Perdita in Sicily will "grow / Faster than thought or time" (4.4.557–58). In a state of bliss, where "immediacy" overrides any temporal pressure,[30] the king feels that "twenty years together" could pass in an instant as he gazes enraptured at the "statue" of Hermione (5.3.71).

More objectively, Time's dualities are part of a predictable revolution, the turning of a wheel or the rising and falling of a wave; it is impossible for anyone to remain "boy eternal" (1.2.65). On the downward side, Time acts as destroyer, having the power to "o'erthrow law" and "o'erwhelm custom," "make stale / The glistering of this present" (4.1.8, 13–14), and inevitably transform "the freshest things now reigning" into something as stale as the old "tale" (Shakespeare's wry comment on his own play)[31] now seems in comparison to the latest dramatic trends (13–15). Happily, Time's ravages are compensated for by an upward cycle into renewal again. In the same ("self-born") hour that he destroys old customs, he can "plant" new ones, just as he is able to give the scene "growing" simply by turning his hour glass (8–9, 16). Temporal cycles, like seasonal ones, bring regeneration. And while Time enables the mistaken assumption that Hermione is dead, he will "unfold" the very "error" that he "makes" (2) when he reveals the truth at the end of the play—that the queen is still alive.

While Time explains his role in turning past into present, present into past, he refuses to give away, or "prophesy" the future of Perdita: "let Time's news / Be known when 'tis brought forth" (26–27). What "ensues" and what "follows after" for Perdita will become a living present, the dramatized story or "argument" of Time (25, 28–29). And so Time's persona merges with that of the dramatist—the "I" who "mentioned"(22) but did not name the son of Polixenes in act 1, and who now "earnestly" hopes that the audience may "never" spend time "worse" than in the current moment of watching *The Winter's Tale* in the theater (30–32).

## FROM DIPTYCH TO TRIPTYCH: ACT 5

Split into two halves until the end of act 4, *The Winter's Tale* becomes a triptych once the action returns to the court of Leontes 16 years after his terrible mistake. While the first portion set in Sicily drives toward tragedy, act 4 provides an antidote in the expansive pastoral comedy of Bohemia, a "predominantly creative and restorative phase."[32] The final movement (act 5) incorporates both in a romantic resolution. Describing the dramatic pattern as thesis-antithesis-synthesis is something of a simplification, since comedy intrudes in Sicily and somber notes in Bohemia. The last phase of the play nevertheless resolves conflicting elements in an almost miraculous, but not impossible chord. The audience can now perceive the upward movement of the play, in that the terrible crisis of act 3—Leontes's mistake and Hermione's apparent death—has not resulted in permanent tragedy. The past informs the king's present, but once Perdita and Florizel arrive in Sicily, hope for the future becomes the dominant strain.

The mood of act 5, scene 1 is both resigned to devastating loss and forward looking. Cleomenes and Dion couch their hopes for the kingdom's future in religious terms. These advisers echo the Lord's Prayer in the linking of "done trespass" with "forgive yourself" (4, 6), acknowledging the "saintlike sorrow" and "penitence" that have redeemed the king's "fault" (2, 4) while arguing that it would now be "holier" for him to "bless the bed of majesty" (31–33) with a new queen who could produce a royal heir. But Leontes is still fixed in the past with Hermione. Just as later, in a tone of religious fervor, he recalls Polixenes as "holy," "sacred," and "blessed" (170–74), so he idealizes his supposedly dead wife as a "sainted spirit" who had amazing "virtues" (57, 7). Encouraging Leontes to believe that Hermione's ghost would chastise him if he found a second wife, Paulina appears to stymie his regeneration by proposing an impossible bargain: he can remarry only with her blessing and only when his "first queen's again in breath; / Never till then" (83–84). Yet as soon as he reacts to the fresh presence of Florizel and Perdita, Leontes's sense of loss is balanced by resurgent "wonder" in his bittersweet observation:

> I lost a couple that 'twixt heaven and earth
> Might thus have stood begetting wonder as
> You, gracious couple, do. (132–34)

Again he ponders what might have been, the conditional future perfect, had his own children survived: "What might I have been, / Might I a son and daughter now have looked on" (176–77). His sudden attraction to Perdita (quickly nipped in the bud by Paulina) shows that he is still responsive to "youth" and beauty; she and her prince are as welcome to him as "spring" is to the "earth" (152). And by scene's end he is moving from a past of regret to a plan for the future ("I will to your father" [229]), promising to help the couple win Polixenes over to accept their marriage.

Thus we are prepared for the report, in the following scene, of the various reunions—Leontes with Camillo, Polixenes, and daughter, Perdita—that paradoxically all combine Time's comic "joy" (4.1.1) with tragic "Sorrow," as if "joy were now become a loss" (5.2.48, 54–55). Act 5, scene 2 also contains the key piece of information, a hint of the big surprise to come, that Paulina has been visiting the site of the queen's statue "privately, twice or thrice a day, ever since the death of Hermione" (113–14). The gathering of all the main characters in the final scene continues the superb modulation of past grief into present joy. Seeing the statue, Leontes at first is caught up in an ideal image of Hermione in the past, when she was "as tender / As infancy and grace" (5.3.26–27). But Paulina leads him into accepting the conditional future perfect of aging, wrinkles and all (for the statue looks "As now she might have done"), and from there into an active participation in the ritual of bringing her back to "warm" life (32, 109). Thus he moves into a future of desire, resolving "Let no man mock me, / For I will kiss her" (79–80).

The "majesty" of the statue, a reminder of Hermione's dignity in the past and a reality in the present, both conjures the king's past evils to "remembrance" (40) and exorcises them, dissipating a sorrow that would otherwise keep him perpetually locked in the past. For it is, as Camillo points out, a grief that could be endless, one that "sixteen summers cannot blow away, / So many summers dry" (50–51). In a play shot through with awareness of temporal process, its renewals as well as its destructions, Paulina's simple command to the statue, "'Tis time" (99), is especially poignant.[33] The young, too, play a role in the redemption of time through the revival of Hermione, for it is Perdita who induces her mother to "speak" (118). Nor are other members of the older generation left out of the romantic reunion when Leontes makes an impromptu match between his two counselors, Camillo and Paulina, before urging the assembly to "Hastily lead away" (155).

## THE QUESTION OF GENRE

Discussing with Hamlet the Players who have arrived in Elsinore, Polonius comes up with an amusing catalogue of dramatic combinations (*Hamlet,* 2.2.396–99). "Tragical-comical-historical-pastoral" describes Shakespeare's *Cymbeline* (1609–10), a tragicomic romance set in Roman

Britain and pastoral Wales. Without the "historical" label it would fit *The Winter's Tale* too. Even while acknowledging the rich mixture of dramatic forms available, Shakespeare satirizes the Renaissance passion for categorization; many of his contemporaries, partly because of their respect for classical forms and desire to imitate them, took "concepts of genre" very seriously indeed.[34] In our century, the exercise of trying to match plays to certain formulae may appear outdated and arid. After all, Shakespeare himself never seemed hidebound by rules or shackled by formal constraints in his plays. Nevertheless, it is important to know the range of established conventions—patterns an audience might have come to expect—that the dramatist was either drawing on or flouting in *The Winter's Tale*.

The early seventeenth century was a time of dramatic innovation as playwrights experimented with new combinations. What we find in the period are generic overlaps: romance trades on adventures, surprises, and reunions, but this (with fuller emphasis on near-catastrophe) is also the stuff of the newer form of tragicomedy. Pastoral, exploring contrasts and connections between court and country, either provides a leisurely interlude within tragicomedy and romance[35] or is itself a mode where tragedy and comedy become "inseparable."[36] The blend of elements in *The Winter's Tale* is unique; yet assessing these elements in wider contexts helps to increase an understanding of the play's particular achievement.

### Late Plays and Theatrical Experimentation

The least controversial label for *The Winter's Tale* is Late Play. Along with *Pericles, Cymbeline,* and *The Tempest,* it forms part of the group of four that the dramatist composed between 1607 and 1611. Although Shakespeare later collaborated with John Fletcher on *Henry VIII* and *The Two Noble Kinsmen,* the four works constitute the last plays (*Pericles* from act 3 on) that he wrote unaided. There is no need to probe into Shakespeare's biography or psyche to account for why he progressed from the dark visions of *King Lear, Macbeth,* and *Timon of Athens* to the relative optimism of the Late Plays.[37] Whether we find in these works a logical progression from Shakespeare's tragedy[38] or a development of his earlier writing of comedy, it is clear that the artist was now fascinated by the challenge of modulating disaster into comic resurgence and the reuniting of royal families.

The four plays are linked in both subject matter and motifs. All of them include a royal father's relationship with or rediscovery of his daughter. Whereas *King Lear* (1605–1606) ends in Lear's agonizing loss of Cordelia—"She's gone forever!" (5.3.260)—*Pericles* dramatizes the king's ecstatic discovery that his daughter, Mariana, is actually alive, and Cymbeline is also reunited with his estranged daughter, Imogen, at the close of that play. Prospero is not parted from his only child, Miranda, in *The Tempest,* but he imposes tests before allowing her to marry. In *The Winter's Tale,* Leontes welcomes the return of Perdita, the cast-out daughter he presumed dead, after 16 years. While the plots of these plays also trace the temporary setbacks of young lovers, *The Winter's Tale* is unusual in concentrating most dramatic energy on reuniting a husband and wife from the older generation. Pericles is amazed to find that his wife Thaisa, thought to have died in childbirth, is still alive, but it is Leontes, in the brilliant denouement of *The Winter's Tale,* who is most focused on re-discovering the wife he lost. With an added twist, the mother-daughter (as opposed to the father-daughter) relationship gains some prominence in *The Winter's Tale,* for it is apparently Perdita, not Leontes, who has inspired Hermione to stay alive.

As these crucial changes in emphasis remind us, slotting *The Winter's Tale* into a category called the Late Plays risks homogenizing its themes and dramatic form, losing a sense of its uniqueness. It is also a mistake to perceive the first three of the four plays as a process of artistic trial and error leading up to the "final success"[39] of *The Tempest,* which is the most coherent in terms of unity of time and place. *The Winter's Tale,* for instance, must forgo that unity in order to include Leontes's slow regeneration and the fortunes of the mature Perdita. Each of the Late Plays in fact uses different strategies to handle the challenges of transforming potentially tragic destruction into romantic reconciliation.

To achieve this, *The Winter's Tale* is frankly experimental in dramaturgy. It conveys the sense of Shakespeare being adventurous, trying something different as he pours old wine (the narrative stuff of romance and fairy tale) into the new bottles of theatrical form.[40] He underlines the improbability of the plot of this "old tale" and breaks the illusion through play metaphors, distancing the audience by refusing to hide what S.L. Bethell calls the "deliberate creaking of the dramatic machinery,"[41] yet working to make the final transformation of statue into woman a moment where they can willingly suspend disbelief. Rather than becoming "half bored to death"[42] with his craft, as Lytton Strachey asserts, Shakespeare composes what Barbara Mowat calls "open form drama."[43] While the play lacks a tight causal structure and often develops what is "monstrous to our human reason" (5.1.41), the overall dramatic effect is far from "naive";[44] it encourages the audience to see within its shifting expectations a reflection of life's strangeness, its promise of the unexpected.

One twentieth-century theory is that Shakespeare wrote these plays with a particular playhouse in mind—the indoor, private theater at Blackfriars.[45] In 1608 Richard Burbage took over this Blackfriars Theatre, a property first acquired in 1596, for Shakespeare's company, the King's Men. From late 1609 it became their venue for winter performances, while they continued to use their public playhouse, the Globe, during the summer season. Offering a roofed theater that could seat only about 500 as opposed to over 2,000 in the Globe, the Blackfriars had better acoustics and lighting, when required, by candles. The boys' companies who used the private theater before the King's Men had also established the custom of music between acts—instrumental arrangements incorporating lutes, pipes, flutes, and violins.[46] Certainly parts of *The Winter's Tale* might benefit from the more intimate setting of Blackfriars. As he watches Polixenes and Hermione conversing further upstage in act 1, scene 2, Leontes could deliver his contorted asides with quiet intensity in such a theater. Subtle lighting, as well as delicate music, might enhance the magical effect of the statue scene. On balance, though, most of the play's sequences could have worked equally well at the Globe; and since the King's Men's winter repertoire coincided with works performed at the Globe in the summer, they needed to be adaptable.[47] The song and dance pageantry of act 4, scene 4, where several groups interact, would come across strongly on a large open-air stage, as would Hermione's trial and the final scene, where several onstage spectators witness the statue's metamorphosis.

Scenes of supernatural intervention in the Late Plays—Jupiter descending on an eagle to set the divine record straight in *Cymbeline,* or Ariel, terrifying as a harpy, disrupting the banquet for the court party in *The Tempest*—might have benefited from more sophisticated technology than was available at the Globe.[48] But because *The Winter's Tale* contains no deus ex machina (the sudden "burst" of Apollo's oracle is reported, not shown in 3.1.8), it could be staged relatively simply. To a lesser extent than *The Tempest,* where spirits impersonate rustics and goddesses in a ceremony to mark the betrothal of Miranda to Ferdinand, *The Winter's Tale* shows the influence of the court masque. This spectacular entertainment, in which masked revelers celebrated the triumph of royal and cosmic order, was often preceded by an antimasque representing chaos or disharmony.[49] The sheep-shearing festival, with its disguisings and revelry, offers the masque's brand of fast-moving pageantry, while the dance of the satyrs is the feast's antimasque, a rough counterpoint to the more civilized dancing of Perdita and Florizel among the shepherds and shepherdesses.

Such virtuoso spectacle suggests how Shakespeare, always a theatrical opportunist and by now adept at presenting his plays at the court of King

James, could "utilize the new and fashionable resources"[50] of the masque even late in his career. Spectacle never takes over *The Winter's Tale,* however. And just as Shakespeare was not simply catering to the tastes of the aristocrats at court when he composed this play, it is unlikely that he turned to this challenging new dramatic material just to gratify the clientele at the private Blackfriars Theatre.[51] We deduce that the audience there would be fairly sophisticated, composed mainly of gallants, young lawyers, gentlemen, and some gentlewomen—well-off spectators who could afford sixpence to sit in the galleries as opposed to two pence for gallery seats at the Globe. Such spectators might be expected to enjoy bizarre shifts in dramatic perspective, such as the grotesque moment in *Cymbeline* when Imogen mistakes the headless body of the brutish Cloten for that of her husband, Posthumous, or when Antigonus's dream-vision of Hermione is rudely terminated by the bear that kills him.[52] Yet John Fletcher's sophisticated pastoral tragicomedy, *The Faithful Shepherdess,* was a failure when it was performed at one of the private theaters in 1608. And *Pericles,* Shakespeare's first experiment in turning a rambling narrative romance into tragicomic drama, must have been performed at the Globe before being registered for publication in 1608. Beaumont and Fletcher's *Philaster,* a mixture of courtly intrigue, pastoral, and romantic tragicomedy written about the same time as *Cymbeline* (critics disagree on which play influenced which), also most likely made its debut at the Globe in 1610. This suggests that the subject matter of Shakespeare's experimental Late Plays appealed to the audiences of the public playhouses as much as to coterie tastes. If, with their self-conscious artifice and disturbing mix of fantastic and realistic, these plays were "fashioned to the sophisticated taste of the private theatergoer, the masses did not stay away."[53]

## ROMANCE

Northrop Frye calls romance the "structural core of all fiction."[54] Depicting an "idealized world,"[55] it represents a quest toward some higher goal or source of happiness. Frye stresses, too, the strong sense of wish-fulfilment with which romance offers up an "imaginative model of desire," depicting "the world we want."[56] Our own age associates romance with love stories, but the genre denotes more than simply journeys that end (as Feste sings in *Twelfth Night*) in "lovers meeting" (2.3.43). In the Middle Ages and Renaissance, romance encompasses strange and wonderful adventures over a long period of time, ending in the reuniting of families or the union of lovers. The "pain of separation" is followed by the "rapture of discovery."[57] Because of romance's emphasis on plot—disguisings, sea

journeys, shipwrecks in exotic places, and even hair-raising pursuits by
wild animals—characters in romance are usually depicted as good or evil
rather than complex. Improbable coincidences that result in the eventual
recovery of lost ones are often felt to be part of an overarching supernatural design,[58] a fortunate outcome that may be predicted by oracles or
foreseen in dream visions. Acts 3, 4, and 5 of *The Winter's Tale* contain
many of these formulae. There is the casting out of a royal child, Perdita,
who grows up (during a gap of 16 years) in another country believing that
she is the daughter of a shepherd; a storm, shipwreck, and savage attack
by a bear; the oracle of Apollo that predicts the return of a natural "heir"
to the kingdom; and, after another sea-journey, the marvelous reunion not
only of the princess with her father, but of the king with the queen he has
long thought dead.

    In fact the genre of romance was not labeled as such in Shakespeare's
time. The early modern period drew its "romance" material from several
forms of fiction or folk tale—classical, medieval, and contemporary.[59]
The classical strand[60] included Heliodorus's Greek romance *Aethiopica*,[61]
translated by Thomas Underdowne in 1569, and Longus's *Daphnis and
Chloe*. Both of these influenced Philip Sidney's *Arcadia* (1580–1585), an
immensely popular, elaborate prose work detailing the adventures of the
princes Pyrocles and Musidorus as they try to win the love of the princesses
Philoclea and Pamela.[62] Among medieval chivalric romances, in which the
knights of King Arthur quest for honor and rescue damsels in distress in the
process, *Guy of Warwick, Amadis de Gaule,* and Malory's *Morte D'Arthur*
served as inspirations for Spenser's *Faerie Queene* (1590–1596), though
less so for Shakespeare's Late Plays. Miracle and late medieval morality
plays, such as *The Castle of Perseverance,* also utilized the quest form, with
trials leading to a happy resolution or spiritual redemption.[63] In addition,
Renaissance writers were able to tap into the more recent fiction of Ari-
osto and Tasso and the novellas of Boccaccio, Bordello, and Montemayor.
This was material that Shakespeare used mainly in his earlier comedies.
The playwright's immediate source for *The Winter's Tale* was the prose
romance *Pandosto* by Robert Greene, who also wrote the romantic plays
*Friar Bacon and Friar Bungay* (1594) and *James IV* (1598).

    What we now call romance was a staple of early Elizabethan drama.
Stephen Gosson, a Puritan outraged by licentious theatrical material,
notes in his *Plays Confuted in Five Actions* (1582) that "the *Aethiopian
historie, Amadis of Fraunce,* the *Rounde table* … have beene thoroughly
ransackt to furnish the Playe houses in London."[64] Most of these early
plays have been lost, but to this period belongs *The Rare Triumphs of Love
and Fortune* (1582), which contains a male character called Hermione,

and, a little later, the popular *Mucedorus* (c. 1590), featuring a clown and a bear. Rather than concocting an original dramatic recipe, Shakespeare was adapting an old one, combining the ingredients of romance into a newer tragicomic dish.

Romantic narrative rambles, meandering into ancillary adventures. Turning "potentially endless"[65] fiction into coherent drama with a logically related beginning, middle, and end is a challenge for the playwright. Applying higher standards to plays than to his own prose fiction, Sidney in his *Defence of Poesie* berates what he calls "absurd" violations of the unity of time as well as place. In current drama, he says, a prince and princess may "fall in love," and, after many tribulations, "she is got with childe, delivered of a faire boy: he is lost, groweth a man, falleth in love, and is ready to get an other child, and all this in two houres space."[66] It is true that Shakespeare's early romance *Pericles* is frankly episodic; not only does it contain rapid shifts of location (crisscrossing among the cities of Antioch, Tyre, Tharsus, Pentapolis, Ephesus, and Mytilene), but it traces the progress of Marina from a newborn in act 3 to a young woman about to be married by the end of the play. In *The Winter's Tale*, though, the technique for traversing time is more sophisticated. Time as chorus allows the playwright to bypass Leontes's 16-year repentance in Sicily so that act 4 can concentrate exclusively on the romantic love between Perdita and Florizel in Bohemia. Thus Shakespeare retains romance's longtime span but keeps audience attention focused by dramatizing two relatively short periods—the first a crisis in the marriage of Leontes and Hermione, the second the courtship of Perdita and Florizel, which then extends into the play's conclusion in Sicily.

Scholars stress the "shock of surprise"[67] inherent in romance narrative, which often features supernatural visitations or other incredible happenings. Ben Jonson, who was deeply committed to surface realism, took a swipe at his rival's plays *The Winter's Tale* and *The Tempest* in the Induction to *Bartholomew Fair* (1614) when he confidently proclaimed himself "loth to make Nature afraid in his playes, like those that beget *Tales, Tempests,* and such like drolleries." Now, nearly 400 years later, Kiernan Ryan defends Shakespeare's romances as a "frontal assault" on "the tyranny of realism itself,"[68] pointing to their "absurd predicaments and outrageous coincidences; the violent simplifications of character and motive; the scandalous liberties taken with time and place; the fortuitous interventions of supernatural forces and pagan divinities; and the benign resolutions contrived in frank contempt of the laws of likelihood."[69] Granted, *The Winter's Tale* revels in discontinuities and waywardness. Yet Ryan may underestimate the convincing, hard-won resolution that Shakespeare achieves within its romantic framework. As Howard Felperin puts it, by the play's end "romance" is "redeemed by life."[70] Perceiving his past afresh after a long period of suffering, by act 5 Leontes has become appropriately receptive to the restoration of his lost wife. And no god arrives to engineer this romance's spectacular "surprise"; instead, Paulina's "lawful" magic (5.3.105), a byproduct of her role as Leontes's conscience, brings about the "wonder" of metamorphosis.

Romance in *The Winter's Tale* is therefore more than dreamlike fantasy or an excuse for staging "drolleries." The play, with its grounding in everyday reality—it includes a little prince whose "smutched" nose must be wiped and a princess who gets seasick[71]—achieves a "romantic verisimilitude"[72] in which even bizarre situations change or mature the main characters. Northrop Frye captures well the way that "quest romance," while both fantastic and idealistic, does not have to be unnatural. It is, rather, the search of the "desiring self for a fulfilment that will deliver it from the anxieties of reality but will still contain that reality."[73] On one level the romantic conclusion of *The Winter's Tale* is ideal, part of a "new and impossible"[74] world. But the living Hermione exhibits realistic wrinkles. She, like Leontes, has been transformed by the realities of time and experience.

## PASTORAL

Pastoral had enjoyed a long literary history before it was reworked in *The Winter's Tale*. The term itself came from "pastor" (Latin for shepherd); and in classical times both the idylls of Theocratus and Virgil's eclogues established the convention of the singing, often lovesick poet-shepherd.[75] The tradition flourished in the Renaissance writings of Petrarch, Ronsard, and Montemayor and it helped to shape the drama of Tasso and Guarini.[76] Initially the shepherd represented a quiet life in tune with nature, a retreat into a green world governed by the rhythms of the seasons rather than the hectic pace of the city or court. Shakespeare's overburdened King Henry VI, for instance, yearns for the peaceful life of the shepherd who could measure time simply in how "many hours" he needed to "tend" his "flock" (*Henry VI,* Part 3, 31, 40). Such a world looked back nostalgically to the Golden Age.

Pastoral, though, was not merely escapist. Increasingly it became a forum in which to explore, often with a satirical edge, the competing values of country and city, or the life of contemplation versus action.[77] To facilitate this genre's debate between the relatively unsophisticated world of nature and a highly civilized, courtly society, the protagonist usually had a foot in both camps. Like the princes in Sidney's *Arcadia,* he was often an aristocratic lover disguised as a shepherd. His sojourn in the country, during which he had opportunities both to pursue his love interest and to mix with genuine countryfolk, could be learning experience before this "courtly pastoralist"[78] returned to court.[79] More likely, though, it would be presented as a series of fabricated adventures, a literary jaunt that allowed, as Frank Kermode puts it, a highly "cultivated" consciousness to reflect in an "artificial way" on the "natural life."[80]

Act 4 of *The Winter's Tale* revitalizes and modifies these traditional elements of pastoral. On one level the Bohemian countryside serves as a healing environment an ocean away from the tyranny of Leontes. But it offers no bucolic paradise, no mythological golden world or Arcadia. It is not the Edenic state that Polixenes associates with childhood, when he and Leontes frisked like "twinned lambs" (1.2.67). Nor does it contain the stylized, literary shepherds and shepherdesses of pastoral tradition,[81] such as Silvius and Phoebe, who balance the yokels William and Audrey in Shakespeare's earlier pastoral comedy *As You Like It* (1599). Instead this is a tough rural community in which Dorcas wishes garlic breath on her rival Mopsa, and a Clown wonders where his adopted sister acquired a taste for rice. Replacing the courtly commentators Jacques and Touch-stone of *As You Like It* is the predatory rogue Autolycus, a "refugee-pirate from the city" who exposes the "naivete and gullibility of the shepherd's restricted life"[82] by fleecing the rustics at their sheep-shearing. Yet the oc-togenarian Shepherd is no fool; he (like some wealthy farmers in Jacobean England) has shrewdly turned a profit from plentiful wool after purchas-ing grazing land with the gold that accompanied Perdita. He remains a hard-working man who, fearing that King Polixenes will take away his livelihood, asks little more than to be buried next to the "honest bones" of his father (4.4.460). Meanwhile his son, the Clown, a pragmatic social climber, happily exchanges rural life in Bohemia for that of the Sicilian court at the end of the play.

This partial crossover between court and country, discussed earlier in this chapter as a means of linking the separate worlds of Sicily and Bo-hemia, complicates the pastoral world of *The Winter's Tale.* Infiltrated by aristocrats, rural Bohemia cannot be an entirely "accurate reflection of the material conditions of an agrarian society."[83] Prince Florizel, only playing at being a rustic, brings romantic idealism to the rural community. Unlike Calidore, a courteous knight in Spenser's *The Faerie Queene* who falls in love with the shepherdess Pastorella, the prince does not need to take on the persona of a shepherd in order to win his lady. Nevertheless his disguise as swain proves both a liberation and a testing ground.[84] Through it Florizel must learn to temper his passion, or hotter "lusts" (34), with reason and forbearance, two qualities that the Old Shepherd displays.[85] Near the end of the play we hear that Florizel has embraced the Clown as his new "brother," thus confirming the idealized "relation between rich and poor"[86] that pastoral often promotes. But this salutary "trip to the real countryside," as Peter Lindenbaum calls it,[87] works only briefly to soften the attitudes of King Polixenes, the other royal who enters this world in disguise. The king is impressed with Perdita as a "low-born lass" who combines "noble" demeanor (156, 159), as she dances and distributes flowers, with spontaneity and a passion for life; but his courtly values surface with a vengeance when he rejects any union between "bark of baser kind," the supposed shepherdess, and "bud of nobler race," the prince (94–95).

Apart from Perdita's brief discussion of art and nature with Polixenes, the relative merits of court and country are never directly debated in *The Winter's Tale*. But the princess-as-shepherdess, combining the tough realism of "I told you what would come of this" (451) with aristocratic graciousness when she welcomes guests and dances "featly" (176), seems a perfect blend of the two worlds. She voices the wholesome bias of the country, defending nature against the tampering art of grafting; at the same time, though, she upholds the aristocratic status quo by condemning cross-breeding. Technically, because she is a true princess, courtly and rustic values need never coalesce in her. Yet the virtues of honesty and simplicity, presumably imbibed from the Old Shepherd as part of her rural upbringing, have become an integral part of Perdita's character, reinforcing her inborn gentility. This means that when she and Florizel make their way to Sicily, as welcome as "spring" is to the earth (5.1.152), Perdita can legitimately bring not only royalty but pastoral strengths to renew the court of Leontes.[88]

## TRAGICOMEDY

In his *Defence of Poetry* (1595), Philip Sidney decries "mongrell Tragicomedie." He claims that with its indecorous mingling of hornpipes and funerals, clowns and monarchs, it fails to achieve the "sportfulness" of comedy or the "admiration and Commiseration" of tragedy.[89] Yet English drama in the early modern period was never constrained by neoclassical rules; from medieval mystery plays to late sixteenth-century romances, it reveled in a farrago of the comic and serious. Thomas Preston's *Cambises* (c. 1561), for instance, advertised itself as a "lamentable Tragedie mixed full of pleasant mirth." "Pyramus and Thisbe," performed by the artisans near the end of *A Midsummer Night's Dream* (1595–1596), is billed as "tragical mirth," and Shakespeare experiments with tonal incongruity in his early tragedy *Romeo and Juliet* (1595–1596), where the music planned for Juliet's wedding must quickly transform into a "merry dump" (4.5.107) when her parents think she is dead. Verbal images in Shakespeare's plays often trade in startling incongruities. In *The Winter's Tale,* Paulina's tragicomic mix of sorrow and joy in having "one eye declined for the loss of her husband, another elevated that the oracle was fulfilled" (5.2.79–81), is anticipated in the equally strange collocations of celebration and mourning—"mirth in funeral, dirge in marriage"—with which Claudius glosses over his hasty marriage to the widow Gertrude in *Hamlet* (1.2.11).

In many of his dramatic plots, too, Shakespeare is interested in how joy can suddenly darken, or a potentially tragic configuration of events may find a happy resolution. Samuel Johnson's observation that Shakespeare's plays are not pure comedies or tragedies but a "mingled drama" of "good and evil, joy and sorrow"[90] is well taken when it comes to the balancing of the two modes in the late tragedy *Antony and Cleopatra,* where the queen turns death into a wedding celebration. By the same token, dark elements intrude in the romantic comedies. *Much Ado about Nothing* (c. 1599) resembles *The Winter's Tale* in using the potentially tragic motif of a slandered woman who is thought to have died but is discovered to be alive at the end of the play. Even *Comedy of Errors,* possibly Shakespeare's earliest (and in some ways most ebullient) experiment in comic form, provides a tragic frame in its opening act. The merchant Egeon, sentenced to be executed in Ephesus unless he can be ransomed by sundown, appears to be a character "whom the fates have mark'd / To bear the extremity of dire mishap" (1.1.140–41). But by act 5 not only are his long-lost twin sons found, but his supposedly dead wife turns up as the Abbess in the local priory. Her jubilant summation, "After so long grief, such nativity!" (5.1.407), looks forward to the fuller movement from near-tragedy to comic birth in the Late Plays.

*The Comedy of Errors* was largely based on the *Menaechmi* of Plautus, who used the term "tragicomedia" to justify the mixture of high and low characters in another of his plays, *Amphityron.* Promoters of tragicomedy as a genre in the late sixteenth century could point to a classical heritage not only from Plautus but from Euripides, who provides a set of happy outcomes to offset catastrophe in his tragedies *Alcestis* and *Iphigenia in Tauris.* This "double" plot, in which one set of characters reverses the tragic pattern by moving from misfortune to good fortune,[91] was discussed by Aristotle in his section on tragedy in the *Poetics;* it provides a precedent for the single plot that Shakespeare follows in *The Winter's Tale,* where an action that seemed headed for catastrophe ends with a comic resolution.

By the time Ben Jonson's plays were published in a folio collection in 1616, the illustrated frontispiece placed "tragicomoedia" in a prominent position. Shown with the simple tunic and sock of comedy but carrying the scepter of tragedy, this figure stands between and slightly above Satyr and Pastor (the satirical and the pastoral), with Tragoedia and Comoedia, one on each side, supporting her from below. Her position at the top suggests that tragicomedy was now an artistically respectable form.[92] It was also an eclectic one. The genre includes Marston's satirical play *The Malcontent,* registered in 1604 as "Tragicomoedia." This drama wrenches potential tragedy into a finale in which errant characters are not punished by death but scourged by the virulent tongue of the satirist Malevole. Jonson's *Volpone* (1606) resembles *The Malcontent* in being harshly satiric in emphasis, neither pure comedy nor tragedy.[93] Shakespeare's problem plays or dark comedies, *Troilus and Cressida* (1601–1602), *All's Well That Ends Well* (1602–1604), and *Measure for Measure* (1604), written close in date to his tragedies, are also dark in tone. They too are sometimes labeled tragicomedies (by modern critics, not in Shakespeare's time) because they incorporate potentially tragic material but waive final disaster.

As a romantic tragicomedy, *The Winter's Tale* avoids the satirical edge and deeply ambivalent endings of the dark comedies. Although there is no evidence that Shakespeare deliberately followed the model provided by the Italian playwright and commentator Guarini, his later tragicomic form does show some affinities with it. Guarini's influential defense of pastoral tragicomedy as a genre in its own right sprang from discussion of his own play *Il Pastor Fido* (1590). In his *Compendio* (1601) he upheld tragicomedy as a legitimate genre by defining it as an original blend of comic and tragic. Not simply a binary structure, or tragedy with a happy ending tacked on, tragicomedy is envisaged as a unique compound, a "third thing that will be perfect in its kind."[94] It takes from tragedy "its danger but not its death" and from comedy its complex plotting and "happy reversal."[95] Fletcher, who succeeded Shakespeare after 1612 as the King's Men's leading dramatist, adopted Guarini's terms in support of his own pastoral tragicomedy, *The Faithful Shepherdess.* In his preface to that play (1608), Fletcher echoes Guarini's danger-without-death formulation when he argues that tragicomedy is not an indiscriminate hodgepodge of "mirth and killing"; rather, "it wants [lacks] deaths, which is enough to make it no tragedy, yet brings some near it, which is enough to make it no comedy."[96] The form that Fletcher and his colleague Francis Beaumont produced in *Philaster* (1610) manipulates audience emotions by taking the characters to the brink of dramatic disaster—in one scene a series of stabbings provides the "danger" of violent deaths for the lovers—but rescues them at the last moment. In *The Winter's Tale,* too, Shakespeare's tragicomic effects are sometimes sensational. "Exit pursued by a bear" is notorious,[97] but in this case there is no reprieve; danger more realistically turns into death when Antigonus is killed and eaten by the bear.

Shakespeare seems closer to Guarini's model for tragicomedy when he prepares the audience early in the play for an upturn to comedy; Antigonus predicts an outcome of eventual "laughter" (2.1.198), and the pastoral episodes prove restorative. But most of the play produces not a "tempering of extremes"[98] or a "fusion of the two modes"[99] as much as bifurcation of elements, an oscillation between contrary perspectives. What Rosalie A. Colie calls the "unvarnished conjunction of tragedy with comedy"[100] is most pronounced in the pivotal scene at the very center of the play (3.3). This is a "volatile mix"[101] in which the Old Shepherd discovers baby Perdita even as his son is witnessing "souls" perishing in a shipwreck and the bear eating Antigonus (90). Something closer to Guarini's "blending of tones"[102]—the double effect of "doleful matter merrily set down; or a very pleasant thing indeed, and sung lamentally," as the Clown puts it (4.4.188–90)—is achieved through the style of act 5, scene 2. Here the Third Gentleman reports a tragicomic mix of jubilation and sadness where "joy waded in tears" (49). Yet even at this point opposites may remain in paradoxical tension, as in the almost absurd image of Paulina's eyes, one elevated, one declined, gazing in two directions.

In Shakespeare's romantic tragicomedies it is the climactic moment of discovery that signals a decisive shift in mode from tragic to comic. The shock of the final revelation in *The Winter's Tale,* the statue coming to life, is felt acutely by the audience because they, too, have been lured into believing that Hermione is dead. They are nevertheless able to accept the wonderful event as what Guarini calls a "credible miracle"[103] appropriate to act 5 of a tragicomedy. While Shakespeare's brand of tragicomedy often sharply juxtaposes the ultra-serious with the comic, it also develops as a cycle of renewal that can happen only after a destructive movement—the jealous tyranny of Leontes leading to the apparent demise of Hermione and the actual death of Mamillius—has come as close as possible to absolute tragedy. Even in the play's finale there is still the double sense of a "world ransomed, or one destroyed" (5.2.16–17). The promise of second chances is strong, but the future is regained at some cost.[104] Because neither Mamillius nor Antigonus can be restored to life, the play retains traces of tragedy even within its final comic resolution.

Some critics have suggested that tragicomedy's experimental quality, its shifts of perspective and deliberate flouting of expectations as it refuses to adhere to one form or mode, make it a political vehicle sympathetic to "revolution."[105] In the years leading up to the English Civil War (1642–1645) the form may have challenged aristocratic assumptions;[106] yet later tragicomedy, building toward the restoration of the monarchy in 1660, more closely reflects royalist sympathies.[107] Similarly *The Winter's Tale,* despite some qualifications in its happy ending, remains essentially conservative in its ideological bias. The play engineers a romantic (though not naively ideal) resolution through the preservation of the royal family.

## MYTH, ALLEGORY, AND SYMBOLISM

Pagan fertility myth[108] or Christian allegory? Even more than Shakespeare's other romantic tragicomedies, *The Winter's Tale* has lent itself to such readings. The very title of the play indicates the low point of the seasonal cycle before winter—with Leontes as the death-oriented man who dwells "by a churchyard" (2.1.30)—turns to spring, with Perdita alluding, through the flowers of Proserpina, to Ovid's myth of metamorphosis.[109] Northrop Frye, among others, finds that this mythical "Proserpine figure" symbolizes the move from death to "rebirth"[110] and, in line with his theory of myths,[111] discusses how *The Winter's Tale* contains the "spring" of comedy within the maturer "summer" of romance. Certainly "great creating Nature" (4.4.88) pulses through the play, preparing us for the renewal at its close more than does the Greek god Apollo and his oracle. Yet the chastened tone of the final act, as Leontes consolidates his "saint-like sorrow," seems more conducive to Christian than pagan mysteries (5.1.2). In such a context even Perdita, previously associated with Proserpina and the pagan goddess Flora, might begin a "sect" and "make proselytes" (107–8); we are prepared for the king to be redeemed as he awakens his "faith" in the statue's ability to return to life (5.3.95). Thus S. L. Bethell discusses the restoration of Hermione as a "carefully prepared symbol of spiritual and actual resurrection,"[112] while E. M. W. Tillyard tends to allegorize the play as a progress from "hell and purgatory" to the "motive of paradise" in the statue scene.[113] More eclectically, G. Wilson Knight explores the "pagan naturalism" of the play as well as its myth of "immortality."[114]

Stressing the visionary quality of the last scene, as Knight does, seems wise if we are to avoid reducing the play to a set mythological pattern. Although readers and audiences may respond strongly to its mythic and religious undertones, the play is not doctrinal. Watching the statue transform into the living Hermione can become a shared ritual. It is a collective gasp of "wonder" (5.3.22), a renewed faith in how miraculous life can be once a flawed human being (in this case Leontes), having reached an appropriate emotional and mental state, is given a second chance at happiness.[115] No surprise, then, that some critics have interpreted the play through in-depth psychology, relating it to archetypes of human experience, or seeing it as a Jungian quest toward individuation.[116] Leontes must move from boyhood to manhood; in this interpretation Mamillius might represent that youthful part of the psyche that must forever be relinquished or integrated into the mature individual.[117]

Such interpretations can open windows on the play. Yet it is important to note that "nothing in the dramatic world of *The Winter's Tale* exists purely or simply for its archetypal dimension,"[118] just as the play's particular presentation of a tragicomic experience, its detail and texture as it unfolds in time, goes beyond any neat theological formulation. Thus Philip Edwards, alert to the dangers of "sentimental religiosity," warns against interpreting the plots of Shakespeare's romances as "symbolic vehicles" for what may (shorn of their nuanced presentation) turn out to be very obvious, "trite and colourless" ideas.[119]

The raging bear that pursues Antigonus in act 3, scene 3 is nothing if not colorful. It kills the one remaining Sicilian courtier who could report what has happened to Perdita, and is also pivotal in shifting the dramatic tone away from tragedy into grotesque comedy.[120] More than a device to move along the plot and bridge the two halves of the play, however, the bear has proved a rich source of symbolic meanings. Like the storm, it seems to represent a "violent unleashing of the irrational forces of nature,"[121] a destructive counterpoint to nature's creative aspects. Dennis Biggens mor-alistically considers the savage animal an "instrument of divine wrath" to punish Antigonus for agreeing to perform Leontes's "savagely cruel er-rand."[122] An interpretation less damning to Antigonus views the bear as a surrogate for Leontes[123] (the Clown later compares "authority" to a "stub-born bear" [4.4.808–9]); in this reading the old courtier suffers the deadly consequences of the king's mistake in casting out his child. It is appropri-ate, too, that a bear becomes what Michael D. Bristol calls a "temporal marker"[124] between wintry Sicily and the summer of Bohemia, enabling a transition from "destruction to rebirth."[125] Hibernating all winter and emerging with its cubs in the spring, the bear has traditionally symbolized "springtime rebirth."[126]

## NOTES

1. Richard Proudfoot, "Verbal Reminiscence and the Two-Part Structure of *The Winter's Tale*," *ShS* 29 (1976), 67–78, discusses the "sharp division" of the action into two halves (67).

2.  S.L. Bethell, The Winter's Tale: *A Study* (London: Staples Press Ltd., 1947), remarks that a modern parallel to this "old joke of international reputation" would be jesting about the Swiss navy (33).

3.  Robert M. Adams, *Shakespeare: The Four Romances* (New York and London: W.W. Norton & Co., 1989), suggests that Bohemia, in some ways "unsophisticated and downright provincial," is a "kind of transposed England" and Sicilia "a surrogate Italy" (93–94).

4.  Graham Holderness, "*The Winter's Tale:* Country into Court," in *Shakespeare: Out of Court,* ed. Graham Holderness, Nick Potter, John Turner (New York: St. Martin's Press, 1990), p. 228. Craig Horton, "The Country Must Diminish: Jacobean London and the Production of Pastoral Space in *The Winter's Tale,*" *Paragon* 20, no. 1 (2003): 85–107, also points to the "dissolution of clear boundaries between city and country" in early seventeenth-century London that is mirrored in rural Bohemia (88).

5.  See Edward M. Moore (ed.), Harley Granville-Barker, *More Prefaces to Shakespeare* (Princeton, N.J.: Princeton University Press, 1974), *Preface to* The Winter's Tale (1912), where Granville-Barker comments on how "the very suddenness of the catastrophe leaves us, paradoxically enough, expectant of some happier resolution" (20).

6.  Barbara A. Mowat, *Dramaturgy in Shakespeare's Romances* (Athens, Ga.: University of Georgia Press, 1976), discusses in detail how the "Leontes-story" is not a tragedy (8–20).

7.  Kathleen Latimer, "The Communal Action of *The Winter's Tale,*" in Louise Cowan (ed.), *The Terrain of Comedy* (Dallas, Tx.: The Dallas Institute of Humanities and Culture, 1984), pp. 125–42, discusses how the efforts of this larger community help to deflect "the protagonist's potentially tragic action" into "an ultimately comic pattern" (139).

8.  Charles Frey, "Tragic Structure in *The Winter's Tale,*" in Carol McGinnis Kay and Henry E. Jacobs (eds.), *Shakespeare's Romances Reconsidered* (Lincoln and London: The University of Nebraska Press, 1978), suggests that Leontes "out Herods Herod," the tyrant of the Mystery play cycles, by "pointing Hermione offstage, forcing Paulina's exit, stalking around the infant Perdita, plucking Antigonus's beard" (122–23).

9.  Nevill Coghill, "Six Points of Stage-Craft in *The Winter's Tale,*" *ShS* 11 (1958): 31–41, comments on how the audience, in a technique of "prepared surprise," is prepared for what "it is about *not* to see" (32).

10.  In contrast, Derek Traversi, *Shakespeare: The Last Phase* (Stanford, Calif.: Stanford University Press, 1953), thinks that "hidden seeds of division" are suggested by the "branch" image (107–8).

11.  Among other critics, Ralph Berry, "*The Winter's Tale:* A Dance to the Music of Time," in *Shakespearean Structures* (Totowa, N.J.: Barnes and Noble Books, 1981), comments on the "stealthy advance of the comic spirit" (133).

12.  Coghill, "Six Points of Stage-craft in *The Winter's Tale,*" p. 35.

13.  Adams, *Shakespeare: The Four Romances,* comments on how "authorial indirection" here is calculated to make the reversal of act 5 "more amazing" (99).

14.  For ways in which Autolycus is a "restorative, antitoxic" counterpart to Leontes, see Berry, *Shakespearean Structures,* p. 132. Howard Felperin, *Shakespearean Romance* (Princeton, N.J.: Princeton University Press, 1972), also comments on how Leontes's "insane dreams" are reworked and "rendered into harmless fantasy" by Autolycus (234).

15.  Mowat, *Dramaturgy of Shakespeare's Romances,* p. 25.

16.  See Ernest Schanzer (ed.), William Shakespeare, *The Winter's Tale,* The New Penguin Shakespeare (London and New York: Penguin, 1986), pp. 30–35. Proudfoot, "Verbal Reminiscence," also discusses how both "minuteness of detail" and the "broadest effects of repetition and contrast" provide continuity in the play (68). J.H.P. Pafford (ed.), *The Winter's Tale,* The Arden Shakespeare (London: Methuen & Co. Ltd., 1963), notes that none of the play's three main parts is a "true dramatic unit" but that all cohere in a "clear unity of design" (lv).

17.  Schanzer (ed.), *The Winter's Tale,* p. 35.

18.  Clifford Leech, "The Structure of the Last Plays," *ShS* 11 (1958): 19–30, argues that *The Winter's Tale* provides both a resolution to the crisis of the Leontes-Hermione plot and the suggestion of a "recurrent pattern" (19) in the "unfinished story" of the next generation, Florizel and Perdita (25).

19.  Noted by Proudfoot, "Verbal Reminiscence," 69. James Edward Siemon, "'But It Appears She Lives': Iteration in *The Winter's Tale,*" *PMLA* 89, no. 1 (1974): 10–15, also notes the "mistaking of true value" in the parallel situations of Hermione and Perdita, and how the "negative possibilities" explored in the first part of the play give way to "positive possibilities," gain from loss, in the second part (15).

20.  Frey, "Tragic Structure in *The Winter's Tale,*" points how out Leontes treats Hermione like a statue in the trial scene (122).

21.  Also discussed by Schanzer (ed.), *The Winter's Tale,* p. 36. Offering a slightly different perspective on the play's mirrorings, William Blissett, "This Wide Gap of Time": *The Winter's Tale,*" *ELR* 1 (1971): 52–70, notes that the two parts of the play, based on "nothing" and "nature" respectively, are like the "positive and negative of a photograph" (55).

22.  Proudfoot, "Verbal Reminiscence," 69.

23.  Charles R. Forker, *Fancy's Images: Contexts, Settings, and Perspectives in Shakespeare and His Contemporaries* (Carbondale and Edwardsville: Southern Illinois University Press, 1990), discusses in detail how Perdita's lyrical "flower aria," as well as spanning the seasons and bridging youth and age, calls on the "memory of past events and subtly anticipate[s] future ones" (117, 123).

24.  See David Young, *The Heart's Forest: A Study of Shakespeare's Pastoral Plays* (New Haven and London: Yale University Press, 1972), p. 134. G. Wilson Knight, "'Great Creating Nature': An Essay on *The Winter's Tale,*" in *The Crown*

*of Life* (London: Methuen and Co., Ltd., 1948), also finds that events move ahead with a "whirling, sickening speed" in the first part of the play (96).

25.   Pafford (ed.), *The Winter's Tale,* The Arden Shakespeare, points out that sheep-shearing should take place in mid-June (lxix).

26.   Coghill, "Six Points of Stagecraft in *The Winter's Tale,*" 35.

27.   Inga-Stina Ewbank, "The Triumph of Time in *The Winter's Tale,*" *REL* 5 (1964): 83–100, explores the "pivotal image" of the Triumph of Time (90), with a final emphasis on Time the Revealer (86).

28.   Coghill, "Six Points of Stagecraft in *The Winter's Tale,*" 36.

29.   Felperin, *Shakespearean Romance,* p. 230. L. G. Salingar, "Time and Art in Shakespeare's Romances," *RenD* 9 (1966): 3–35, also points out how Time communicates an "imaginative, subjective" experience of time "to the minds of the audience" (6).

30.   Stanton B. Garner, Jr., "Time and Presence in *The Winter's Tale,*" *MLQ* 46 (1985): 347–67, explores how the play counterpoints the "immediacy" of the moment with time "understood through its effects of change and consequence" (353, 361).

31.   Young, *The Heart's Forest,* notes how Time's speech touches on "the artist's attitudes toward his materials" (144). Like Time, Shakespeare has defiantly overthrown "law" and "custom" in his unusual dramatic structuring of *The Winter's Tale*.

32.   Schanzer (ed.), *The Winter's Tale,* p. 30.

33.   See Charles Frey, "The Play in Time," in *Shakespeare's Vast Romance: A Study of* The Winter's Tale (Columbia and London: University of Missouri Press, 1980), p. 163.

34.   See Rosalie A. Colie, "Genre-Systems and the Functions of Literature," in *The Resources of Kind: Genre Theory in the Renaissance* (Berkeley, Los Angeles, London: University of California Press, 1973), p. 3.

35.   In "Perspectives on Pastoral Romance, Comic and Tragic," in *Shakespeare's Living Art* (Princeton, N.J.: Princeton University Press, 1974), Rosalie A. Colie equates Renaissance "pastoral drama" with "tragicomedy" (267), while R. S. White, *"Let Wonder Seem Familiar": The Endings of Shakespeare's Romances* (Atlantic Highlands, N.J.: Humanities Press, 1985), notes that in romance the pastoral is "cradled as a parenthesis within the unending process of time" (5).

36.   Stephen Orgel (ed.), William Shakespeare, *The Winter's Tale,* The Oxford Shakespeare (Oxford: Oxford University Press, 1994), p. 37.

37.   The idea of Shakespeare reaching serenity (reflected in the Late Plays) after a spiritual crisis is explored by Edward Dowden, *Shakespeare: A Critical View of His Mind and Art* (New York and London: Harper and Brothers, 1881), p. 338. More recently, Kiernan Ryan (ed.), *Shakespeare: The Last Plays* (London and New York: Longman, 1999), speculates that the "peculiar intensity and resonance of these parables of expiation may owe much" to Shakespeare's "prospective retirement" to dwell with his wife and daughters (5).

38.   E.M.W. Tillyard, *Shakespeare's Last Plays* (London: Chatto and Windus, 1954), finds in the Late Plays the "final, regenerative phase of the tragic

pattern" (21), while Robert Uphaus, *Beyond Tragedy: Structure and Experience in Shakespeare's Romances* (Lexington: University of Kentucky Press, 1981), stresses the plays' "emphasis on the cycle of life and death as a continuation of the larger processes of life itself" (5).

39.   This view is challenged by Tillyard, *Shakespeare's Last Plays,* p. 48.

40.   Fitzroy Pyle, The Winter's Tale: *A Commentary on the Structure* (New York: Barnes and Noble Inc., 1961), calls these plays a "sophistication" of romance, "deliberate exercises … made from a more self-conscious artistic standpoint" (183).

41.   S. L. Bethell, *Shakespeare's* The Winter's Tale, p. 50.

42.   Lytton Strachey, "Shakespeare's Final Period," in *Books and Characters* (London: Chatto and Windus, 1922), p. 60.

43.   See Barbara A. Mowat, "The Romances as Open Form Drama," in *The Dramaturgy of Shakespeare's Romances,* pp. 95–110. Stephen J. Miko, "Winter's Tale," *SEL* 29 (1989): 259–75, also discusses how Shakespeare's attitude, as he tests the limits of romantic conventions, is "not merely experimental but playful" (260). John Greenwood, *Shifting Perspectives and the Stylish Style: Mannerism in Shakespeare and His Jacobean Contemporaries* (Toronto, Buffalo, London: University of Toronto Press, 1988), discusses *The Winter's Tale,* with its "deliberate cultivation of illusory awareness," as an "archetypically mannerist play" (187).

44.   Bethell, *Shakespeare's* The Winter's Tale, p. 20.

45.   See G. E. Bentley, "Shakespeare and the Blackfriars Theatre," *ShS* 1 (1948): 38–50.

46.   See R. A. Foakes, "Playhouses and Players," in A. R. Braunmuller and Michael Hattaway (eds.), *The Cambridge Companion to English Renaissance Drama* (Cambridge: Cambridge University Press, 1990), pp. 1–52, 27, and Pyle, The Winter's Tale*: A Commentary,* Appendix II, "The Blackfriars Theatre, and the Question of Genre," pp. 171–90.

47.   See Daniel Seltzer, "The Staging of the Last Plays," in J. R. Brown and Bernard Harris (eds.), *Later Shakespeare,* Stratford-upon-Avon Studies 8 (New York: St. Martin's Press, 1967), pp. 127–65, 128.

48.   Bernard Beckerman, *Shakespeare at the Globe, 1599–1609* (New York: The Macmillan Company, 1962), conjectures that "no machinery for flying" existed at the Globe (94).

49.   Northrop Frye, "Romance as Masque," in Kay and Jacobs (eds.), *Shakespeare's Romances Reconsidered,* suggests that the "ascending movement from chaos and absurdity to peace and order" in Shakespeare's Late Plays resembles the "polarity of the antimasque and masque" (30).

50.   J. M. Nosworthy, "Music and its Function in Shakespeare's Romances," *ShS* 11 (1958): 64–68, 68.

51.   Bentley, "Shakespeare and the Blackfriars Theatre," argues that Shakespeare produced a "new kind of play for the new theatre and audience" at the private Blackfriars (49).

52.   Roger Warren, *Staging Shakespeare's Late Plays* (Oxford: Clarendon Press, 1990), thinks that rather than alienating the audience, these theatrical de-

vices "seem to act as a kind of shock tactic, to focus maximum attention upon the individual human emotions and situations that are displayed on stage in an extreme form—love, despair, jealousy, death and burial, reconciliation and forgiveness" (6).

53.  Felperin, *Shakespearean Romance,* p. 289.

54.  Northrop Frye, *The Secular Scripture: A Study of the Structure of Romance* (Cambridge, Mass., and London: Harvard University Press, 1978), p. 15.

55.  Northrop Frye, *The Anatomy of Criticism* (1957; Princeton, N.J.: Princeton University Press, 1971), p. 151.

56.  Northrop Frye, "The 'Triumph of Time,'" in *A Natural Perspective* (New York and London: Columbia University Press, 1965), pp. 116–17.

57.  Cyrus Hoy, *The Hyacinth Room: An Investigation into the Nature of Comedy, Tragedy, and Tragicomedy* (New York: Alfred A. Knopf, 1964), p. 273.

58.  Marco Mincoff, *Things Supernatural and Causeless: Shakespearean Romance* (London and Toronto: Associated University Presses, 1992), argues that in Greek romance human beings are more "playthings of fortune" than guided by Providence (22), and R. A. Foakes, *Shakespeare, The Dark Comedies: From Satire to Celebration* (London: Routledge and K. Paul, 1971), also emphasizes the sense of "inscrutable providence" in *The Winter's Tale* (128). In contrast, John F. Danby, *Elizabethan and Jacobean Poets* (London: Faber and Faber Ltd., 1965), finds that in Romance the "sphere of the transcendent" encloses the sphere of "non-human accident, chance, or misfortune"; human patience is rewarded with a providential outcome (80).

59.  These are outlined in White, *"Let Wonder Seem Familiar,"* pp. 177–82.

60.  See Hallett Smith, *Shakespeare's Romances: A Study of Some Ways of the Imagination* (San Marino, Calif.: The Huntingdon Library, 1972), pp. 8–9. Salingar, "Time and Art in Shakespeare's Romances," also points out how Euripidean romance focuses on recognition and "the re-establishment of a divided family" (8).

61.  Carol Gesner, *Shakespeare and the Greek Romance: A Study of Origins* (Lexington: The University of Kentucky, 1970), p. 119, finds *Aethiopica,* with its shipwrecks and "exposure and restoration" of a royal child, an influence on *The Winter's Tale,* but mainly through Greene's *Pandosto.*

62.  This is discussed as part of the romance tradition by E. C. Pettet, *Shakespeare and the Romance Tradition* (New York: Staples Press, Ltd., 1949), pp. 23–32.

63.  See Felperin, *Shakespearean Romance,* pp. 12–16, and Robert Grams Hunter, *Shakespeare and the Comedy of Forgiveness* (New York and London: Columbia University Press, 1965). Louis L. Martz, *"The Winter's Tale:* Trilogy of Redemption," in *From Renaissance to Baroque: Essays on Literature and Art* (Columbia: University of Missouri Press, 1991), 131–45, argues that the third part of the play is "miracle" (138). H. W. Fawkner, *Shakespeare's Miracle Plays:* Pericles, Cymbeline, *and* The Winter's Tale (London and Toronto: Associated University Presses, 1992), also finds an "extraordinary concentration on the idea

of miraculous recovery" in the play (24), where the resurrection of Hermione is divorced from any "logically causal context" (65).

64.   Cited in White, *"Let Wonder Seem Familiar,"* p. 22.

65.   Ibid., p. 2. Patricia Parker, *Inescapable Romance: Studies in the Poetics of a Mode* (Princeton, N.J.: Princeton University Press, 1979), observes the principle of deferral in romance, a "form which simultaneously quests for and postpones a particular end, objective or object" (4). J.M. Nosworthy (ed.), William Shakespeare, *Cymbeline,* The New Arden Shakespeare (London: Methuen, 1963), also points out the "structural challenge" of romance, where "problems of space and time" are transferred to the stage (xxxii).

66.   *The Defence of Poesie,* in Albert Feuillerat (ed.), *The Prose Works of Sir Philip Sidney,* vol. 3 (1912; Cambridge: Cambridge University Press, 1963), p. 38.

67.   Pettet, *Shakespeare and the Romance Tradition,* p. 27.

68.   Kiernan Ryan (ed.), "Introduction," *Shakespeare: The Last Plays* (London and New York: Longman, 1999), p. 15.

69.   Ibid., p. 5.

70.   Felperin, *Shakespearean Romance,* p. 244.

71.   These and other details are pointed out by Mincoff, *Things Supernatural and Causeless,* p. 84.

72.   Felperin, *Shakespearean Romance,* p. 220.

73.   Frye, *The Anatomy of Criticism,* p. 193.

74.   Frye, *A Natural Perspective,* p. 117.

75.   Frank Kermode (ed.), *English Pastoral Poetry from the Beginnings to Marvell* (London: George Harrap & Co. Ltd., 1952), notes that in this tradition the shepherd, as a "natural piper and singer," is "easily made to stand for the poet" (18).

76.   See Thomas McFarland, *Shakespeare's Pastoral Comedy* (Chapel Hill: The University of North Carolina Press, 1972), pp. 22–24.

77.   Outlined by Young, *The Heart's Forest,* p. x.

78.   Paul Alpers, *What Is Pastoral?* (Chicago and London: University of Chicago Press, 1996), p. 204.

79.   Holderness, *The Winter's Tale:* Country into Court," discusses how the court could thus become "regenerated and reconstructed" (196). Peter Marinelli, *Pastoral* (London: Methuen & Co., Ltd., 1971), also notes how the "courtly invaders" are expected to return to the city or court and "renew and regenerate it by the knowledge they have gained" from their experience in the country (62).

80.   Kermode, *English Pastoral Poetry,* p. 12.

81.   See Walter W. Greg, *Pastoral Poetry and Pastoral Drama* (London: A.H. Bullen, 1906), p. 411.

82.   Colie, "Perspectives on Pastoral," in *Shakespeare's Living Art,* p. 272. Bethell, The Winter's Tale: *A Study,* also thinks the play shows the "shortcomings of country life" but that it nevertheless asserts the "priority of the agrarian life in the scale of social values" (93).

83.   Louis Adrian Montrose, "Of Gentlemen and Shepherds: The Politics of Elizabethan Pastoral Form," *ELH* 50, no. 3 (Fall 1983): 415–59, 418. Montrose

finds that in pastoral "agrarian social relations" are "reinscribed within an ideology of the court" (431).

84. Castiglione's recommendation in *The Book of the Courtier* that the courtier dress as a "rustic shepherd" to release his natural charm and grace, since "masquerading carries with it a certain freedom and licence" is pointed out by Harold E. Toliver, "Pastoral Hierarchy and Entelechy" in *Pastoral Forms and Attitudes* (Berkeley, Los Angeles, London: University of California Press, 1971), p. 27.

85. Philip M. Weinstein, "An Interpretation of Pastoral in *The Winter's Tale*," *SQ* 22 (1971): 97–109, also discusses how Florizel's progress shows how "passion … when informed by reason, can become creative" (109).

86. William Empson, *Some Versions of Pastoral* (1935; Harmondsworth: Penguin, 1966), p. 17.

87. Peter Lindenbaum, "Time, Sexual Love, and the Uses of Pastoral in *The Winter's Tale*," *MLQ* 33, no. 1 (1972): 3–22, 6. Lindenbaum contends that Perdita's healthy attitude toward the progress of sexual love repudiates Polixenes's regressive definition of sexuality in terms of the Fall (14–16).

88. Derek Traversi, *Shakespeare's Last Phase* (Stanford, Calif.: Stanford University Press, 1953), comments on how "pastoral simplicity" must be assimilated into "the courtly order" before the end of the play (140–41).

89. *The Defence of Poesie,* in Feuillerat (ed.), *The Prose Works of Sir Philip Sidney,* vol. 3, p. 39.

90. Samuel Johnson, Preface, *The Plays of Shakespeare,* in *Dr. Johnson on Shakespeare,* ed. W. K. Wimsatt (Harmondsworth: Penguin, 1969), p. 62.

91. Sixteenth-century English plays of the "Christian Terence" school, written in Latin, were also tragedies with a happy ending. See Marvin T. Herrick, *Tragicomedy: Its Origin and Development in Italy, France, and England* (Urbana: University of Illinois Press, 1955), pp. 16–62, 62.

92. The "Introduction" to Gordon McMullen and Jonathan Hope (eds.), *The Politics of Tragicomedy: Shakespeare and After* (London and New York: Routledge, 1992), points out that tragicomedy became enormously popular, "arguably the most important dramatic genre of the period 1610–50" (1).

93. R. A. Foakes, "Tragicomedy and Tragic Form, " in A. R. Braunmuller and J. C. Bulman (eds.), *Comedy from Shakespeare to Sheridan* (London and Toronto: Associated University Presses, 1986), pp. 74–88, discusses how "The growth of satirical drama fed into the development of tragicomedy" (77).

94. Discussed by Joan Hartwig, *Shakespeare's Tragicomic Vision* (Baton Rouge: Louisiana State University, 1972), p. 17.

95. Madeleine Doran cites and discusses the *Compendio* in *Endeavors of Art: A Study of Form in Elizabethan Drama* (Madison: University of Wisconsin Press, 1964), pp. 203–9, 207. David L. Hirst, *Tragicomedy* (London and New York: Methuen, 1984) also discusses Guarini's theories in helpful detail (6).

96. "To the Reader," *The Faithful Shepherdess,* in *Beaumont and Fletcher: Select Plays,* introd. M. C. Bradbrook (London: Dent, 1962), p. 242.

97. Louise G. Clubb, "The Tragicomic Bear," *CompLit Stud* 9 (1972), 17–30, notes how in Italian pastoral tragicomedy the bear is associated with both

the "civilized and savage" and is therefore "appropriate to the tragicomic genre" (24–25).

98. Discussed by Barbara Mowat in "Shakespearean Tragicomedy," in Nancy Klein Maguire (ed.), *Renaissance Tragicomedy: Explorations in Genre and Politics* (New York: AMS Press, 1987), p. 85. In this chapter Mowat argues that Shakespeare's dark comedies are closer to Guarini's recommendations on tragicomedy than are his Late Plays.

99. Hartwig, *Shakespeare's Tragicomic Vision*, p. 17.

100. Colie, "Perspectives in Pastoral," in *Shakespeare's Living Art*, p. 268.

101. Hirst, *Tragicomedy*, applies this term to one type of tragicomedy that has become popular in the twentieth century (xi).

102. This is Doran's term, in *Endeavors of Art*, p. 206.

103. Mowat discusses this term in "Shakespearean Tragicomedy," p. 83.

104. John T. Shawcross, "The Generic Context: Tragicomedy as Genre, Past and Present," in Maguire (ed.), *Renaissance Tragicomedy*, comments on the "provisional" nature of the play's ending (29).

105. Nancy Klein Maguire, "Introduction: Towards Understanding Tragicomedy," in *Renaissance Tragicomedy*, ed. Maguire, p. 2.

106. Walter Cohen, "Prerevolutionary Drama," in Gordon McMullan and Jonathan Hope (eds.), *The Politics of Tragicomedy: Shakespeare and After* (London and New York: Routledge, 1992), finds oppositional stances in some popular tragicomedy of the period but admits that it is not the "most fertile ground for identifying a prerevolutionary tradition" (124–25).

107. See Lois Potter, "'True Tragicomedies' of the Civil War and the Commonwealth," in *Renaissance Tragicomedy*, ed. Maguire, pp. 196–217.

108. Suggested in F.C. Tinkler, *"The Winter's Tale,"* *Scrutiny* 5 (1936–37): 344–64, 358.

109. See David Armitage, "The Dismemberment of Orpheus: Mythic Elements in Shakespeare's Romances," *ShS* 39 (1987): 123–37, 130.

110. Frye, *The Anatomy of Criticism*, p. 183. F. David Hoeniger, "The Meaning of *The Winter's Tale*," *UTQ* 20 (1950–51): 11–26, finds in the play's Persephone myth a symbol of "man's hope in a blissful immortality" (23).

111. Frye, *The Anatomy of Criticism*, pp. 131–239.

112. Bethell, The Winter's Tale: *A Study*, p. 103.

113. Tillyard, *Shakespeare: The Last Plays*, p. 84.

114. Knight, *The Crown of Life*, pp. 128, 30.

115. William T. Matchett, "Some Dramatic Techniques in *The Winter's Tale*," *ShS* 23 (1969): 93–107, discusses how Shakespeare manipulates audience response so that "we participate in the loss and we participate in the miracle of restoration" (106). Robert R. Hellenga, "The Scandal of *The Winter's Tale*," *ES* 57, no. 1 (1976): 11–18, emphasizes the sheer fact of Hermione's return in the flesh—"an impossible desire has been satisfied"—above any symbolic interpretation (18).

116. Elizabeth Bieman, *William Shakespeare: The Romances* (Boston: Twayne Publishers, G.K. Hall & Co., 1990), finds "transformative reorderings

of persons, events, and societies" in the play (5); in particular, she explores the "puer-senex" archetype as it operates in Leontes (86).

117.   Other symbolic interpretations are just as convincing. Susan Snyder, "Mamillius and Gender Polarization in *The Winter's Tale*," *SQ* 50, no. 1 (1995): 1–8, points out how Mamillius, whose name stems from *mamilla* (meaning "breast" or "teat"), appears to represent the feminine principle. He becomes a victim of a world that, through the actions of Leontes, "ruthlessly polarizes male and female" (8).

118.   Felperin, *Shakespearean Romance,* p. 221.

119.   Philip Edwards, "Shakespeare's Romances: 1900–1957," *ShS* 11 (1958): 1–18, 11.

120.   Coghill, "Six Points of Stage-Craft in *The Winter's Tale*," notes the modulation from tragedy to comedy through the bear's combination of the "terrible" and the "grotesque" (34–35).

121.   A. D. Nuttall, *William Shakespeare:* The Winter's Tale (London: Edward Arnold, 1966), p. 36.

122.   Biggens, "'Exit Pursued by a Beare': A Problem in *The Winter's Tale*," *SQ* 13 (1962): 3–13, 12, 11.

123.   In "'Bearing Hence': Shakespeare's *The Winter's Tale*," *SEL* 44, no. 2 (2004): 333–46, Maurice Hunt explores the "figurative metamorphosis of Leontes into the Bohemian bear" through the series of puns earlier in the play that "make Leontes bearish" (336).

124.   Bristol, "In Search of the Bear: Spatiotemporal Form and the Heterogeneity of Economies in *The Winter's Tale*," *SQ* 42 (1991): 145–67, 159. Bristol relates the bear to the feast of Candlemas in the early modern era, in which a "carnivalesque bear-man" participated in a range of "observances that mark the end of Christmastide and the beginning of the agricultural work year" (159).

125.   Biggens, "'Exit Pursued by a Beare,'" 13.

126.   David Rockwell, *Giving Voice to the Bear* (Niwot, Colo.: Roberts Rinehart Publishers, 1991), notes that Native American tribes such as the Delaware associated the bear with the birth of the new year (7).

# 4

# DRAMATIC LANGUAGE AND CHARACTER PRESENTATION

Shakespeare's contemporary Ben Jonson, realizing how significantly words define us as individuals, offered the challenge "speake that I may see thee."[1] Our impressions of dramatic characters are partly built through their actions and what other people report about them; but what they say and how they say it is paramount. While image patterns and verbal motifs in *The Winter's Tale* perform several functions—they tap into underlying themes, contribute to dramatic form and texture, and help to define and connect the play's two locations—Shakespeare's poetry and prose are also crucial in revealing his dramatis personae.

## IMAGES AND KEYWORDS

Reiterated images bridge the gap between the worlds of Sicily and Bohemia. The "twinned lambs" reference to the king's boyhood, for instance (1.2.67), prepares us for the shepherds' lives in act 4. In a play that foregrounds "great creating nature," it is not surprising that human emotions mirror the "fundamental rhythmical movements" of the natural world.[2] Leontes's misconception in act 1 is so rooted that, as Camillo tells Polixenes, "You may as well / Forbid the sea for to obey the moon" as change the king's mind (1.2.427–28). In a reworking of the image with a more positive twist, Florizel is described as so in love with Perdita that he stands and reads her eyes like "the moon" gazing upon "the water" (4.4.172–73). The crossover of images and motifs from one part of the drama to the next often signals a transformation for the better.[3] While the "infection" in the opening scenes spreads from Leontes's "diseased opinion" (1.2.297) that he is playing the ignominious role of cuckold to his unfaithful wife, "play" in Bohemia is a form of life-renewing recreation. By act 5, Sicily's infection is purged once Perdita, who extends the idea of "grace" first introduced by Hermione, returns to be reunited with her father and to fulfill the oracle. It is appropriate that this child or "issue" of Leontes and Hermione brings the plot to a "gracious ... issue" that is crowned by the revelation that Hermione is also alive.

Leontes initiates the image cluster on "infection" as soon as his sick delusion begins.[4] Convinced that he has been tainted by his wife's adultery, he extends his situation to embrace that of other husbands: "Many thousands on's / Have the disease, and feel't not" (1.2.206–7). He proposes that if the queen's "liver" were as "infected" as her honor, she would not live an hour (304–5); Hermione, forcibly removed from her son, finds herself treated "like one infectious" (3.2.96). So warped has the king's perception of reality become that he would welcome poison given to Polixenes as "cordial" (1.2.318) and the sight of a venomous spider in his own cup—an emblem of "infected" knowledge—as a blessed sign of certainty (2.1.42). Camillo correctly observes that it is Leontes's opinion that is "diseased" while Hermione is pure; yet "fear / ... oft infects the wisest" (1.2.261–62). At first this cautious servant cannot "name the disease," except to tell Polixenes, who is "well," that he is part of its transmission (387–88). Horrified when he discovers the true situation, Polixenes pledges that his blood may be turned to "infected jelly" if he is in any way guilty (419). When the "sickness" of Mamillius (2.3.11) proves fatal, the boy becomes a scapegoat for his father's sin, a permanent reminder of the repercussions of tyrannical jealousy. It is Paulina who not only tries to explode the king's "rotten" fantasy (88) but acts as a physician, though a stern one who keeps his guilt fresh until she can cure him by producing the living Hermione.

The king's fantasy centers on his playing the ignominious role of cuckold. When Leontes first acknowledges the "infection" of his "brains" (without realizing that he is responsible for poisoning his own mind), he connects this infection with the "hardening" of his "brows," the creation of those invisible horns supposed to grow from the forehead of the husband whose wife is deceiving him (1.2.145–46). Expanding the horn/cuckold image, Leontes moves from comparing the love sighs of his friend and his wife with the "mort o' th' deer" to obsessing over other horned or "neat" animals—an association of ideas that follows his innocuous advice to his son to be "neat" in its primary sense of clean (118, 123). Now the steer, heifer, and calf grotesquely parallel his own family group. He likens Mamillius to the "wanton calf" who does not yet have "shoots" (budding horns) but whose "dam" has created cuckold's horns for her mate (126–28, 137).

Leontes's gross image of being immersed in a vile part—"Inch-thick, knee-deep, o'er head and ears a forked one!" (186)—proliferates new meanings of "play" for him.[5] Mamillius the child can play innocently (recalling the boy kings who "frisk[ed] i' th' sun"). But Leontes sees Hermione as indulging in a dalliance, a harmful form of deceit with Polixenes, while Leontes the cuckold is like an actor adopting such a disgraceful and graceless role that he will be hissed from the stage. This final instance of "play" in a theatrical context is one of the play's self-conscious, metadramatic images. It is continued in Hermione's claim that her situation at trial is more "unhappy" that any story "devised / And played to take spectators," (3.2.34–36)—an image later echoed by the penitent Leontes in act 5, when he imagines the ghost of Hermione, offended if he re-marries, haunting "this stage / Where we offenders now appear" (5.1.58–59). The king shatters the dramatic illusion most completely in act 1 when he invites husbands in the theater to ponder whether they too may be cuckolds: "And many a man there is, even at this present, / Now, while I speak this, holds his wife by th' arm," little dreaming that she has been intimate with "Sir Smile, his neighbor" (192–96). The alienation effect of this is disturbing, not primarily because Leontes is reaching out to the real audience, but rather because he is encouraging them to share in an unfounded suspicion.

Playing a role in his own mad scenario, Leontes has lost the healthy sense of play that M. M. Mahood defines as "holiday freedom," or the "instinctive life" that children enjoy in their games.[6] Bohemia offers a regenerative counterbalance to Leontes's crippled sensibility. To defend his disguise as shepherd, Florizel recalls how classical deities transformed themselves into those horned animals, Jove a "bull" and Neptune a "ram" (4.4.28–29), that Leontes painfully associates with cuckoldry. These gods at play are sexual but nonthreatening, since Florizel promises to be more "chaste" in his desires than they were in pursuing love; his image of metamorphosis is an exhortation to "jollity" (33, 25). Perdita still distrusts role-playing, but she spontaneously expresses her desire for Florizel by imagining a game in which she would strew him with garlands, not "like a corse" but "like a bank for Love to lie and play on" (131–32). Later she accepts disguise as a necessary stage in her quest to be married to the prince, telling Camillo, "I see the play so lies / that I must bear a part" (659–60).

In addition to embracing creative forms of play, Perdita manifests natural grace and physical comeliness. As act 4 opens, Time tells us that she is "grown in grace / Equal with wond'ring" (4.1.24–25), and when she plays flower goddess, the princess wishes "Grace and remembrance" to Polixenes and Camillo by giving them the herbs rosemary and rue (4.4.76). Dancing with the prince she moves gracefully, like a "wave o' th' sea" (141); in Sicily Leontes greets her and Florizel as a "gracious couple" (134). It is appropriate that Hermione's first words to her daughter take the form of a prayer that the gods will "pour [their] graces" on Perdita's head (5.3.122), since it is Hermione who has first developed the keyword "grace." In act 1 she fondly recalls her promise of marriage to Leontes after a long courtship as "Grace indeed" (1.2.105), and she turns the hardship of being falsely accused into a means of achieving a "better grace" (2.1.122). As with her appeal to the gods' "graces," the word has spiritual overtones here. But it also emerges from Hermione's entire persona as a woman who displays social graces (being courtly in the best sense) and who has the healing capacity to forgive freely and love unconditionally.

*The Winter's Tale* also deals with consequences. It builds to an outcome or "issue" that, depending on whether grace comes into play, may or may not be tragic. The play's opening scenes hold little promise that future time will match up to the past; Archidamus worries that no degree of munificence ("magnificence") will repay the debt Bohemia owes to Sicily (1.1.12), just as Polixenes fears that no amount of time, however "long," can express his thanks for Leontes's hospitality (1.2.3). In the second part of the play, however, this compulsive calculating of periods of time ("nine changes of the wat'ry star" [1]) and tallying of costs, whether it is Polixenes fearing that he will forever be "in debt" to his host (6) or Hermione talking of earnings and wages (94, 107),[7] is replaced by a sense of things maturing through temporal process and seasonal cycles. Perdita needs the 16 years telescoped by Time to grow in grace and become an agent of her father's recovery. The age of adolescence between "ten and three-and-twenty" cannot, as the Old Shepherd wishes, be bypassed (3.3.58–59); it too is "owed" to "Time," which tries "all" (4.1.1–3).

The word "issue" appears 14 times in the drama—more than in any other of Shakespeare's plays. Just over half of these instances refer to offspring; Leontes resolves not to "rear another's issue" after convincing himself that Perdita is the "issue" of King Polixenes (2.3.92), while in the final act the Sicilians fear that the kingdom will not survive Leontes's "fail of issue" (5.1.27). The other instances of the word denote issue as outcome,[8] as when fear over the "foul issue" of Leontes's jealousy (2.3.151) follows Emilia's hope that Paulina's bringing the baby to Leontes will prove a "thriving issue" (2.2.44), and Dion trusts that the oracle of Apollo will bring a "gracious ... issue" to the trial of Hermione (3.1.22). In an ironic echo that returns to the sense of issue as offspring, Polixenes laments in act 4 that his "issue" (Florizel) has failed to be "gracious" by leaving court to visit a shepherdess (4.2.28–29). Hermione's declaration when she turns from statue to woman—that she has "preserved" herself "to see the issue" (5.3.127–28) because the oracle gave hope that her daughter has remained alive—poignantly combines the two meanings of this keyword.

It reinforces, too, the importance of the eye motif in the play's final scenes. References to seeing are pronounced in the verbal report of the royal reunions ("that which you hear you'll swear you'll see"), where Leontes and Camillo seemed to "tear the cases of their eyes" by staring at one another, and several parts of the scenario "angled" for the "eyes" of the Third Gentleman now narrating it (5.2.34–35, 14, 89). At the play's finale, prolonged gazing at the statue leads to its reanimation. Leontes, who a scene or two earlier could only remorsefully imagine how he might have "looked upon [his] queen's full eyes" (5.1.53), now observes "motion" in the eye of what appears to be a work of art (5.3.67). Perdita too might "live by gazing" (Camillo's compliment to her in 4.4.110), a reverend "looker-on" of the statue for 20 years (5.3.85). Until, that is, the icon so appealing to the eye comes to life and communicates with her daughter through speech.

## PROSE AND POETRY

Most of the play, depicting royal families, is written in blank verse, but the language of those scenes exclusively in prose (1.1, 4.2, and 5.2) is often courtly too. Carol Thomas Neely notes the euphuistic style, the deliberate setting up of antitheses and weighing of alternatives through parallel phrases.[9] We find it in Archidamus's hope that the Sicilians' "senses" will be so drugged when they visit Bohemia that they "may, though they cannot praise us, as little accuse us" (1.1.14–16). It shapes the way that Polixenes persuades Camillo to stay on as his counselor after 15 years in Bohemia: "Better not to have had thee, than thus to want thee" (4.2.13–14). This carefully structured speech with its ornate figures of speech—possibly a parody of the elaborate style of Shakespeare's source, Greene's *Pandosto*—peaks in act 5, scene 2, where the Third Gentleman tries to recreate in words "a sight which was to be seen, cannot be spoken of" (45–46). Personified emotions convey either excess ("one joy crown[ed] another" [47]), antithesis ("joy and sorrow" wage a "noble combat" in Paulina [78–79]), or fusion ("joy waded in tears" [49]). Such language expresses paradoxes, opposites that never quite merge but are central to the tragicomic experience. We learn of a "world ransomed, or one destroyed"

(16–17) and how Paulina, awkwardly torn between grief and rejoicing, has one eye "declined for the loss of her husband," another "elevated" at the discovery of Perdita (79–80). Something of the same poetic effect—this time compounded by the dramatic ritual itself—is created in the art/nature, death/life dichotomies of the statue scene, though now the first half of each pair transforms into its opposite rather than both remaining in equilibrium.

The prose spoken by the shepherds in the second half of the play is not as finely wrought as that of the courtiers. The Clown describes the shipwreck in vivid images taken from ordinary life (the ship "boring the moon with her mainmast" and the sea and sky divided by less than a "bodkin's point" [3.3.91, 85]) while the Old Shepherd discerns some "stair-work ... trunk-work ... behind-door-work" underlying the arrival of the abandoned baby (72–73). It is not quite the case, though, that "no parallelism, ... no traces of euphuism"[10] emerge in the rustics' style. To the Old Shepherd are given the choric lines expressing a transition from near-tragedy to pastoral comedy, "Now bless thyself; thou met'st with things dying, I with things new-born" (112–13), where the neatness of the antithesis is only partly offset by the homely benediction introducing it. He also, unlike his son the Clown, makes a smooth transition to blank verse in front of the disguised Camillo and Polixenes, though it remains blunt and colloquial in diction, as when he recalls his late wife, hostess of the feast, "her face o' fire / With labor and the thing she took to quench it" (4.4.60–61).

Autolycus, who never speaks in verse, turns prose into a vehicle of colorful wit. He packs it with energetic images—gelding a codpiece of a purse, scaring the choughs (rustics) away from the chaff—and cynically puts down the Old Shepherd as an "old sheep-whistling rogue, a ramtender" (782–83) and Perdita as a "clog" at Florizel's "heels" (684). Masquerading as a courtier for the two shepherds near the end of act 4, scene 4, he bombards them with a series of euphuistic questions to convince them that he is indeed "courtier cap-a-pé" (741): "Seest thou not the air of the court in these enfoldings?" "Receives not thy nose court-odor from me?" (735–36, 737). His rhetorical pièce de résistance comes when he delineates the cruelest possible punishment that the king could impose on the Shepherd's son. He builds from the rustic's being "flayed alive, then 'nointed over with honey" and stung by wasps, to his being revived with a "hot infusion" (790–94). Finally, personifying the punishing sun as a wry observer of this ritual, Autolycus provides the graphic detail (horrific for the listeners on stage, hilarious for the audience) of how the Clown will be "set against a brick wall, the sun looking with a southward eye upon him, where he is to behold him with flies blown to death" (796–98).

At this late stage in his dramatic career, Shakespeare's blank verse is flexible, with many more run-on lines, frequently closing with weak, unstressed, syllables such as "of" or "and," instead of endstopped ones. The poetic language itself is far from slack. It is crammed with evocative metaphors and similes, as when Polixenes boasts that his young son "makes a July day short as December" (1.2.169), and Leontes rants that his wife "deserves a name / As rank as any flax wench, that puts to / Before her troth-plight" (276–78). But metrically the poetic line remains "remarkably free."[11] Colloquial rhythms often override the basic iambic pentameter, and sentences spread over several lines to accommodate the digressions and ellipses of ordinary conversation. Russ McDonald suggests that this effect of grammatical "suspension," as we wait for the sense to be completed within the convoluted verse paragraph, mirrors "suspensions in the action," turns and counterturns, before we reach tragicomedy's final clarification.[12]

Individual speeches are often "impassioned."[13] Frank Kermode comments on how Shakespeare's "late style is peculiarly well suited to disturbed mental states";[14] thus we pass quickly from Polixenes's courtly hyperbole in "There is no tongue that moves, none, none i' th' world / So soon as yours could win me" (1.2.20–21) to a rhythm that is similar, but more ominous through its pronounced repetition of strongly stressed monosyllables, in Leontes's troubled, "My heart dances, / But not for joy, not joy" (110–11). Increasingly a "spasmodic, interjectory, explosive"[15] style characterizes the king's soliloquies and speeches after he becomes jealous. When Leontes grills Camillo on whether he has witnessed the love-play of Polixenes and Hermione, his speech, culminating in the hissed sibilant of the unpleasantly graphic "slippery," is one huge sentence that extends over nearly seven lines and contains three parentheses, each stretching over a line and a half. Our impression is of a torrential obsession briefly stanched with self-serving pieces of dubious proof:

> Ha you not seen, Camillo—
> But that's past doubt, you have, or your eyeglass
> Is thicker than a cuckold's horn—or heard—
> For to a vision so apparent, rumor
> Cannot be mute—or thought—for cogitation
> Resides not in the man that does not think—
> My wife is slippery? (1.2.267–73)

Also disrupting any smooth progression of sound or sense is the series of 11 sharp questions within 8 lines in Leontes's intense "Is whispering nothing?" tirade, where intangible "nothing" turns agonizingly concrete in the imagined details of "Kissing with inside lip?" and "Horsing foot on foot?" (284–96).[16] Even in public, the king almost loses control. His disjointed language reflects how he is torn apart by the contrast between the genteel appearance of Hermione (her "without-door form") and the reality, which the lords evade with their "shrugs … hum's … ha's":

> Praise her but for this without-door form,
> Which on my faith deserves high speech, and straight
> The shrug, the hum or ha, these petty brands
> That calumny doth use—oh I am out!
> That mercy does, for calumny will sear
> Virtue itself—these shrugs, these hum's and ha's,
> When you have said she's goodly, come between,
> Ere you can say she's honest. (2.1.69–76)

Again, parentheses interrupt the logical sequence, with a virtual break-down at "oh I am out." Increasingly he speaks a "language" that Hermione fails to "understand" (3.2.78) and that the audience finds it difficult to follow.[17]

Leontes's tyrannical need to retain authority is reflected in the way that he coats his sexual obsession with a veneer of reasonableness. His emotional "Affection" speech (1.2.138–46) mixes direct, native monosyllables ("can thy dam, may't be?") with polysyllabic abstractions ("intention," "coactive," "commission").[18] Later, trying to offer the assembled court a formal justification for his irrational position, Leontes packs the latinate terms "familiarity," "conjecture," "approbation," "circumstances," "proceeding," and "confirmation" into just six lines of verse (2.1.175–80).

Paulina's role as a stern moralist who must enforce the horror of what Leontes has done is underlined in her "Do not repent" diatribe:

> A thousand knees,
> Ten thousand years together, naked, fasting,
> Upon a barren mountain, and still winter
> In storm perpetual, could not move the gods
> To look that way thou wert. (3.2.208–12)

Each hyperbole, part of a complex double subject, spills over into the next line, progressing in gravity from "ten thousand years" through "storm per-petual" until the bleak verbal phrase "could not move" clinches the prospect of a hopeless future for Leontes. Contrast the simpler diction and slower pacing of Hermione's firm defense of her innocence in the trial scene. Her prizing of "honor" over "life" is foregrounded by the word's position, after a series of monosyllables, at the end of the line, which leads without pause into Hermione's claiming of it and her determination to "stand for" it:

> For life, I prize it
> As I weigh grief, which I would spare; for honor,
> 'Tis a derivative from me to mine,
> And only that I stand for. (3.2.41–44)

The character of the verse shifts noticeably in the second half of *The Winter's Tale*. Counteracting the contorted expression and "sheer turbulence"[19] of Leontes's "tremor cordis" are the "wave o' th' sea" rhythms of Florizel's tribute to Perdita (4.4.135–46), created by delicate shifts of the midline caesura.[20] As the prince elaborates on how each of Perdita's acts "betters what is done," he reaches the peak of wishing she could "move still, still so, / And own no other function" when she is dancing (142–43): a chiasmic balance that holds the surge of continuous movement against its arrest, suggesting his desire to retain the perfection of the moment. The verse line flows again as Florizel pays tribute to Perdita's innate royalty, equating all her "doing[s]" and "acts" with "crowns" and "queens":

> Each your doing,
> So singular in each particular,
> Crowns what you are doing in the present deeds,
> That all your acts are queens. (143–46)

That Leontes is a somber and chastened man in act 5 is reflected in his language. Although his diction still balances abstract against concrete, his verse is purged of the portentous, "pseudo-rational phraseology,"[21] the "old habits of abstraction and categorization"[22] with which he justified his tyranny. Continuing the shift that began at the end of the trial scene ("Come, and lead me / To these sorrows" [3.2.240–41]), the tenor of his speeches is lucid and dignified, the pace more "measured."[23] His explanation of how he cannot "forget" his "evil" sets Hermione's "virtues" against his own "blemishes" and "wrong"—nouns that are all placed before the caesura in each line, while "remember" at the end of the first line, instead of being set against "forget," is paired with "cannot forget":

> Whilst I remember
> Her and her virtues, I cannot forget
> My blemishes in them, and so still think of
> The wrong I did myself ... (5.1.6–9)[24]

The tone of "reverend awe"[25] in the final scene results partly from the incantatory, mesmeric rhythms of Leontes's address to the statue, where supernatural "magic" is linked by alliteration and assonance to Hermione's "majesty":

> O royal piece!
> There's magic in thy majesty, which has
> My evils conjured to remembrance, and
> From thy admiring daughter took the spirits
> Standing like stone with thee. (5.3.38–42)

Evil in the past, beneficent magic in the present; the coldness of stone set against the warmth of flesh—these are just two of the poetic opposites that are united and resolved when the statue transforms into Hermione.

## DRAMATIC CHARACTERS

In Shakespeare's tragedies the main protagonists are portrayed as complex individuals whose choices help to determine the ultimate catastrophe. The case is altered in tragicomic romance. Since *The Winter's Tale* pushes toward a happy ending through strange and surprising twists of plot, characters need not be presented as entirely consistent, nor do their mistakes always lead to a disastrous outcome. This is not to say that the play always "subordinates character to situation,"[26] or that speech patterns express the "truth of the situation"[27] rather than the essence of personality. The female protagonists, especially, are impressive as many-sided individuals; as Granville-Barker remarks, "No play of Shakespeare boasts three such women as Hermione, Perdita, Paulina."[28] But coherent character development is not at a premium. Indeed at times all the dramatic characters are shown in terms of some human trait or archetype of behavior rather than as complex personalities. Hermione foregrounds this dimension when she extends her own situation in the trial scene into a mini-allegory, confident that

> Innocence shall make
> False Accusation blush, and Tyranny
> Tremble at Patience. (3.2.29–31)

Yet apart from the relatively indistinguishable First and Second Gentlemen of act 5, characters in the play are never purely types. While the Old Shepherd and his son the Clown go unnamed, they are clearly differentiated. The father is both shrewd and kind, suspecting that the baby he finds is the result of some "behind-door-work" but compassionate enough to "take it up" (3.3.73–75). While he would like his grown foster daughter to "quench [her] blushes" (4.4.67) and try to be the hearty, robust hostess that his wife once was, he recognizes her innate quality (177) and is receptive to her love for the youth he thinks is the shepherd Doricles. His subsequent sense of betrayal when Doricles turns out to be Prince Florizel—"You have undone a man of four score three" (457)—is moving in its simple dignity. His son the Clown sometimes plays the role of the naive rustic, easily robbed by Autolycus and gulled by the peddler's ballads and knickknacks; yet he seems to have an eye on the main chance, opportunistically welcoming both the gold accompanying Perdita and, 16 years later, the favors of Mopsa and Dorcas. In Sicily he happily exploits his new status as "gentleman," even if it means swearing falsely that Autolycus is a reformed character (5.2.166–67). In these ways he is shown to be of somewhat "cheaper metal"[29] than his father. For it is the Old Shepherd who finally insists that the lowborn should become "gentle" in behavior once they have been received at court (162).

Because characters in *The Winter's Tale* interact as part of a social or family group and closely reflect on one another, they are best analyzed together rather than in isolation. The two "brother" kings, Leontes and Polixenes, mirror each other even after the rift in their friendship; in a closer intergenerational link, the characters of Hermione and Perdita turn out to be strikingly similar. The one outsider, Autolycus—rogue, creative entrepreneur, and merry wanderer—offers comic parallels and contrasts to royal tyranny. And in a fitting "symmetry,"[30] Camillo and Paulina, who both serve as consciences to their kings, are married at the end of the play.

## LEONTES, POLIXENES, AND FLORIZEL

### Leontes

Leontes's change from cordial friend to jealous, irrational tyrant is extremely abrupt. In this play Shakespeare seems more interested in exploring the psychology of jealousy rather than, as in *Othello,* presenting a vulnerable individual who is plausibly made suspicious through the skillful suggestions of a false friend. Yet many readers, as well as actors approaching the role, have not been satisfied with the notion that Leontes's jealousy descends on him "like a terrible dream."[31] Several, including the nineteenth-century actor Charles Kean, conclude that Leontes's suspicions about his wife, like those of King Pandosto in Shakespeare's source, have been hatching over time. Others prefer to ground the emotion more realistically.

If Leontes has "long since been jealous," as Nevill Coghill claims,[32] then at the beginning of act 1, scene 2 he is simply testing Hermione by asking her to persuade Polixenes to stay longer. This interpretation might be supported by Leontes's laconic, even grudging remark, "At my request he would not" (86) when he discovers that Hermione's "tongue," and not his, has succeeded in persuading Polixenes to stay (20). But the line does not offer decisive evidence that Leontes is suspicious before the play opens. It could just as easily be played as sudden flaring resentment of the fact that his wife has more power over his friend than he does,[33] a moment that ignites his suspicion of an affair between the two. Taking a deconstructive stand, Howard Felperin deftly shows how the "indeterminacy" of the dramatic language blurs any certainty for the audience, for "much of what Hermione says may be construed either within or outside the bounds of royal hospitality and wifely decorum."[34] William T. Matchett goes even further in contending that Leontes's jealousy appears credibly motivated to the audience. Shakespeare, he argues, provides so many misleading signs—sexual innuendoes in the speeches of Polixenes and Hermione, plus the fact that Polixenes has been in Sicily for nine months and the queen is heavily pregnant—that not only Leontes but those watching the spectacle are bound to suspect adultery. Thus Leontes's jealousy "comes less as a surprise than as a confirmation."[35] For Ernest Schanzer, the most telling provocation comes shortly before Leontes's outburst "Too hot, too hot!" (108), when Hermione announces that her powerful words in the past earned her a "royal husband" and now, "for some while, a friend" (107–8),[36] a word whose secondary Elizabethan meaning was lover. In fact Leontes picks up on the word's sexual implication in his first full line after that, "To mingle friendship far is mingling bloods" (109). And it may be particularly galling for Leontes to see his wife open her "white hand" to Polixenes when he himself had to wait "three crabbèd months" (102–3) before she would give him her hand in marriage.[37]

Linguistic indeterminacy aside, it seems unlikely that Shakespeare would go out of his way to present a tarnished image of Hermione only to reverse it completely a short time later. While the queen's language is often sensual (as in "you may ride's / With one soft kiss a thousand furlongs" [94–95]) and even somewhat provocative, her badinage can be read as appropriate courtly "entertainment" (111).[38] Similarly, Bohemia's suggestive double meanings—he says that he is "standing in rich place" and fears that something may "breed" during his absence from his country (7, 12)—need not be misconstrued, except by a husband disposed toward jealousy.

One disagreement hinges on how much Leontes hears of the conversation in which Hermione teases Polixenes for implying that women are "devils." She claims that the two wives, she and the queen of Bohemia, will forgive him for this insult only "If you first sinned with us, and that you slipped not / With any but with us" (82, 84–86). If Leontes hears only the final lines of this conversation,[39] he might think that she is using the singular "you" and the royal "we," alluding to Polixenes having a first-time affair with the wife of his "brother" king. If Leontes *does* hear the whole conversation between his friend and his wife, Douglas L. Peterson argues, the guilt evoked in him by Polixenes's account of lost boyhood innocence triggers both a resurgence of pubertal sexual desire ("stronger blood") and a transfer of that desire onto Leontes's "double," Polixenes.[40] Indeed some 80 lines later Leontes himself recalls an idyllic time when his phallic "dagger" was "muzzled / Lest it should bite his master" (156–57), as though he, like Polixenes, is all too aware of the fall from purity with the advent of sexual awareness. A Freudian reading would go further in inferring a triangular relationship in which Leontes substitutes Hermione for himself in a homoerotic attraction to his male friend.[41] Or it might deduce that Leontes's jealousy, stemming from his fear of rejection by the nurturing mother, functions at the "deepest level of oral anxieties."[42] Whatever the subconscious cause, the king's emotional conflict results in a terrible jealousy.

This is to come full circle, from accepting that Leontes is being completely irrational (since people susceptible to jealousy, as Emilia observes in *Othello,* have no real "cause" for that emotion [3.4.160]) to finding prompts in the text that can show exactly where Leontes's latent fears progress into full-blown jealousy. The situation is complicated by our having no real knowledge of Leontes's character before jealousy strikes. Whereas Othello is shown to be a respected general, calm and confident in a crisis at the opening of his play, we remain convinced by Leontes as a study of an all-consuming emotion rather than a character changed by it.[43] Coleridge, who finds in Leontes a "morbid suspiciousness," a "vice of the mind" that is never shown in Othello, notes in the person suffering from jealousy an "eagerness" to snatch at inadequate "proofs," a "grossness" in imagining the sexual infidelity, and a "selfish vindictiveness."[44] All these are indeed conveyed through the tortuousness of Leontes's increasingly impressionistic language. Most pronounced is Leontes's illogical jump from what he takes to be the empirical evidence of "paddling palms and pinching fingers" (115) to the certainty that he is "o'er head and ears a forked one" (186)—a cuckold. As with Macbeth, once "horrible imagin-

ings" take root, "nothing is / But what is not" (*Macbeth,* 1.3.138, 141–42);
by the time Leontes confronts Camillo he is angrily asserting that if the
signs he sees are irrelevant, then "The covering sky is nothing, Bohemia
nothing, / My wife is nothing" (294–95). Fueling the fire of suspicion is
his misogynistic assumption that women are habitually "false" (131):

> No barricado for a belly. Know't
> It will let in and out the enemy,
> With bag and baggage. (204–6)

Leontes even needs to be reassured of his paternal claim to Mamillius—
that he is indeed "like" his own son (130).

What may distinguish Leontes's paranoid jealousy from the merely typical is the degree of his masochism. Although he tells Camillo that he is
not so "muddy" and "unsettled" as to bring this "vexation" (326) on himself, his need to confirm his own worst fears emerges strongly from his
"I have drunk and seen the spider" speech (2.1.36–45). A superstition in
Shakespeare's time held that individuals could be poisoned by a spider in
a drink only if they actually saw it, presumably lurking at the bottom, after
drinking from the cup. Leontes notes that "violent hefts" (retching) occurs
only if "one present / The abhorred ingredient to his eye, make known /
How he hath drunk." There is something very deliberate about this making "known" (to the world at large, perhaps) how he been infected, and the
word "blest" ("How blest am I / In my just censure") implies that Leontes
has masochistically embraced his own destructive belief that his wife is
adulterous. The "spider" has no grounding in reality; yet Leontes wants to
give credence to his sick fantasy by elaborating this little parable.[45]

In the space of two scenes Leontes has traveled far: from urging Polixenes to stay longer to wanting to poison him, and from recalling how
Hermione pledged she was his own "forever" to the conviction that she
has betrayed him in the worst way (1.2.105). As he succumbs to "infection" of the "brains" (145), he becomes a solipsist who ironically makes
all "true that is mistrusted" (2.1.48). Believing that "there is a plot against
[his] life, [his] crown" and that Polixenes has "pre-employed" Camillo,
the jealous husband transforms into the paranoid king (47–49). Now his
wife is not only a "bedswerver" but a "traitor" who may be planning to
assassinate him (93, 89). As his paranoia grows—he believes that he can
both "see" and "feel" what he has only imagined (152)—he convinces
himself that his "rest" might be restored if his wife were "Given to the
fire" (2.3.1, 8).

This is brutal indeed. Yet it is also grotesquely comic. Something of the
"schoolboy coward"[46] is there in Leontes's petulant bullying of Camillo

("You lie, you lie" [1.2.299]) and his threat to put Antigonus to death if he disobeys his king (2.3.135); and he is ineffectual against the strong woman Paulina. What makes him a "feather for each wind that blows" (2.3.152) is his residual humanity. He cannot quite bring himself to destroy the newborn Perdita, just as his obvious affection for his "dear'st" Mamillius, even at the height of his passionate delusion ("Mine honest friend, / Will you take eggs for money? [1.2.137, 160–61]), goes some way toward retaining the audience's sympathy.[47]

And because Leontes appears to be in the grip of a disease beyond his control, the turnaround in his character at the end of the trial scene is like the breaking of a fever. As soon as he hears that Mamillius is dead, Leontes recognizes his "profaneness" against the oracle and his misjudgment of those closest to him, especially Camillo. Once Paulina brings news of Hermione's death, his aggression crumbles completely. Instantly he welcomes Paulina's bleak vision of despair ("Go on, go on") and accepts the penance of visiting the tombs of his wife and son once a day as part of his "shame perpetual" (3.2.312, 236).

This willingness to be chastised by Paulina is the keynote of his "penitent" (4.2.24) character in act 5. The two work in tandem, she sternly reactivating his "memory" of the peerless Hermione, he somewhat masochistically accepting the burden of guilt and regret: "She I kill'd! I did so; but thou strik'st me / Sorely, to say I did" (5.1.50, 17–18). Over the question of whether he should marry again to produce an heir, Leontes meekly promises, "We shall not marry till thou bidd'st us" (82), even though he is clearly attracted to Perdita and prepared to beg the "precious mistress" (223) of Florizel for himself if she is not yet married. The final scene continues the pattern. The king's response to the statue is both elicited and controlled by Paulina: "behold, and say 'tis well," "No longer shall you gaze on't," "It is required / You do awake your faith" (5.3.20, 60, 94–95). Some masochism remains as he yearns to be tormented further by the lifelike statue—"For this affliction has a taste as sweet / As any cordial comfort" (76–77). As if in a trance, he is simultaneously pulled back into the past, his "evils conjured to remembrance," and drawn into the "pleasure" of the present (40, 73), sensitive to the minute details of the artwork. The veins, the eye, the illusion of "breath"(79) in the statue draw him ever closer to the "sweet'st companion" he once knew (5.1.11), now rediscovered as a living woman: "O, she's warm!" (5.3.109). After the physical reunion, Leontes humorously turns the tables on Paulina by commanding her to take Camillo as an "honorable husband" (143), and his "O peace, Paulina" (135) may be read as a final silencing of the unruly woman.[48] Yet in bidding her "Lead us from hence" (152), he echoes his own much earlier "Come, and lead

me / To these sorrows" (3.2.240–41), seeming to defer again to Paulina
as his "good" counselor (5.3.151).

It is, of course, impossible to speculate on the future of the marriage
between Leontes and Hermione or what degree of mutual affection can
be restored. We may feel, along with Peter Erickson, that Leontes has reformed his masculinity by learning to value Hermione's "nurturant presence," just as in the interim he has benefited from Paulina's. Or we may
sense some conflict between a psychological level on which Leontes still
plays "boy eternal"[49] to the maternal queen and a social hierarchy in which
he again takes up his position as the patriarch to a subdued, possibly estranged, wife.

### Polixenes

At the beginning of the play Polixenes is more prolix, yet much more
opaque than the terse Leontes. His language expresses a conventional,
elaborate courtliness—he will be "for perpetuity … in debt" to his host—
even though he is evidently trying to extricate himself from a visit that
has already gone on too long: "My affairs / Do even drag me homeward"
(1.2.5–6, 23–24). In the event it is his reluctance to be impolite that makes
him concede to Hermione's threat to make him her "prisoner" if not her
"guest," since "To be your prisoner should import offending" (57). His
exaggerated idealism appears in his nostalgic memory of when he and
Leontes were "boy eternal," free even from original sin; in his reference
to Hermione as "sacred lady" (76);[50] and in his allusion to Judas: if he
is guilty let his "name / Be yoked with his, that did betray the Best!"
(1.2.418–20). Sensing how violent the king's jealousy may be (453), he
quickly accepts Camillo as his "pilot" back to Bohemia (449). We might
wonder why he does not stay to defend or protect the "gracious Queen"
(460). Is he cowardly, as "Fear o'ershades me" suggests (458)? Here situation tends to override character. Polixenes clearly needs to leave in order
to let Leontes direct his "revenges" solely against his wife (2.3.18).

Sixteen years later Polixenes is in some ways a changed man, "graver,
less impetuous, less romantic, less idealistic."[51] He is still being polite,
however, studying how to be more "thankful" to Camillo in order to keep
him in Bohemia (4.2.20). Mostly he functions as a surrogate for Leontes (Stephen Orgel calls them "two versions of the same psyche")[52]; he
feels keenly the loss of Sicilia's queen and son, "even now to be afresh
lamented" (26), and is unhappy about his own son's absence from court.
Just as Leontes was "angling" to discover a hidden affair between friend
and wife (1.2.180), so now Polixenes will use his spy system to discover

the "angle that plucks" his son to the house of a shepherd (4.2.49). Receiving from Perdita the "flow'rs of winter" (4.4.79) at the sheep-shearing festival—rosemary, for remembrance, and rue, signifying repentance—he is a living reminder of his counterpart, the King of Sicily.

For the purposes of pastoral debate, the king becomes the civilized spokesman for how nurture can improve nature; he defends the hybrid gillyvors against Perdita's label, "Nature's bastards" (83). While he senses that everything about this graceful shepherdess "smacks of something greater than herself" (158), his role as the stern patriarch dictates that he must "divorce" her from his son Florizel and reimpose the traditional social hierarchy. Like Leontes, he has jealously watched and felt excluded from a warm relationship. The perennial envy of age for youth compounds the father's resentment at being left out of his son's betrothal, as he sarcastically inquires, "Is not your father grown incapable / Of reasonable affairs? Is he not stupid / With age and alt'ring rheums?" (401–3). Echoing the irrational harshness of Leontes, he threatens to bar his own son from royal succession, to ensure a "cruel" death for Perdita (444), and, we later discover, to impose "diverse deaths in death" on the shepherds (5.1.202). In the Bohemian countryside Polixenes speaks with a scathing directness that never emerges when he is a guest in Sicily.

We do not hear much from the Bohemian king in the final scene, where the focus is directed toward the reunion of Leontes with Hermione. It is amusing, though, to note how much he has reverted to his former courtly politeness. When Leontes remarks that the statue's face looks "wrinkled" and "aged," it is Polixenes who gallantly interjects, "O, not by much!" (5.3.29). Reconciled with his closest friend, Polixenes now again calls Leontes "brother," graciously offering to take on the burden of the king's grief since he himself was the "cause" of it (53–54).

### Florizel

Florizel, in act 1 the unseen "double" of the young prince Mamillius, is first mentioned in the words of his biased father. Polixenes claims that this much-loved and versatile son ("He's all my exercise, my mirth, my matter") can make a July day short as December and cure melancholy in an instant (1.2.166–71). When we actually see the Bohemian prince in act 4, scene 4, he is enjoying his disguise as a "poor humble swain" while retaining all the brightness and stature of "Golden Apollo" (the sun-god), insulated by his royal birth from Perdita's more mature, well-grounded anxiety about the king's reaction. But if there is something naive about Florizel's exhortation to "Be merry" and "Apprehend / Nothing but jol-

lity" (46, 24–25), it is offset by the strength and idealism of his love
for Perdita. This devotion resonates strongly because it is expressed so
simply:

> For I cannot be
> Mine own, nor anything to any, if
> I be not thine. (43–45)

Whereas Polixenes excludes women from his idyllic memory of being
"boy eternal," Florizel here "embraces the female."[53] He matches his lady
in chastity, since he will not let his "desires" outpace his "honor" (33–34),
and he is immune to Autolycus's "knacks" (353) because Perdita already
has the gift of his heart. The audience is bound to warm to a young man
who can celebrate his beloved's speaking, singing, and dancing as abso-
lutely as Florizel does in his eulogy "What you do / Still betters what
is done" speech (135–46). Youthful enthusiasm makes him want his betrothal to be witnessed not only by the disguised Polixenes but by the
entire cosmos, "men; the earth, the heavens, and all" (375).

As courtly lover, Florizel sometimes resorts to conventional hyperbole,
as when he compares Perdita's white hand to "the fanned snow that's
bolted / By th' northern blasts twice o'er" (368–69). But when tested by
his father's threats, he uses language more in tune with nature than with
courtly "ceremony" (519), swearing that he will never "break" his "oath"

> for all the sun sees or
> The close earth wombs or the profound seas hide
> In unknown fathoms … (493–95)

Prepared to renounce his "paternal inheritance,"[54] he is proud to be "heir"
to his "affection" (485). Yet part of his progress is to reaffirm his total
commitment to his beloved without succumbing to the "madness" of his
"fancy" (486–88). Gradually his initial recklessness ("let myself and Fortune / Tug for the time to come" [500–501]) and despairing fatalism ("we
profess / Ourselves to be the slaves of chance" [543–44]) are tempered by
Camillo's reasonableness. Florizel allows himself to "be advised" (485),
agreeing to set sail for Sicily.

Once there this paragon of sincerity suddenly becomes very adept at
lying. It is as though dressing in Autolycus's garments as part of the escape
plan has given Florizel some of the shape-shifter's powers, or returned
him to the boyish chameleon talents ("parasite … soldier, statesman, all"
[1.2.168]) that so delighted his father. In quick succession the prince tells
Leontes that he has come on the command of King Polixenes (too infirm to

make the trip himself, but full of loving messages for Sicily); that his new wife is the daughter of the Libyan king Smallus; and that he has dismissed his best train back to Bohemia. When his tall tales are discredited by the sudden appearance of Polixenes, Florizel quickly regains his former candor. Admitting that he is not married, he pledges his continued devotion to Perdita despite the hostility of Fortune, and opportunistically asks Leontes to relive the "affections" of his own youth in order to serve as the prince's advocate to Polixenes (5.1.220). Florizel remains silent in the concluding scene. But we receive a testimonial to his warm generosity and freedom from class snobbery when the Clown recounts how "the King's son took me by the hand and called me brother; and then the Prince, (my brother) … called my father father; and so we wept …" (5.2.149–53).

## AUTOLYCUS AND ANTIGONUS

### Autolycus

Although he does not appear until act 4, Autolycus affords an actor a "clown's star performance";[55] his is the third longest part in the play following those of Leontes and Paulina. In discussing *The Winter's Tale,* Samuel Johnson commends Autolycus alone as a "very naturally conceived and strongly represented" character.[56] In fact this shape-shifter and master of illusions, entirely Shakespeare's creation, is less a character than a series of roles. In his first appearance he transforms effortlessly from a singing comedian, celebrating thievery and promiscuity, to the conman in action. Pretending to be a gentleman whose own clothes have been stolen and replaced by the "detestable" rags of the rogue Autolycus, he wickedly thanks the Clown for his "charitable office" even as he picks his pockets (4.3.63, 77). By stepping outside his own persona he can comment, with mock gravity, on the "knavish professions" of this "fellow" who haunts wakes and fairs (100, 87). For the sheep-shearing he dons a false beard ("peddler's excrement" [4.4.718]), again warning his rustic victims that "there are cozeners abroad" (254) at the same time that he touts fantastical ballads claiming to be authentic reports and passes off counterfeit trinkets as the "new'st and fin'st" (325). All this, of course, is his cover for more filching of "festival purses" (619). When opportunity knocks in the form of Florizel's relatively plush outfit, Autolycus reverts to the role he once had as the prince's servant, impersonating a courtier to fool more gold out of the two shepherds. His name, meaning "wolf by himself," is appropriate for his character, as are his origins in classical myth, recounted in Ovid's *Metamorphoses*.[57] There Autolycus, the son of light-fingered Mercury by the nymph Chione, is the grandfather of the wily Ulysses, and his fraternal

twin is the son of Apollo, the god whose oracle predicts the conclusion of
*The Winter's Tale*.

The functions of Autolycus are as difficult to pin down as his personae.
Wilson Knight calls him "spring incarnate,"[58] and indeed when this vagabond enters singing of the "sweet o' the year" (4.3.3) he quickly becomes
a refreshing comic antidote to the paranoia and winter tyranny of Leontes.[59] As the king's parodic double (turning "cruel manipulative actions"
into "comic turns"),[60] Autolycus is the spirit of fun and freedom in Bohemia, a reminder that "red blood reigns in the winter's pale" (4) and that it
is pointless to fret over "the life to come" (30). At the same time, though,
he is a recognizable figure on the margins of Shakespeare's own society,
a "feigned" beggar or rogue who survives by exploiting and preying on
his countrymen.[61] In a juxtaposition that is telling on stage, Autolycus's
planned hoodwinking of the rustics at the festival is followed by a dance
of satyrs—another reminder of rougher, antisocial elements that may
disrupt the pastoral community. The rogue himself cynically views his
gulls as beasts, branding them as "choughs," and "puppies," while to him
"Honesty" is a "fool" and "Trust" a "very simple gentleman" (4.4.622,
710, 599–600). Can this subversive "trickster-archetype"[62] ever be integrated into the social hierarchy at the court of Sicily? He may remain the
rootless outsider, the incorrigible opportunist for whom every public gathering—whether at a hanging or in a church—furnishes a clever man with
"work" (689–90). Like Shakespeare taking up and transforming Greene's
material (the *Conny-Catching* pamphlets as well as *Pandosto*), Autolycus
is a "snapper-up of unconsidered trifles" (4.3.26) for his own benefit. But
while he is "parasitic"[63] and more "predatory"[64] than Shakespeare's other
Fools and jesters (such as Touchstone in *As You Like It* or Feste in *Twelfth
Night*), he is never as actively destructive as his villainous counterpart,
Leontes. Since his stealing seems to do no lasting damage, and Fortune
favors him by dropping "booties" in his mouth (4.4.838–39), the audience
is encouraged to collude with Autolycus, not to censure him as a "master
of deception and exploiter of unsanctioned sensuality."[65]

As part of the upswing from tragedy to comedy in act 4, Autolycus
embodies an inveterate optimism—the "merry heart" that "goes all the
day" while a "sad" heart tires quickly (4.3.129–30). And true to his creed
of "when I wander here and there / I then do go most right" (16–17),
he hovers on the margins not only of rural society but of the plot, too.
Shakespeare seems deliberately to exclude the trickster from any role that
might entail honest behavior or guarantee him a place in the "book of
virtue" (125–26).[66] Granted, at the end of act 4 Autolycus appears all set
to become an active agent in the revelation that Perdita is a princess. Ini-

tially deciding not to inform King Polixenes about the flight of his son because it might be a "piece of honesty" that runs counter to his profession of "knavery," he soon finds himself "honest" by "chance," seizing the opportunity to help Florizel by steering the shepherds away from the king and onto the prince's ship (4.4.686, 716–17). In this he serves as a comic facilitator, enabling the shepherds to reach Sicily and participate in the final revelation. But what motivates Autolycus is always mercenary, never altruistic. He squeezes gold out of the shepherds by falsely promising to bring them to the king, and he definitely expects "advancement" from his former master, Florizel (843). Ironically, because the discovery of Perdita's origins takes place without him, he never benefits financially from bringing the rustics to Sicily; it turns out that the young couple were too distracted by seasickness during the voyage to open up the "fardel" and see the precious tokens. Autolycus ruefully admits that it is just as well he was not the "finder-out of this secret," since his other "discredits" would have cast grave doubts on its authenticity (5.2.124, 130–31). In fact Autolycus's chicanery in act 4, in which "hallowed" trinkets and knickknacks are treated as though they were religious mysteries (4.4.606), throws into relief the "lawful" magic of Paulina when she brings the statue of Hermione back to life in the final scene (5.3.105). The peddler's "trumpery" art (601) has given way to the creative illusion, the "high art"[67] that concludes *The Winter's Tale*.

## Antigonus

Autolycus is a lone wolf; and yet the sound and shape of his name echoes that of Antigonus, Sicilian courtier and husband of Paulina. As these characters (both invented by Shakespeare) never appear on stage together, one actor could have played both roles.[68] If that were the case, Autolycus's complaint to the Clown that his "shoulder-blade" is "out" (4.3.74) would be an amusing in-joke for Shakespeare's audience, for it is not long in stage time since the Clown has matter-of-factly described how the bear "tore out" the "shoulder bone" of Antigonus (3.3.94–95). Such doubling might have been more than theatrically expedient. In fact the two dramatis personae, at first glance so different, play similar roles in advancing the tragicomic momentum of the play. Antigonus, the stalwart adviser in part 1 of the play, at first strongly opposes the tyranny of the king; he warns that such perverted "justice" may prove "violence" and extravagantly offers to geld both his daughters and himself if ever Hermione proves "honor-flawed" (2.1.127–28, 143). Nevertheless, when he agrees to abandon the "innocent" baby in some desert place and dies in Bohemia himself, Antigonus becomes a tragic scapegoat for the cruelty of Leontes.[69]

The way he dies, killed and eaten by a bear, is pivotal in tone. It is both grim and grotesque, a reminder that we are watching a play that is tragicomic in mode. What if the actor of Antigonus were to metamorphose into Autolycus in act 4? Even more than the old courtier, the rogue who enters "singing" is an antidote to Leontes's claustrophobic obsession, a strong signal that the play is taking a different turn. If Antigonus (like Hermione) was not in fact "gone forever" (3.3.57) but instead resurrected as Autolycus,[70] the audience would not only register a decisive shift in mode—away from tragedy and into the healing pastoral of Bohemia—but be subtly prepared for another resurrection, unexpected but crucial: that of Hermione in act 5.

## HERMIONE AND PERDITA

### Hermione

It is tempting to call Hermione a "symbol of perfection achieved."[71] This "gracious lady" (2.2.20), who is so "sovereignly … honorable" (1.2.323) that even the anonymous Lord would wager his life she is "spotless" (2.1.131), appears in a vision to Antigonus wearing "pure white robes, / Very like sanctity" (3.3.21–22). Leontes remembers her as a "sainted spirit" (5.1.57). Even before her appearance as a statue there is something magisterial about her in the trial scene, "like Patience on a monument" (*Twelfth Night,* 2.4.114). Yet in the early scenes she will strike audiences not as an icon but as a "vibrant, feisty"[72] woman whose strength is quickly put to the test. The keynotes of her character are grace under pressure and a strong sense of integrity or "honor"—a word she underlines five times when she is on trial. She combines these attributes with a wit and physical warmth that are appealing in their directness.

In the process of persuading Polixenes to stay she is charming and forthcoming,[73] perhaps just enough to exacerbate Leontes's anxieties; yet she begins her campaign only at her husband's bidding ("Tongue-tied, our Queen?" [1.2.27]), and he encourages her with "Well said, Hermione" (33). While her obvious pregnancy—she is close to term with her second child—may be a threatening reminder to Leontes of the "sexualized female body,"[74] it gives her the freedom to be open, even pleasantly flirtatious, with a close family friend.[75] Obviously Hermione enjoys the challenge of rhetorical oneupmanship, reminding Polixenes that "All in Bohemia's well" (31), that he does not need to see his son again yet, and that she has the power to be his gaoler if not his hostess. Relishing the courtly game, she teases him with "A lady's 'Verily' is / As potent as a lord's" (50–51).[76] Her language is a compelling mixture of down-to-earth, often sensual idiom ("We'll thwack him hence with distaffs," "cram's with praise, and make's / As fat as tame things" [37, 91–92]) and stately, though never overelaborate, language: "Yet of your royal presence, I'll adventure / The borrow of a week" (38–39).

She may again be luxuriating in her pregnancy and the license it gives her to indulge her whims ("I long") when she angles for praise by asking Leontes to remind her of her first "good deed," that of agreeing to marry him, before the current one of persuading Polixenes to stay (101, 97).[77] Her seriously spoken response to his narrative, "'Tis Grace indeed" (105), should reassure him, as should her concerned "Are you moved, my lord?" (150) when he appears "unsettled" (147). Far from insensitive, she is confident in extending her largesse simply because she loves Leontes "not a jar o' th' clock behind / What lady she her lord" (43–44). As she explains in her trial scene, it would have shown "disobedience" and "ingratitude" to her husband not to be graciously hospitable to his closest friend, Polixenes (3.2.67).

Hermione's fortitude is tested to the quick in the scene where Leontes tears her away from Mamillius and publicly accuses her of adultery. Circumstances force her change from "spirited and witty" to a woman of "dignity and deep generosity."[78] Shocked at the roughness she first takes for "sport," Hermione refuses to call her husband a "villain" for impugning her honor. Instead she generously foresees how his terrible "mistake" may "grieve" him when he comes to "clearer knowledge" and blames his error on some "ill planet" (2.1.58, 79–81, 96–97, 105). Asking the lords to "measure" her justly and her women to stay calm, she remains supremely dignified even while burning with "honorable grief" that cannot be assuaged by tears, since she herself is not "prone to weeping" (108–14). She accepts the challenge to her moral integrity with stoicism ("I must be patient" [106]) and a courageous resolution to create something good, even spiritually beneficial, out of her plight: "this action I now go on / Is for my better grace" (121–22). Obedient and loyal—"The King's will be performed!" (115)—she allows herself one parting reproach that underlines her own need for personal vindication:

> Adieu, my lord.
> I never wished to see you sorry; now
> I trust I shall. (122–24)

In Greene's *Pandosto,* Bellaria is spirited in defending herself at trial. But in Hermione Shakespeare magnifies the impression of courage in a woman determined to prove her moral "integrity" even though she lacks physical "strength" after giving birth to Perdita (3.2.25, 104). The forensic skills she used to cajole Polixenes come to the fore in three great speeches; Hermione turns out to be her own best defense lawyer.[79] Knowing that what she says will be counted "falsehood" (indeed Leontes has earlier declared that women will "say anything" [1.2.131]), she makes her ultimate appeal to "powers divine" and the oracle—an audience beyond the one in front of which she must "prate and talk for life and honor" (3.2.27, 40). With a royal dignity befitting the Emperor of Russia's daughter, the queen reminds Leontes of her "chaste" and "true" past life, a time she was in his "grace," before justifying the correctness of her behavior toward Polixenes (33, 46). She is not afraid to label her feeling for their friend "love." It is, though, "such a kind of love as might become / A lady like [her]" (63–64), never going "one jot beyond / The bound of honor" (49–50).

In her third long speech in the trial scene, Hermione eloquently reminds the tyrannical Leontes why death can be no punishment for her; a touch of passionate scorn flashes in her rejoinder, "Sir, spare your threats: / The bug which you would fright me with, I seek" (89–90). Methodically she outlines her reasons for disdaining life: she has lost her husband's love, the "crown and comfort" of her life; she is separated from her first-born; her newborn baby has been "Haled out to murder"; and she herself is branded a strumpet, deprived of the physical comforts that any new mother of her rank deserves (92, 99–102). She now lives only to vindicate and "free" her "honor" (108). Hermione is stern in denouncing a verdict based purely on jealous surmises as "rigor, and not law" (112). Yet her final words, an aside, are again magnanimous; she wishes her father were alive to observe his daughter's trial, but with eyes of "pity, not revenge!" (121). In her generosity toward her husband she resembles Desdemona, who rejects any philosophy of "revenge" in dealing with a wayward husband (*Othello,* 4.3.93). Yet Hermione is more mature and clear-sighted in her judgment, more passionately intent on vindicating her own integrity. As Wilbur Sanders comments, the queen's voice is full of "feeling and flexibility, yet at the same time implacable as steel."[80]

Remarkably Hermione remains a figure of forgiveness, warming back in the final scene from "cold" stone to a life of renewed relationship with Leontes; she "hangs about his neck" (5.3.112). If we assume that her silence to her husband is not hostile, then Hermione represents a "benignly generative maternal presence," able to restore the male's "generativity"[81] once he recognizes that he has been "more stone" than the statue (38). Several feminist critics, though, argue that the queen's transformation from monument to living woman fails to restore her vibrancy since she remains "tongue-tied." In this reading Hermione's return serves mainly to reestablish masculine authority at the cost of female autonomy, putting the patriarchal Leontes back in a position of "kingly command of all social relations."[82]

## Perdita

After the sheep-shearing festival Perdita never dominates the stage. She speaks only two lines in act 5, scene 1, expressing pity for her "poor father," the Old Shepherd, who is being hounded by Polixenes, and disappointment that the heavens seem opposed to her marriage to Florizel (202–4). In the final scene she is given two short speeches, in which she first hopes to kiss the hand of the statue (5.3.42–46) but then states she is content to be a "looker on" (84–85) before she kneels again, silently, to seek the blessing of the living woman. As proof of Perdita's royal identity, the Third Gentleman cites the "majesty of the creature, in resemblance of the mother" (5.2.38–39); and in the long pastoral scene of act 4, Perdita shows that she does indeed possess not only the demeanor but the grace, wisdom, and integrity of her mother. Because she has been brought up as a shepherdess, believing that she is low-born, these qualities emerge in her spontaneity, warmth, and directness rather than as courtly attributes. We are nevertheless constantly made aware of her royal disposition, of the princess in counterpoint with the countrified young woman.

Even Perdita's pronounced respect for social rank, the mirror image of Hermione's acute sense of what "become[s]" an aristocratic "lady" (3.2.63–64), seems to point to her royal roots. It suggests a belief in a fixed hierarchy that was part of ruling class ideology in Shakespeare's society, as when Leontes defends the "mannerly distinguishment" between "prince and beggar" (2.1.86–87). Perdita defers to Prince Florizel as "sir," "gracious lord," "high self," "gracious mark o' th' land," and is almost ashamed that she, a "lowly maid" (as she thinks), is "goddesslike pranked up" (4.4.5–10). She predicts that the "power of the King" will forestall the couple's plans to be married (37), and when the showdown arrives she does not quite have the courage to tell Polixenes "plainly," to his face, that the sun shines on high and low alike (447–49). Instead she resolves to "queen it no inch farther" (453). Her conviction that social classes should be kept separate, the status quo decorously upheld, is shown most fully in her refusal to follow the principle of grafting the "gentler scion" to the "wildest stock" by cultivating hybrid gillyvors in her garden (93, 100).

Meanwhile all who come in contact with her sense that she is more innately refined and wise for her years than her country environment would warrant; everything she does "smacks of something greater than herself" (158). Physically graceful, she dances "featly" (176), standing out from the crowd. Camillo, charmed by her blushing modesty, terms her "queen of curds and cream" (161). Later in the scene he finds that her wise fortitude makes her "mistress / To most that teach" (586–87), while the Servant who first sees her in Sicily calls her a "creature" who might "make proselytes / Of who she but bid follow" (5.1.108–9). When Perdita confirms her constancy and commitment to Florizel by making it clear that "affliction" will never "take in" her "mind" (4.4.580–81) she echoes Hermione's gracious stoicism and moral courage,[83] prompting Florizel to remark on how far this apparent shepherdess goes beyond ("is forward of") her upbringing ("breeding").

In tune with her country values, Perdita aligns herself with "great creating Nature" (88); with Polixenes she is firm in defending unadulterated nature over art. Hating pretense, she deplores Florizel's disguise as shepherd, and her refreshing lack of sophistication comes through most strongly in her sexual frankness.[84] While Perdita lacks her mother's playful, courtly wit, she uses earthy idiom similar to Hermione's when she insists that she would not want Florizel to "Desire to breed by [her]" were she to disfigure her own natural appearance by cosmetics (101–3). Without doubt Perdita is chaste, and she holds Florizel to his vow of being an "unstained shepherd" (149). Yet she is not coy about expressing physical desire for her swain. Having lamented the "malady / Most incident to maids" (124–25)—dying, like primroses, before they have a chance to go to bed with the sun—she passionately imagines Florizel strewn with flowers, "quick" and in her arms. "Not like a corse" (131–32): Perdita's rejection of death, part of this young woman's forthright wish to procreate, paves the way for Hermione's revival from "dead likeness" (5.3.15).

Coppélia Kahn notes the wider significance of Perdita's chaste sexuality when she discusses how the princess's reconciling of "virginity and erotic appeal" is symbolically able to unite Leontes's "divided attitudes toward women."[85] As with Hermione, we become aware of what Perdita represents within the larger pattern of the drama, though the presentation of her character never becomes overly schematic. When she imaginatively conjures up the spring flowers that Proserpine was gathering when she was abducted by Dis, Perdita embodies the life force and fertility that will renew Leontes and barren Sicily. Returning there, she is as welcome as "spring" is "to th' earth" (5.1.152). By prompting Hermione to speak in the final scene, Perdita also plays a crucial role in the reanimation of the queen. Her alliance with her mother, and her own projected future as royal matriarch now that she is about to marry Florizel, guarantee what Janet

Adelman calls the promise of "female continuity and generativity"[86] at the end of the play.

## PAULINA AND CAMILLO

### Paulina

Presented as the toughest of the three, Paulina completes the triumvirate of strong women in the play. Whereas Hermione and Perdita take shape from Bellaria and Fawnia in Greene's *Pandosto,* Paulina is Shakespeare's original.[87] This "unruly"[88] woman who defies the dictates of her patriarchal society is unusual in the degree to which she wields power over Leontes and in how fully she takes control of the play's denouement. First introduced as the staunch defender of the "good queen," she becomes Hermione's guardian—both physically during the 16 years that the queen is supposedly dead and, less tangibly, when she keeps the memory of Hermione alive for Leontes. Most significantly, she breaks female stereotypes to become the "conscience"[89] of the king. At first his stern critic, she takes on the roles of physician, counselor, and guide in act 5, facilitating Leontes's reunion with his wife by stage-managing the final scene of *The Winter's Tale.*

Paulina can play these roles only because she is so outspoken. Unlike the gentler Hermione and Perdita, this "audacious lady" (2.3.41) combines "wit" with "boldness," determined to "use" her tongue—the female instrument of power—not to flatter Leontes but to trumpet her "red-looked anger" by defending the queen "to th' loud'st" (2.2.51–52, 33–38). Her very first words, the ringing command "The keeper of the prison, call to him," project authority. As she positions herself as advocate for Hermione, a "good lady" of "honesty and honor," both Emilia and the Jailer comment on Paulina's own "honor" and "goodness" (2, 9, 6, 42). Firm in her resolve to correct Leontes's delusion—"He must be told on't, and he shall" (30)—Paulina is also tender in hoping that the king may "soften" at the sight of the newborn (39). Unlike the subservient Jailer, she is not afraid to transgress against the king's arbitrary decrees. Instead she uses the precedent of the "law and process of great Nature," which has already freed the baby from her mother's womb, to justify removing the child from prison (59).

Bringing the newborn to the king is a risky mission, but Paulina is up to the task. She is scornful of the male courtiers who "creep like shadows," cowed by the king (2.3.33). In this scene she combines the comic stereotype of the aggressive, shrewish scold[90] (she threatens "Let him that makes but trifles of his eyes / First hand me" [61–62]) with the stern, female adviser figure from medieval tradition[91] who comes with "words as medicinal as true" (36), again aligning herself with "good goddess Nature" in pointing out that the baby reveals the "very mold" of her father (101–2). She wishes she were a "man" who could champion Hermione's honor by physical "combat" (59–60). Instead she "abrogate[s] masculine power"[92] by defying her husband Antigonus and refusing to obey the king for as long as possible. She taunts Leontes with her insistence that Hermione is the "Good queen, my lord, good queen, I say good queen" (58), adding three more instances of "good" in the next few lines to bait him further. Defiantly, she even terms the king not only a madman whose "rotten" opinion is based on "weak-hinged" fancy, but a "heretic" (88, 117, 113). But while strongly suggesting that the king's "cruel rage something savors / of tyranny" (117–18), this truth-teller stops short of a direct accusation that could be deemed treasonous.

When she returns to the trial scene after Hermione's swoon, however, she frankly labels him "O thou tyrant" and asks with scathing sarcasm, "What studied torments, tyrant, hast for me?" (3.2.173).[93] Like Hermione, Paulina is a skilled rhetorician. Her strategy to make Leontes "run mad" with guilt is to rehearse the sequence of his errors—defaming Polixenes, destroying Camillo's reputation, throwing out his infant daughter, even indirectly causing the death of his son—only to dismiss such clearly heinous actions (for "a devil / Would have shed water out of fire" rather than abandon a newborn) as "nothing" (181–97). In this way she builds to his one unforgivable crime: causing the death of the "sweet'st, dear'st" creature, Hermione (197–99). Ramming home the horror, she declares that no repentance, however intense, could induce the gods to take pity on him. Her excoriation magnificently releases the outrage the audience feels at what they believe to be the death of an innocent woman.[94] Does Paulina in fact know that Hermione is alive, and is she manufacturing a worst-case scenario in order to show Leontes that superficial repentance is not enough? Or does she, along with the audience, think at this point that Hermione is really dead? The tone of outrage suggests the latter; but the very flamboyance of her "rhetorically embellished" tirade may convey "contrivance" instead.[95]

An actress must also decide what drives Paulina's abrupt capitulation and apology after Leontes submits to her chastising:

> Alas, I have showed too much
> The rashness of a woman; he is touched
> To th' noble heart. What's gone and what's past help
> Should be past grief; do not receive affliction
> At my petition. (218–22)

Is she being disingenuous here? While it would be hard to deliver these lines as biting "irony,"[96] they may be part of Paulina's clever disclaimer; in a strategy of "calculated tactlessness,"[97] she goes on to remind him that he has lost his wife and both his children even while vowing to speak of them "no more" (227). And her final lines, "Take your patience to you, / And I'll say nothing" (229–30) could be delivered as a bargaining gambit, even a threat, rather than a promise that she will remain silent now he is becoming penitent. Alternatively, she may be genuinely compassionate (never purely a scold, she has shown tenderness before)[98] in her quest to teach Leontes penitence by her own example when she tells him, "all faults I make, when I shall come to know them, / I do repent" (217–18).

If she is using a calculated technique in this scene, it certainly "smacks rather of sadism."[99] Sixteen years later, Paulina continues to revive painful memories, and Leontes continues to respond somewhat masochistically; when she slyly slips in the word "kill'd" he obediently responds, "She I killed! I did so" (5.1.16–17). In the role of Leontes's physician (as Paulina claims in 2.3.53), hers is a process of "caustic healing"[100] that may at this stage appear counterproductive. As guardian of Hermione's memory, reiterating that the queen lived "peerless" (5.3.14), she resents Perdita's being praised as the "rarest of all women" on her arrival at court (5.1.112). And when Leontes is attracted to Perdita, she reminds him that Hermione was "more worth such gazes" (226). Only retroactively can she be seen to be preparing both Leontes and the audience for a miracle—the return of Hermione—when she makes the king swear that he will marry again only with her permission, and never until his first queen is again "in breath" (83).

Unless we already know the ending, Paulina will seem too severe. She locks Leontes into his old grief, preventing his ritual of repentance from progressing, as it naturally would, into renewal, and discouraging any possibility of royal succession. But having firmly aligned herself with the gods and the oracle of Apollo at the beginning of act 5, she now has the authority to work what seems to be divine magic. This she does by enticing as well as tormenting the king. In her "chapel" she urges him to admire the statue as an incredible likeness but twice will not let him touch it; she tempts him to imagine "it moves," but twice threatens to draw the curtain to hide it (61, 68, 83). In an echo of her earlier ironic "do not receive affliction / At my petition" (3.2.221–22), she now offers to "afflict" him further by making the statue "move indeed" and take him by the hand (75, 88).

Managing the transformation of statue into woman is an awesome responsibility, recalling how in act 3 Paulina offered to "serve" Leontes as she "would do the gods" if he could bring "Heat outwardly or breath within" to the apparently dead body of Hermione (3.2.204–5). Yet she insists that she is not "assisted" by the "wicked powers" of witchcraft (5.3.90–91). While Paulina is reticent about where Hermione has been for 16 years, allowing her "living" to remain as improbable as an "old tale," it is clear that the queen is not "stol'n from the dead" (115–17). Paulina is a superb stage-manager and artistic director, a surrogate for the playwright rather than a Neoplatonic mage; her magic is as "lawful as eating" (111). This "grave and good" (1) conjurer matches a "death that is no death"— the demise of Hermione that she affirmed in act 3—with a "revival that is no revival."[101] She alone is responsible for contriving an amazing spectacle, for despite the earlier praise given to the supposed sculptor, Julio Romano, Paulina is careful to assure everyone that "the stone is mine" (58). And now, appropriately for a woman who has appealed to the "great goddess Nature," her work of art turns out to be nature itself, the flesh and blood Hermione whom she has helped to preserve.[102] As producer of this long-designed reunion, Paulina first insists that Leontes must "awake" his "faith" (95) and then directs him to "present" his "hand" to the queen and woo her afresh (107–8). In a final choreographic touch, this promoter of women makes sure that Perdita will "interpose" herself to kneel for her mother's blessing and thus prompt Hermione to speak again (119).

### Camillo

At this point Paulina's work as facilitator of the solemn reunion of royal husband and wife is over. But the moment she indulges in self-pity, seeing herself as an "old turtle" (132) who must forever mourn her lost mate, Leontes produces his own trump card: Camillo is to be her new husband. Somewhat glibly, and with "touching clumsiness,"[103] Paulina is absorbed into the comic finale of marriages. She appears to accept her "proper status to be that of obedient wife—to somebody, to anybody, to whomever the king chooses."[104] Yet, as Carol Thomas Neely comments, this betrothal solves "two potentially problematic triangles"—Paulina as the queen's rival, since she has served almost as surrogate wife for Leontes during Hermione's absence, and the "rivalry of Polixenes and Leontes for Camillo's services."[105] The match is also appropriate because the two serve much the same function, as counselors and consciences. In act 1 Leontes recalls how "priest-like" Camillo has cleansed his "bosom" in the past (1.2.237–38), and in act 4 Camillo seems to Florizel a "medicine" that can work "almost a miracle" in arranging the flight of the lovers (4.4.591, 538).

Like Paulina, Camillo not only acts as a "physician" to the king (2.3.54) but is noted for his "honor" and "honesty." Defending his integrity to Leontes in act 1, scene 2, he is careful to separate any charges that he has been "negligent, foolish, and fearful" from his overall "honesty" (250, 263). And when Polixenes appeals to the "honor" of this respected man to tell him what is amiss, Camillo cannot resist being "charged in honor" by an "honorable man" (402, 408–9); because he could never countenance killing a king, whatever the reward, he quickly entrusts his "honesty" to a new master (435). Twice Leontes refers to the "honor" of the "most humane" Camillo when he deeply regrets having alienated his trusty servant (3.2.163–64). At the end of the play he commends Camillo to Paulina as an "honorable husband" to whose "worth and honesty" a "pair of kings," Bohemia as well as Sicilia, can now attest (5.3.143–46).

While never as sharp-tongued as Paulina, Camillo can be outspoken to those in authority. He cuts through the courtly circumlocutions of Archidamus (anxious about matching Sicilia's hospitality in Bohemia "next summer") with "You pay a great deal too dear for what's given freely" (1.1.17–18). Horrified by Leontes's suspicions about Hermione, he chides his monarch with "You never spoke what did become you less" (1.2.282). And when Leontes tries to force him to "Say it be, 'tis true," Camillo firmly insists, "No, no, my lord" (298–99).

Overall, though, Camillo is much more tactful and circumspect than his "audacious" female counterpart. He speaks riddlingly to Polixenes about the hidden "disease" afflicting Sicilia (387). In an effort to curb Florizel's recklessness in act 4, he is less than candid when he compliments the prince's ill-conceived plan as "ponderous and settled" (4.4.528). Leontes accuses his servant of being a "hovering temporizer" (1.2.302) when Camillo is reluctant to agree that Hermione is false. Indeed there is something very shrewd and canny about the way that Camillo sees how the land lies and acts accordingly; he goes from a vehement denial of what the king suspects to allowing "I must believe you, sir," while agreeing that he could poison Polixenes with a "lingering dram" if necessary (334, 320). He is clearly temporizing here—having recognized, as he later tells Polixenes, that nothing will "shake / The fabric" of the king's "folly" (429–30)—and is playing the careful diplomat when he urges Leontes to take back his queen for the sake of the prince as well as to exert some damage control over what the neighbors ("courts and kingdoms / Known and allied" to Sicily [339–40]) will say. When he realizes that Leontes is a lost cause, he rapidly turns his "fortunes" over to the service of Polixenes (441).

Similarly, when he advises Florizel on how to escape from Bohemia, he admits in two asides that he plans to "serve" his own "turn," too (4.4.513, 666–71). Steering Florizel towards his own "dear Sicilia" (515) will give him a pretext to return to his homeland and to his old master. Accordingly, despite promising that he will "strive to qualify" the wrath of Polixenes

(536), he secretly plans to tell the king the whole scheme so that together they can pursue the runaways to Sicily. Yet ultimately Camillo's duplicity[106] works toward a happy reconciliation, just as Paulina's concealment of Hermione for 16 years—shocking on a realistic level—is accepted without criticism as part of the larger providential scheme.

In the same way that Paulina stage-manages the statue episode, so Camillo, another internal dramatist, carefully scripts the lovers' departure. Promising that Florizel will be "royally appointed as if / The scene you play were mine" (596–97), he also directs Perdita to "disliken / The truth of [her] own seeming" (656–57) in order to escape to the waiting ship. Opportunistically, he discerns in Autolycus an "instrument" who can furnish clothes to disguise the couple, chivying along the rogue with "discase thee instantly" (629, 637–38). Camillo even supplies precise directions for how Florizel should greet Leontes when he and Perdita reach Sicily: "What you … shall deliver … I'll write you down" (563–64). Impressed, Florizel praises "worthy" Camillo as "Preserver of my father, now of me" (558, 590). For her part, during the 16-year gap Paulina has helped Hermione "preserv[e]" herself to bless the future of her daughter (5.3.127). Whether we view them as honorable guardians or "inveterate artists and contrivers,"[107] Camillo and Paulina seem destined to be part of the re-couplings in the play's finale.

## NOTES

1. In C. H. Herford, Percy Simpson, and Evelyn Simpson (eds.), *Ben Jonson,* vol. 8 (Oxford: Clarendon Press, 1947), p. 625.

2. Caroline E. Spurgeon, *Shakespeare's Imagery and What It Tells Us* (Cambridge: Cambridge University Press, 1935), p. 305.

3. Maurice Hunt, *Shakespeare's Romance of the Word* (London and Toronto: Associated University Presses, 1990), points out the "redemptive" mirroring technique in the play (89).

4. See W. H. Clemen, *The Development of Shakespeare's Imagery* (London: Methuen, 1966), pp. 196–98.

5. M. M. Mahood, *Shakespeare's Wordplay* (London: Methuen, 1969), discusses the extensive *"double-entendres"* here (149).

6. Ibid., p. 154.

7. Stanley Cavell, *Disowning Knowledge in Seven Plays of Shakespeare* (Cambridge: Cambridge University Press, 1987), links this "computational" and "economic" language with the play's emphasis on communication through recounting or telling (201–2).

8. In *Beyond Tragedy* (Lexington, Ky.: University Press of Kentucky, 1989), Robert W. Uphaus expands the range of significant meanings of "issue" in *The Winter's Tale* to include the legal (Time's tests and the "trial between the

vying forces of tragedy and romance" [89]) and the medicinal—the discharging of disease effected by the younger generation and by Paulina's enterprise (73, 89).

9. Neely, *"The Winter's Tale:* The Triumph of Speech," *SEL* 15, no. 2 (Spring, 1978): 321–38, 322–23.

10. Ibid., 330.

11. S.L. Bethell, The Winter's Tale: *A Study* (London: Staples Press, Ltd., 1947), p. 20.

12. Russ McDonald, "Poetry and Plot in *The Winter's Tale*," *SQ* 36 (1985): 315–29, 316, 327.

13. Bethell, The Winter's Tale: *A Study,* p. 21.

14. Frank Kermode, *Shakespeare's Language* (London and New York: The Penguin Press, 2000), p. 278.

15. G. Wilson Knight, "'Great Creating Nature': An Essay on *The Winter's Tale*," in *The Crown of Life* (London: Methuen and Co., 1948), p. 82.

16. McDonald, "Poetry and Plot in *The Winter's Tale*," analyzes in detail the "syntactic and prosodic complexity" of this speech (324–25).

17. A.F. Bellette, "Truth and Utterance in *The Winter's Tale*," *ShS* 31 (1978): 65–75, comments on how "Each person speaks in the way which is most directly expressive of his or her nature" (65); in particular, the author contrasts Leontes's "disjointed utterance" with Hermione's "controlled" speech (67).

18. See Jonathan Smith, "The Language of Leontes," *SQ* 19, no. 3 (1968): 317–27, who points out that Leontes retreats into unusual latinate diction as a form of "intellectual circumlocution" (321).

19. Kermode, *Shakespeare's Language,* p. 281.

20. Hunt, *Shakespeare's Romance of the Word,* analyzes stylistically the cresting and suspension effects in Florizel's speech (99). In "'Stir' and Work in Shakespeare's Last Plays," *SEL* 22, no. 2 (1982): 285–304, Maurice Hunt further discusses the "dynamics of motion and fixity" in the style of *The Winter's Tale* (297).

21. Smith, "The Language of Leontes," p. 326.

22. Neely, *"The Winter's Tale:* The Triumph of Speech," p. 332.

23. Kermode, *Shakespeare's Language,* p. 273.

24. Derek Traversi, *Shakespeare: The Last Phase* (Stanford, Calif.: Stanford University Press, 1953), analyzes the delicate rhythmic construction of the speech, where Leontes's "weight of memory" balances the "perfections" of Hermione against the "magnitude" of his own faults (167).

25. Kermode, *Shakespeare's Language,* p. 275.

26. Charles Frey, *Shakespeare's Vast Romance: A Study of* The Winter's Tale (Columbia and London: University of Missouri Press, 1980), p. 28.

27. Anne Barton, "Leontes and the Spider: Language and Speaker in Shakespeare's Last Plays," in *Essays, Mainly Shakespearean* (Cambridge: Cambridge University Press, 1994), pp. 161–81, 171, where Barton argues that the play's language expresses the "truth of the situation" more often than it reveals character.

28. Harley Granville-Barker, "Preface to *The Winter's Tale*" (1912), in *More Prefaces to Shakespeare,* cd. Edward M. Moore (Princeton, N.J.: Princeton University Press, 1974), p. 23.

29.   Ernest Schanzer (ed.), William Shakespeare, *The Winter's Tale* (London and New York: Penguin, 1986), p. 21.

30.   Granville-Barker, "Preface to *The Winter's Tale*," p. 23.

31.   Schanzer (ed.), *The Winter's Tale*, p. 21.

32.   Nevill Coghill, "Six Points of Stage-Craft in *The Winter's Tale, ShS* 11 (1958): 31–41, 33. Roger J. Triemens, "The Inception of Leontes' Jealousy in *The Winter's Tale*," *SQ* 4 (1953): 1–26, also cites Leontes's "remarkably terse and laconic words" at the opening of the scene as evidence that he is "already jealous" (323–24). Louis L. Martz, "*The Winter's Tale:* Trilogy of Redemption," in *From Renaissance to Baroque* (Columbia and London: University of Missouri Press), pp. 131–45, compares Leontes to a Greek tragic protagonist such as Clytemnestra, already "in the grip of a furious jealousy" (137), and S. R. Maveety, "What Shakespeare Did with *Pandosto:* An Interpretation of *The Winter's Tale*," in *Pacific Coast Studies in Shakespeare,* ed. Waldo F. McNeir and Thelma N. Greenfield (Eugene: University of Oregon Press, 1966), pp. 263–79, argues that Leontes is a "victim of a divine curse" (265), like Seneca's hero in *Hercules Furens.*

33.   In "Rhetoric and the Tragedy of *The Winter's Tale*," *Ucrow* 20 (2000): 116–32, Adam McKeown notes that Leontes is "forced to confront Hermione's rhetorical superiority everywhere he looks" (116).

34.   Howard Felperin, "'Tongue-tied our Queen': The Deconstruction of Presence in *The Winter's Tale*," in *Shakespeare and the Question of Theory,* ed. Patricia Parker and Geoffrey Hartman (London and New York, 1985), pp. 8, 9.

35.   William T. Matchett, "Some Dramatic Techniques in *The Winter's Tale*," *ShS* 23 (1969): 93–107, 95.

36.   Schanzer (ed.), *The Winter's Tale*, p. 24.

37.   See Fitzroy Pyle, The Winter's Tale: *A Commentary on the Structure* (New York: Barnes and Noble, Inc., 1969), p. 20.

38.   Graham Holderness, "*The Winter's Tale:* Country into Court," in Graham Holderness, Nick Potter, John Turner, *Shakespeare: Out of Court* (New York: St. Martin's Press, 1990), p. 207.

39.   This idea—that Leontes is otherwise occupied during the speech—was first proposed by Arthur Quiller-Couch and John Dover Wilson (eds.), *The Winter's Tale,* The New Shakespeare (Cambridge: Cambridge University Press, 1931), p. 133. Norman Nathan, "Leontes' Provocation," *ShS* 19 (1968): 19–24, concludes that the jealousy is "sudden" but also "well-motivated" because Leontes legitimately misinterprets the conversation between Hermione and Polixenes (20).

40.   Discussed by Douglas L. Peterson, *Time, Tide, and Tempest* (San Marino, Calif.: Huntingdon Library Publications, 1973), p. 159.

41.   See J.I.M. Stewart, *Character and Motive in Shakespeare* (London: Longmans, 1949), pp. 35–36, and Coppélia Kahn, *Man's Estate: Masculine Identity in Shakespeare* (Berkeley and Los Angeles: University of California Press, 1981), who discusses how it would be "his way of defending against the horrified realization that he too still loves that friend" (215). A. D. Nuttall, *Shakespeare: The Winter's Tale* (London: Edward Arnold, 1966), probes the related Freudian

theory that "Leontes' attitude to Hermione is a disguised projection of his own guilt" (19).

42. This is the thesis of Murray M. Schwartz, "Leontes' Jealousy in *The Winter's Tale*," *AMIAA* 30, no. 3 (1973): 250–73, who analyzes how Leontes projects his "knowledge of maternal malevolence" onto Hermione (273).

43. David Young, *The Heart's Forest: A Study of Pastoral in Shakespeare's Plays* (New Haven and London: Yale University Press, 1972), points out the remarkable tension between Leontes as the "conventional" figure of a jealous husband and the "psychological verisimilitude that bursts out" in his speeches (121).

44. Thomas Middleton Raysor (ed.), Samuel Taylor Coleridge, *Shakespearean Criticism,* vol. 3 (London: Dent, 1960), pp. 110–11.

45. Wilbur Sanders, The Winter's Tale: *Twayne's New Critical Introductions to Shakespeare* (Boston: Twayne Publishers, 1987), also comments that Leontes's jealousy is "both helplessly involuntary *and* ... recklessly chosen" (29).

46. Pyle, The Winter's Tale: *A Commentary,* p. 42.

47. Ibid.

48. This is the view of David Schalkwyk, "'A Lady's "Verily" Is as Potent as a Lord's': Women, Word, and Witchcraft in *The Winter's Tale*," *ELR* 22, no. 2 (1992): 242–72, 268.

49. Peter Erickson, *Patriarchal Structures in Shakespeare's Drama* (Berkeley, Los Angeles, London: University of California Press, 1985), pp. 169, 168.

50. Erickson, *Patriarchal Structures,* calls this a "courtly reflex gesture" (151). Patricia Southard Gourlay, "'O my most sacred lady': Female Metaphor in *The Winter's Tale*," *ELR* 3 (1975): 375–95, comments on Polixenes's "gentlemanly misogyny" (378) at this point.

51. This was Peter Hall's take on the character in his 1988 production for the National Theatre; see Roger Warren, *Staging Shakespeare's Late Plays* (Oxford: Clarendon Press, 1990), p. 129.

52. Stephen Orgel (ed.), William Shakespeare, *The Winter's Tale,* The Oxford Shakespeare (Oxford: Oxford University Press, 1996), p. 25.

53. Janet Adelman, "Masculine Authority and the Maternal Body: The Return to Origins in the Romances," in *Suffocating Mothers: Fantasies of Maternal Origins in Shakespeare's Plays,* Hamlet *to* The Tempest (New Haven and London: Yale University Press, 1992), p. 229.

54. Erickson, *Patriarchal Structures,* p. 164.

55. John Russell Brown, *Shakespeare's Plays in Performance* (New York: Applause Theatre Books, 1966; 1993), p. 97.

56. W. K. Wimsatt (ed.), *Dr. Johnson on Shakespeare* (Harmondsworth, Middlesex: Penguin, 1960; 1969), p. 109.

57. See Orgel (ed.), *The Winter's Tale,* pp. 50–52.

58. Wilson Knight, *The Crown of Life,* p. 100.

59. J.H.P. Pafford (ed.), *The Winter's Tale,* The Arden Shakespeare (London: Methuen and Co. Ltd., 1963), finds that Autolycus serves as a "faint rhythmic parallel to the evil in Leontes in the first part of the play" (p. lxxx). Joan Hartwig, "Bearers of Parodic Burdens," in Carol McGinnis Kay and Henry E.

Jacobs (eds.), *Shakespeare's Romances Reconsidered* (Lincoln and London: University of Nebraska Press, 1978), comments on how Autolycus absorbs some of the "disorderly aspects of Leontes' disturbed imagination" shown earlier in the play (101).

60.   Carol Thomas Neely, "Incest and Issue in *The Winter's Tale*," in *Broken Nuptials in Shakespeare's Plays* (Urbana: University of Illinois Press, 1993), p. 203.

61.   Simon Forman's eyewitness account of the play, 1611, reprinted in Orgel (ed.), *The Winter's Tale,* p. 233. Arthur F. Kinney, *Rogues, Vagabonds, and Sturdy Beggars* (Amherst: University of Massachusetts Press, 1990), points out the zestful tone of the rogue pamphlets; judged within that literary context, Autolycus is more a lovable rogue than a dangerous phenomenon (5).

62.   Richard Hillman, *Shakespearean Subversions: The Trickster and the Playtext* (London and New York: Routledge, 1992), p. 223.

63.   Sanders, The Winter's Tale*: Twayne's New Critical Introductions,* p. 95.

64.   Traversi, *Shakespeare: The Last Phase,* p. 139.

65.   Peterson, *Time, Tide, and Tempest,* p. 183.

66.   In contrast, Lee Sheridan Cox, "The Role of Autolycus in *The Winter's Tale*," *SEL* 9 (1969): 283–301, argues that this "purveyor of falsehood" becomes the "agent of a power for good" (286).

67.   Discussed by Howard Felperin, *Shakespearean Romance* (Princeton, N.J.: Princeton University Press, 1972), p. 237, and also David Kaula, "Autolycus' Trumpery," *SEL* 16, no. 2 (1976): 287–303, 288, 303. In contrast, Walter S. H. Lim, "Knowledge and Belief in *The Winter's Tale*," *SEL* 41, no. 2 (2001): 317–34, argues that Autolycus increases our skepticism about the play's ending by "linking faith directly to superstitious belief and ignorance" (331).

68.   Admittedly the star comic actor with the King's Men, Robert Armin, would most likely be restricted to one role. T. J. King, *Casting Shakespeare's Plays: London Actors and their Roles, 1590–1642* (Cambridge: Cambridge University Press, 1992), deduces that the parts of Antigonus and the Third Gentleman would be doubled (244). Richard Proudfoot, "Verbal Reminiscence and the Two-Part Structure of *The Winter's Tale*," *ShS* 29 (1976): 67–78, speculates that the doubling of Antigonus and Autolycus is at least possible and that it would add another nuance to the artifice of act 5, scene 2, in which Autolycus is a "slightly unexpected auditor of the Third Gentleman's narration of the death of Antigonus" (73).

69.   In a more moralistic interpretation, Dennis Biggens, in "'Exit Pursued by a Beare': A Problem in *The Winter's Tale*," *SQ* 13 (1962): 3–13, argues that Antigonus's violent death is an appropriate punishment for his becoming an "agent of tyranny" (12) and thus an "emblem of broken integrity" (8).

70.   In "'Bearing Hence': Shakespeare's *The Winter's Tale*," *SEL* 44, no. 2 (2004): 333–46, Maurice Hunt also suggests that "in dying Antigonus undergoes a rebirth" as Autolycus (338).

71.   Traversi, *Shakespeare: The Last Phase,* p. 123.

72.   Erickson, *Patriarchal Structures in Shakespeare's Drama,* p. 162.

73. Martine Van Elk, "'Our Praises Are Our Wages': Courtly Exchange, Social Mobility, and Female Speech in *The Winter's Tale*," *PQ* 79, no. 4 (Fall 2000): 429–57, discusses how the conventions of "rhetorical performance" give the queen some freedom to indulge in sexualized "courtly repartee" (438, 436).

74. Adelman, *Suffocating Mothers,* p. 221.

75. Gemma Jones played the role for the Royal Shakespeare Company in 1976. In "Hermione in *The Winter's Tale*," in Philip Brockbank (ed.), *Players of Shakespeare* (Cambridge: Cambridge University Press, 1985), pp. 153–65, Jones notes that "If Hermione is in a state of maternity this can embrace not only the child that she has and the child that she carries but also her husband and his friend in an entirely chaste and compassionate love" (158).

76. A. L. French, *Shakespeare and the Critics* (Cambridge: Cambridge University Press, 1972), finds Hermione's "cajoling charm" a deliberate use of her sexual power (140).

77. Sanders, The Winter's Tale: *Twayne's New Critical Introductions,* instead interprets this more subtly as showing how Hermione, lured into gratifying her husband, is "making her way carefully through the tangled thickets of Leontes' misprision and self-doubt" (37).

78. Pafford (ed.), *The Winter's Tale,* The Arden Shakespeare, p. lxxiii.

79. Bellette, "Truth and Utterance in *The Winter's Tale*," points out that there is "not the least hint of casuistry, sleight of tongue or special pleading" in Hermione's defense, but testimony to "a world of order, value and relatedness" (69).

80. Sanders, The Winter's Tale: *Twayne's New Critical Introductions,* p. 44.

81. Adelman, *Suffocating Mothers,* pp. 196, 236.

82. Valerie Traub, *Desire and Anxiety: Circulations of Sexuality in Shakespearean Drama* (London and New York: Routledge, 1992), p. 45.

83. Granville-Barker, "Preface to *The Winter's Tale*," notes that Perdita has "all her mother's courage and self-possession" (23–24).

84. Neely, "Women and Issue," stresses Perdita's "frank and whole-hearted aceptance of sexuality" (201).

85. Kahn, *Man's Estate,* p. 219. Bill Overton, The Winter's Tale*: The Critics Debate* (Atlantic Highlands, N.J.: Humanities Press International, 1989), also refers to Perdita's "innocent eroticism" (80).

86. Adelman, *Suffocating Mothers,* p. 234.

87. Pyle, The Winter's Tale*: A Commentary,* finds the "germ" of this "masterful woman" in Porrus's shrewish wife in Greene's *Pandosto* (40).

88. Holderness, "*The Winter's Tale:* Country into Court," discusses Paulina in these terms (219).

89. Bethell, The Winter's Tale*: A Study,* notes that Paulina represents this function (100), as does Knight, *The Crown of Life* (95).

90. Overton, The Winter's Tale*: The Critics Debate,* comments on how Shakespeare "disables the stereotype" of the scold or virago by making the deranged king appeal to it (66).

91. See Carolyn Asp, "Shakespeare's Paulina and the *Consolatio* Tradition," *ShakS* 11 (1978): 145–58, 147. Laurie Shannon, *Sovereign Amity: Figures of*

*Friendship in Shakespearean Contexts* (Chicago and London: University of Chicago Press, 2002), comments on how Paulina's role allows the "counselor-friend" to be "gendered feminine" in *The Winter's Tale* (209, 213).

92.    Holderness, "*The Winter's Tale:* Country into Court," p. 217.

93.    M. Linday Kaplan and Katherine Eggert, "'Good Queen, My Lord, Good Queen': Sexual Slander and the Trials of Female Authority in *The Winter's Tale,*" *RenD* 25 (1994): 89–118, 108, note how the play vindicates Paulina's "scolding" when Leontes finally admits "Thou didst speak but well, / When most the truth" (3.2.230–31).

94.    See Thomas McFarland, *Shakespeare's Pastoral Comedy* (Chapel Hill: University of North Carolina Press, 1972), p. 130.

95.    A.P. Riemer, "Deception in *The Winter's Tale,*" *SSEng* 13 (1987–88): 21–38, 28. For differing interpretations, see Warren, *Staging Shakespeare's Late Plays,* pp. 124–26.

96.    Gourlay, "'O My Most Sacred Lady,'" p. 385.

97.    Pafford (ed.), *The Winter's Tale,* p. lxxv. D.J. Enright, *Shakespeare and the Students* (Chatto and Windus: London, 1970), also points out that Paulina must gain Leontes's "unambiguous permission" to tell him the truth so that she can become his spiritual advisor during Hermione's absence (182).

98.    Warren, *The Staging of Shakespeare's Late Plays,* comments that Paulina is "neither a scold nor a railer but a compassionate woman who only becomes a tigress when provoked by Leontes' stubborn inhumanity" (114).

99.    Sanders, The Winter's Tale*: Twayne's New Critical Introductions,* p. 52.

100.    Gourlay, "'O My Most Sacred Lady,'" p. 385. Jane Tylus, *Writing and Vulnerability in the Late Renaissance* (Stanford, Calif: Stanford University Press, 1993), finds Paulina's subversiveness consists in keeping Leontes's wounds "open" and drawing on the "community" of dead "witnesses" to his misdeeds (166, 173).

101.    Pyle, The Winter's Tale*: A Commentary,* p. 135.

102.    Robert Egan, *Drama within Drama: Shakespeare's Sense of His Art* (New York and London: Columbia University Press, 1975), discusses Paulina as an "artificer" who induces in the audience a "passionate readiness" for the project's culmination as she turns her "image to a reality" (81, 84–85).

103.    Sanders, The Winter's Tale*: Twayne's New Critical Introductions,* p. 119.

104.    Orgel (ed.), *The Winter's Tale,* p. 79.

105.    Neely, "Incest and Issue in *The Winter's Tale,*" p. 209.

106.    Robert M. Adams, *Shakespeare: The Four Romances* (New York and London: W.W. Norton and Co., 1989), wryly remarks of the union of Paulina with Camillo that "the sharpness of her tongue will be needed to curtail the excessive suppleness of his" (108).

107.    R.A. Foakes, *Shakespeare, the Dark Comedies to the Last Plays: From Satire to Celebration* (London: Routledge and K. Paul, 1971), p. 144.

# 5

# *THEMES*

Because the plot of *The Winter's Tale* progresses from near-tragedy to comic resolution, several themes—how providence works through time, the "victory of spring over winter,"[1] miraculous second chances—lie at the heart of the play, embedded in its very structure and verbal texture. This chapter focuses instead on concepts that are presented less overtly but that make equal claim to significance within the play's overall vision. The first, arising from Leontes's jealousy, hinges on the polysemous word "affection" and counterposes involuntary emotions with firm faith in the loved one. The second raises the important issue of how far "honor" is innate in a "gentleman born" (5.2.148) and how far it is manifested through good deeds that are not restricted to the aristocracy. The importance of distinguishing true "virtue" from courtly trappings links to a third, the larger question of credibility in the play as a whole. Can this dramatized "old tale" (5.2.65), with its forays into make-believe, impress an audience with an image of truth? One solution is offered in the final scene, where the magic of theater enables the audience to embrace illusion—the restoration of Hermione—as an ideal version of reality. When an admired statue is revealed to be a living woman, art becomes the consort of nature rather than its adversary.

## MULTIPLYING "AFFECTION," UNIFYING "FAITH"

Leontes's private outburst "Affection! Thy intention stabs the center" (1.2.138–46) is probably the most puzzling passage in the play. As has been discussed in chapter 1, it is by no means clear whether Leontes is referring to what he thinks is Hermione's lust for Polixenes or contemplating his own passionate response; the position of "affection" in the verse paragraph allows for both possibilities. Complicating the issue is the nexus of meanings, ranging from "kind feeling" to lustful "passion" to "disease," that the word "affection" carried for Shakespeare and his contemporaries. This semantic indeterminacy enables Leontes's doubts about Hermione, fueling his jealousy as he ponders the painful question: is it not entirely possible that his wife's long-term affection for his friend Polixenes has strayed into sexual desire that has already been consummated?

As Howard Felperin remarks, "verbal duplicity" is rife in the Sicilian court of act 1, reinforcing the sense that there is no stable reality in the world, only an "infinite play of signs."[2] For Leontes the ambiguities inherent in "affection" prove particularly disturbing. In some Shakespearean contexts "affection" signifies what has become its most common meaning today, given as sense 6 in the Oxford English Dictionary (OED): "kind feeling, love, fondness, loving attachment." This is how King Henry uses it in *Henry IV,* Part 2, when he reminds his son Clarence that he holds a "better place" in Prince Hal's "affection" than any of Hal's other brothers do (4.4.22). More frequently, however, Shakespeare uses the word to denote "feeling as opposed to reason; passion, lust" (sense 3 in the OED, now obsolete). Thus Mardian in *Antony and Cleopatra* claims to have "fierce affections, and think / What Venus did with Mars" (1.5.17–18).

*The Winter's Tale* opens with Camillo's reference to the strongly rooted "affection" between the two kings, Sicily and Bohemia (1.1.24–25). Presumably, unless we discern some hidden sexual attachment,[3] this signifies the "kind feeling" and "fondness" they have felt for each other since childhood. But by the time Leontes's jealousy has been triggered, his image of "affection" stabbing the center (getting to the heart of things) springs from his vision of two people lustfully "paddling palms and pinching fingers."[4] A third meaning of "affection" current in the early seventeenth century— OED's sense 10, "An abnormal state of body, malady, disease"—adds to the complexity of what Leontes is experiencing here. Jealousy is one of the "inordinate affections," as Robert Burton puts it in his *Anatomy of Melancholy* (1620), that are difficult to govern and susceptible to "strongest imagination."[5] In his contorted "Affection" speech, Leontes might be speculating on his own "malady" as an involuntary emotion.[6] The irony generated by this reading is that Leontes, even after correctly diagnosing "affection" as a state that, through heightened imagination, makes "possible things not so held" and amplifies what's "unreal" (139–41), quickly convinces himself that, in *his* case, what he has dreamt up is actually happening. The king no longer recognizes, as Camillo does, that his "opinion" is truly "diseased" (297).

Certainly Leontes's difficulty in distinguishing what is true from what is false, and whether or not his wife is "slippery" (1.2.273), is exacerbated by verbal signs that turn out to lack stable referents. The king must also confront the baffling array of meanings of "friendship" and "play." At what point might the close "friend" of a married couple turn into an intimate lover? (OED's sense 4 of "friend" as "lover or paramour," now obsolete, was a common secondary meaning of the word in Renaissance contexts.) Unlike Hermione, who confidently negotiates the different meanings of the tricky, multipurpose word "love," using it (three times within six lines in the trial scene) to denote honorable hospitality toward her husband's friend (3.2.63–64), Leontes cannot disassociate this from "mingling bloods"—adulterous passion (1.2.109). Similarly caught up in the ambiguities of "play," he is unsure where it changes from the harmless games of children ("Go play, boy, play," as Leontes urges Mamillius) to sexual sport ("thy mother plays") or deceptive role-playing ("and I / Play too" [187–88]). Hermione's "bounty" and "fertile bosom" (113) with Polixenes may imply either courtly hospitality or sexual generosity. And because the language of courtesy is often exaggerated and opaque, working against the direct expression of deep feeling, much of what Polixenes says in the opening scene is open to misconstruction.[7] As conveyed by another of the word's proliferating meanings, genuine "affection" could not always be distinguished from "affectation" (cited by the OED as sense 13, now obsolete, of "affection"). Lacking Hermione's understanding of the "fine distinctions of meaning"[8] within different social contexts, faced instead with the horror of "nothing" meaning anything, Leontes grasps at a false certainty by choosing the worst possible interpretation of the signs.[9] In this way he gives "substance and definition" to his "emotional chaos."[10]

As Leontes falls further into the abyss of misperception and "weak-hinged fancy" (2.3.117), it becomes clear that his fixation on negative meanings indicates a failure of faith. Whereas Othello, newly married to Desdemona, vows "My life upon her faith!" (*Othello,* 1.3.294) and loses confidence in his wife only after Iago undermines his sense of security, *The Winter's Tale* opens with Leontes doubting Hermione almost immediately. As Camillo observes, as soon as the king's terrible delusion takes hold, the only thing that is "piled upon his faith" is the "fabric of his folly" (1.2.430–31). His obsession with an evil that does not exist (the spider in the cup), and his passionate assertion "I do see't, and feel't" (2.1.152),

parodies St. Paul's reminder that the real test of Christian faith is to believe in the mysteries that are invisible, for "we hope for that which we see
not" (*Romans,* 8.25).[11]

The rest of the play, though, explores ways of restoring a strong relationship through developing trust or "faith" in the integrity of the loved
one. In Bohemia, the prince's progress toward union with Perdita is the
antithesis of Leontes's rupture from Hermione; Florizel's love for the
princess-as-shepherdess represents the kind of "sound affection" (4.4.383)
to which Leontes must aspire. Florizel assures his lady that his "lusts" do
not "Burn hotter than [his] faith" (34–35), for his commitment to chaste
affection will never give way to violent passion. Yet love is not coolly
rational. After his father threatens to disinherit him, Florizel affirms that
nothing in the whole cosmos will make him break his "oath" to his beloved (495), for the shattering of his "faith" would be unnatural (481–83).
He chooses to be "advised" by his "fancy" (in its now obsolete sense, OED
8b, of "amorous inclination, love"); if reason will not comply, he prefers
"madness," which at least entails "honesty" to his "vow" (486–92).[12]

It is striking how Leontes, too, in the final act is guided by his "fancy"
to reawaken his "faith." When Florizel arrives at the Sicilian court, the
prince trusts that the king's memory of his own youthful "affections" will
make him plead the lovers' cause to Polixenes (5.1.220–21). And Leontes
is clearly receptive to "wonder" (133), since he has feared that the very
sight of the Bohemian prince might "unfurnish" him of "reason" by powerfully reminding him of the dead Mamillius (123).[13] Now, in the play's
finale, Paulina threatens to draw the curtain once she senses that Leontes's
"fancy" (the word here encompasses "imagination," OED's sense 4, as
well as love) may lead him to believe that the statue is about to move
(5.3.60–61). But just as Florizel preferred the "madness" of his love to the
dictates of cool reason, so Leontes prefers the ecstasy of imagining that
the statue lives:

> No settled senses of the world can match
> The pleasure of that madness. (72–73)

The suspension of reason is akin to faith; it is a creative response to events
that defy credibility. When the First Gentleman in act 5, scene 2 reports
on the royal reunions (mysteries that remain unseen and supposedly cannot be described), he stresses how they inspired the "notable passion of
wonder" (5.2.17). The "countenance of such distraction" (51) that accompanies Leontes's discovery of his lost daughter echoes the "brow of much
distraction" that he wore when he first became jealous (1.2.149). Now,

though, "distraction" signals not destructive passion but responsiveness to the kind of "rare" revelation, or "rush to knowledge," promised by the oracle (3.1.20–21) and offered by the spectacle of the statue coming to life.[14]

Paulina's appeal to Leontes before the statue moves—"It is required / You do awake your faith" (5.3.94–95)—resonates on several levels. Like her namesake St. Paul, who maintained that eternal salvation comes through faith alone, she could be urging him to believe in the miracle of Hermione's revival as a religious mystery. It is such faith that enables "Every wink of an eye some new grace [to be] born" (5.2.118–19). Yet in a more direct, human way, Paulina exhorts Leontes to have faith in the lawful "magic" (5.3.39) of renewed physical contact with Hermione.

Whereas Leontes earlier scorned the "ignorant credulity" of his courtiers who believed in the queen's integrity (2.1.192), he must now perform the same act of faith. The "wonder" of Hermione's transformation is thus more an instance of human than divine grace. And if Providence is operating, it is through the good will of individuals, Paulina as well as Hermione. In particular, it works through the queen's faith in "dear life" (5.3.103), her hope for the continuation of her marriage, and her abiding love for Leontes. Belief in such possibilities—the faith, hope, and above all, the love (*agape* or "charity") that St. Paul privileges above the first two in 1 Corinthians 13—need not be naive. Hermione has moved on; she has earned her wrinkles. It must be supposed that her relationship with Leontes could never be restored precisely, only recreated afresh. Nevertheless, the play's romantic ending resolves the theme of affection and faith optimistically. It suggests that the confusing ambiguities of "affection" may be negotiated not primarily through reason or logic, which Leontes has abused during the first part of the play, but through "faith" in the goodness of individuals and in their love.[15]

## "A GENTLEMAN BORN": NOBLENESS, HONOR, AND VIRTUE

Excitedly narrating the reunion of Perdita with her father, Leontes, the Third Gentleman rehearses the evidence for her royal identity: the queen's mantle and jewel found with the baby; the "majesty" of Perdita's demeanor (5.2.38); and, calling on yet another, now archaic, meaning of "affection"—a "disposition towards; bent, inclination" (*OED,* sense 13)—her "affection of nobleness, which nature shows above her breeding" or humble upbringing (39–41). No "bark of baser kind," as Polixenes puts it when he is discussing the art of grafting, she is actually a "bud

of nobler race" (4.4.94–95); nature has triumphed over nurture. One traditional Renaissance viewpoint—that nobleness and honor derive from
"excellencie of birth and lineage"[16]—is boldly upheld in the Gentleman's
report. But the text overall does not endorse such a monolithic view; instead *The Winter's Tale* contests various notions of what it means to be
noble and honorable. While on one level the play affirms that those who
are privileged by birth are naturally "noble" and "gentle," it also suggests
that individual "honor" is less dependent on social rank than on proving
virtue through "good deeds."

In Shakespeare's romance *Cymbeline* (1609), Belarius expounds the
aristocratic position on inborn nobility. Musing on the two princes he kid-
napped from court when they were infants and brought up in the Welsh
countryside, he marvels at their instinctive refinement and courage; he attributes their "royalty unlearn'd, honor untaught" (4.2.178) to the "sparks
of nature" (3.3.79). The assumptions of Leontes are more frankly elitist.
He thinks that if his son, Mamillius (a "gentleman of the greatest promise"
[1.1.36–37]), reacts to his mother's "dishonor" by falling ill, that proves
his inherent "nobleness" (2.3.11–12). The king refuses to call Hermione a
lady on the grounds that she has forfeited her sexual honor. Such a debase-
ment of the linguistic coinage would, he believes, undermine the whole
social hierarchy:

> O thou thing,
> Which I'll not call a creature of thy place,
> Lest barbarism, making me the precedent,
> Should a like language use to all degrees,
> And mannerly distinguishment leave out
> Betwixt the prince and beggar. (2.1.82–87)

But, of course, by crudely and tyrannically indicting Hermione, he for-
feits his own right to be called noble or honorable. As the queen implies,
if Leontes is in his right mind when he makes these accusations, then he
is the "most replenished villain" (where the root word "villein" denotes
low-born)[17] "in the world" (79). Although she continues to address him as
such, he is no longer her "gentle" lord (98).

Hermione herself, daughter of the Emperor of Russia, also endorses
the idea of honor as a birthright, calling it a "derivative from me to mine"
that she hopes to pass on to her son (3.2.43). To this end she repeatedly
"stand[s]" up for her "honor" during her trial and insists on trying to "free"
it from calumny (42, 109). Her assumptions, which are traditional, tally
with those expressed by Count Lewis in Castiglione's popular *The Book
of the Courtier* (1528; translated by Sir Thomas Hoby in 1561): that if a

gentleman "swerve from the steps of his ancestors, hee staineth the name of his familie."[18] But whereas a nobleman or gentleman could validate his good name or that of his lady by chivalrously fighting a duel—and Paulina wishes she were a man who could prove Hermione "good" through "combat" (2.3.59)—a lady, more passively, was expected to uphold her honor through remaining sexually "honest" or chaste. Hermione agrees: if she went "one jot beyond / The bound of honor" and stained her lineage through immodest conduct, her next of kin should "Cry fie upon [her] grave" (3.2.49–53).

Counterbalancing this notion that nobleness and good name are inherited from one's ancestors or, in the case of aristocratic women, simply maintained by being chaste, the play incorporates more egalitarian ideas about acquiring honor. For instance Camillo, the trusted servant to two kings, is frequently commended for his honor and honesty. Although Polixenes calls Camillo a "gentleman," he implies that this courtier has risen to his current position through learning rather than birthright:

> certainly a gentleman, thereto
> Clerklike experienced, which no less adorns
> Our gentry than our parents' noble names
> In whose success we are gentle (1.2.392–95)

Influential sixteenth-century humanist handbooks such as Sir Thomas Elyot's *The Boke Named the Governour* (1531; 1537) gave priority to learning above martial arts in the education of a prince or gentleman, and Castiglione's *Courtier* (in the voice of Lord Octavian) also recommends "studie and diligence"[19] in the art of "letters" (learning).[20]

Even more important, in contemporary discourse as well as in the play itself, is the belief that honor is "the reward due to virtuous action."[21] While Count Lewis in *The Courtier* admits that being a "Gentleman borne" gives an individual an edge,[22] for "noblenesse of birth ... inflameth and provoketh unto virtue,"[23] it is only the starting point. Virtue truly "consisteth in doing and practise."[24] Francis Bacon's similar definition of honor (1597) as the "revealing of a man's virtue and worth"[25] fits Hermione's character well. She does more than simply preserve her married chastity. Although couched in the courtly banter of act 1, scene 2, her eagerness to be given credit for two "good" deeds (1.2.97–98)—persuading Polixenes to stay longer and agreeing to marry her husband—underwrites her bias toward active virtue.

Significantly, the other character most associated with "good deeds," the Old Shepherd, does not have the advantage of noble birth. This virtuous man, who wishes he could have "helped" Antigonus to escape the

bear (3.3.106) and shows "pity" for the abandoned Perdita (75) even before he discovers the wealth that accompanies the child, resolves to make
his "lucky day" an occasion to "do good deeds" (137–38). While he buys
land and becomes prosperous in the intervening 16 years, he remains honorable in his arrangements to marry Perdita to the man he takes to be the
shepherd Doricles. Even after being created a gentleman at the Sicilian
court, the Old Shepherd maintains his integrity. Though concerned by the
"false" oath that his son is proposing, he kindly and courteously agrees
to give a "good report" of Autolycus (5.2.172, 160), telling his son, "we
must be gentle, now we are gentlemen" (162–63).

Perdita mediates between the two versions of being gentle: the aristocratic assumption that nobleness is inherited[26] and the counterview that
honor can be achieved through virtuous actions. Polixenes notes that this
young woman seems "too noble" for her "place" in the Bohemian countryside; he even declares that his own son would be "unworthy" of her were
it not for the prince's inherited royal "honor" (4.4.159, 440–41). Florizel
acknowledges the innate quality of his "gentle" love (46) when he praises
all her "acts" as "queens" (146), though he assumes that his bride's dowry
will consist entirely of her "virtue" (391). Although she herself rejects
the idea of uniting the "wildest stock" to a "gentler scion" (93), Perdita
appears to be a perfect hybrid. Like the honest Old Shepherd, she is down-
to-earth in her abhorrence of being "pranked up" or "painted" (10, 101)
and in her stoical resolve to "milk [her] ewes, and weep" (454) once she
believes she can no longer marry Florizel. Yet she is instinctively courteous. At the sheep-shearing she performs her duties "featly" (176), with an
effortless "Grace" that, according to *The Book of the Courtier,* is "not to
be learned."[27]

The wheel comes full circle, back to "courtly elitism,"[28] the traditional
assumption that nobility is inherited, when Perdita returns to Sicily and
is discovered to be the lost heir of King Leontes. For the kingdom can
survive only through genealogical succession, the royal nature passed on
("derivative") from parent to child. In such a closed community, no grafting of "baser" bark onto the royal tree is permissible, just as Polixenes
strongly denounces Florizel as no longer of his own "blood" (4.4.434)
for proposing to marry a low-born shepherdess. In this vying of "blood"
(ancestry) with achieved "virtue" (*All's Well That Ends Well,* 1.1.62), *The
Winter's Tale* allows ancestry to win out in act 5.

Yet Shakespeare's play manages to have it both ways. It endorses equal
opportunity ways of acquiring "honor" through virtuous deeds even while
it closes with a romantic solution that upholds the aristocracy's unques-
tioned right to govern. As in the discourse of the age, one view does not

displace the other.²⁹ In 1521 Elyot had argued in *The Governour* that "nobility" consists less in "ancient lineage," revenues, and lands than in "wisdom and virtue."³⁰ Yet Henry Peacham's *The Complete Gentleman* (1622), while promoting honor as the "reward of virtue and glorious action," still avers that "in the genuine sense, nobility is the honor of blood in a race or lineage."³¹ In 1596 Shakespeare himself, applying on behalf of his father, John, was finally granted a coat of arms that allowed him to write "gentleman" after his name. Thus the comic sequence in act 5, where the Clown gloats over being a "gentleman born before [his] father" (5.2.148–49), may well be subtle self-parody, the playwright poking fun at his own pretensions. Even this episode cuts two ways, however. It mocks at social upstarts but also satirizes older aristocratic notions of honor. The Clown's semi-aggressive stance, as he challenges Autolycus to a fight to "try whether I am not now a gentleman" (142–43), glances at a code that stressed "martial prowess" as the "chief advancer of gentry"³² and often encouraged dueling to resolve disagreements. Such a code also entailed loyalty to the courtly group, sometimes at the expense of an individual's honesty. Thus the Clown is eager to "swear" that his fellow courtier Autolycus is an "honest" fellow even though he is patently a rogue (166–67), just as Antigonus is earlier forced to swear to his liegelord Leontes that he will cast out the royal baby, an "ungentle business" indeed (3.3.33).

In exploring the question of what finally constitutes "honor," the play thus presents conflicting notions rather than giving priority to one view or embodying a clear thematic message. It ends with the revelation that Hermione has "preserved" herself to see the "issue" in which her royal daughter reclaims her birthright (5.3.124, 128). But it also foregrounds the queen's gesture of active, virtuous forgiveness when she presents her hand as "suitor" (109) to Leontes, a reenactment of her earlier "good deed" in offering her hand to him in marriage.

## "LIKE AN OLD TALE STILL": TRUTH AND FICTION

From the very beginning, when Leontes confuses his own jealous fantasy with reality, *The Winter's Tale* is concerned with credibility. As the play moves deeper into the world of romance, the audience is confronted with the strange and improbable; the uncanny coincidence of Perdita (brought up as a shepherdess) pairing with the prince of Bohemia and then discovering her royal father in Sicily is followed by the marvel of Hermione's reanimation. Still, Shakespeare is concerned about eliciting belief as well as wonder. The play keeps raising the question: how may such an "old tale" be given credit? Even though it is not factually true, can the play succeed in communicating an essential truth about human life and its opportunities for restoration?

In act 2, deciding that "A sad tale's best for winter," Mamillius is eager to entertain his mother with a spooky tale (2.1.25). This framing device alerts us to different degrees of fiction in the play. Introduced so appealingly and never finished, the prince's story turns into a frightening reality when Leontes becomes darkly possessed by the "sprites and goblins" of jealousy (26). Playing a "disgraced" part in earnest (1.2.188), he turns into a destructive tyrant who must "dwel[l] by a churchyard" for 16 years (2.1.30). At her trial Hermione points out how severely she has been victimized by her husband's fictions: "My life stands in the level of your dreams" (3.2.79). These lead, as far as the audience is aware for most of the final two acts, to her own death after Leontes blasphemously rejects the truth of the uncontestable oracle as "mere falsehood" (138).

In Bohemia it is Autolycus who reintroduces the topic of storytelling and credibility. This conman and master of fictions busies himself selling ballads, among his other counterfeit trinkets, at the sheep-shearing festival. Whereas the doomed Mamillius opts to tell a "sad" and not a "merry" tale (2.1.23), Autolycus begins by promoting "doleful" and "pitiful" tales but then, egged on by the enthusiastic rustics, moves to "merry" ones (4.4.263, 283, 290). Although peddling flagrant fiction, he works hard to convince his audience of the ballads' authenticity. When questioned, he claims that the ballad about a celibate woman turning into a "cold fish" (281) has been verified by "Five justices' hands … and witnesses more than my pack will hold" (285–86).

Mopsa naively tells the Clown "I love a ballad in print, a-life, for then we are sure they are true" (261–62). But while in Shakespeare's age licensed books carried the stamp of authority, ballads printed as unlicensed broadsides often tried to pass off outrageous fiction as fact.[33] Mass produced, they were the tabloids of the day, designed to shock and entertain rather than to inform truthfully. The wider play audience, if not Mopsa and Dorcas, will remain suspicious. Even Autolycus ironically deconstructs the ballads' authority. Challenged by Mopsa's insistent "Is it true, think you?" Autolycus asserts that his most preposterous tale, of the usurer's wife "brought to bed of twenty money bags," is "Very true" because it was witnessed by the midwife Mistress Taleporter and "five or six honest wives" who were present at the birth (267–72). The midwife's name gives the game away; like the balladmonger himself, she "carr[ies] lies abroad," her pledge no more trustworthy than his.

The same concern over the validity of "copy" that has no reliable origins underlies Leontes's anxiety, in the early part of the play, about his claims to paternity. With "Art thou my boy?" (1.2.120) he begins to question not only whether he has fathered the unborn Perdita but also his son, Mamillius. He reassures himself that the prince has the royal imprint, his father's nose—"They say it is a copy out of mine" (122)—until he remembers that "they" who report this are women, who "will say anything" (131). Paulina uses a similar printing metaphor when she tries to reassure the king and his courtiers that Perdita is a facsimile of her father:

> Behold my lords,
> Although the print be little, the whole matter
> And copy of the father: eye, nose, lip ... (2.3.97–98)

But Leontes, who has already denounced Paulina as an "intelligencing bawd" (67), obliquely discredits her evidence by again associating her with a gossipy midwife, a "hag" who will not hold her "tongue" (106–8). Nevertheless, after 16 years he uses Paulina's criterion to validate Florizel as the authentic prince of Bohemia and his mother as truly chaste:

> Your mother was most true to wedlock, Prince:
> For she did print your royal father off,
> Conceiving you. (5.1.124–26)

In her role as printer (not, it seems, gestator or coproducer), the Queen of Bohemia has faithfully transmitted the royal copy. Unlike Autolycus's mass-produced ballads, part of a "bastardized ... print commodity"[34] that can make no serious claim to truth, a legitimate noble child in this patriarchal society must carry the print of his or her father.

Like mass-produced print, oral report in *The Winter's Tale* is subject to fraud. The dream of Antigonus, which he reports just before he is killed, misleads the audience into thinking that Hermione is one of the "spirits o' th' dead" (3.3.15).[35] The Clown turned gentleman throws doubt on veracity at court when he asserts that "If it be ne'er so false, a true gentleman may swear it in the behalf of his friend" (5.2.173–74). This raises a question germane to the play itself: can the Gentlemen's report of the royal reunions in act 5 be truly reliable?

The Gentlemen advertise their material as being beyond the ingenuity of the most notorious tale-spinners—"such a deal of wonder ... that ballad makers cannot be able to express it" (5.2.25–27)—even while they strive to convince each other that they are telling the truth. The Second Gentleman, like Mopsa and Dorcas challenging Autolycus's ballad material, plays the skeptic; he voices the possible doubts of the theater audience when he muses that "This news, which is called true, is so like an old tale that the verity of it is in strong suspicion" (29–31). Rising to the challenge, the Third Gentleman reassures his auditors that although what occurred was "Like an old tale still," it is "Most true" (65, 33). Refusing to be defeated by words, he strives to recreate a wonderful happening that "lames report" and "undoes description" (61–62). Truth is made "pregnant by circumstance," full of corroborating details such as the queen's mantle and jewel, which furnish "unity in the proofs" that Perdita is indeed the lost princess (33–35). Even a seemingly fantastic detail such as the death of Antigonus, who is eaten by a bear, should convince the skeptical hearer whose "credit" is "asleep" (66). Autolycus, egregious peddler of fiction, is sidelined; as he later admits, it would be unfortunate if these revelations were to be contaminated by his other "discredits" (131).

Report is such a "highly mediated form of representation"[36] that it can never aspire to the thing itself. For that we need spectacle in the theater, the reanimation of Hermione, which must "be seen, cannot be spoken of" (5.2.45–46), as the "newly performed" (or completed) statue of Hermione (103–4) comes to life in an astounding visual performance. We are prepared to make the leap from hearing about something to witnessing it as "most true" by what the Servant has said about the surprising appearance of Polixenes in Sicily; he tells Leontes in act 5, scene 1 that the "report" of the king's arrival would "bear no credit" were not the "proof"—his physical presence—so "nigh" (179–80).

Seeing is believing in the climactic statue scene. In a total reversal from Leontes's earlier pointing out Hermione as an object lesson in deception—"You, my lords, / Look on her, mark her well" (2.1.64–65)—he must now use his eyes to perceive the perfection of the statue-as-woman. Paulina cuts through the doubts of the spectators with

>                                        That she is living,
> Were it but told you, should be hooted at
> Like an old tale: but it appears she lives ... (5.3.115–17)

Caught up in the illusion, we are prepared to swallow this extreme improbability. It is fitting that Paulina defers more fact-finding, or the mundane "relation" (130) of what the queen has been doing all these years, until later. Likewise, Leontes hurries the spectators away to allow "Each one [to] demand and answer to his part / Performed in this wide gap of time" (153–54). Telling stories, even if they are believable, now belongs offstage.

Autolycus and his counterfeitings have made us skeptical about tall tales,[37] while the Gentlemen underline how difficult it is credibly to report the incredible.[38] On top of this, the amazing sight of a statue coming to life would seem to confirm the words of Fabian when he is reacting to the strange transformation of Malvolio in *Twelfth Night:* "If this were play'd upon a stage now, I could condemn it as an improbable fiction" (3.4.127–28). Yet the romance in *The Winter's Tale* allows us to renounce the solipsistic nightmare world of Leontes in favor of a creative dream that is "monstrous to our human reason" (5.1.41) but that nevertheless, like the "madness" of Florizel's love for Perdita, opens into truth. Succumbing to the magic of theater,[39] the audience imaginatively embraces one final, redemptive fiction—an actor posing as a statue and then playing a woman who returns to her husband after 16 years of being "dead"—as an expression of what life truly *can* be.[40]

## ART, NATURE, AND THE MAGIC OF THEATER

Ultimately Shakespeare's fiction—the dramatic artifice itself—points to a truth about life, or life as it has the potential to be once it is reanimated by faith. Fiction and reality are no longer at odds by the end of the play; neither are art and nature. When what seems to be a perfectly fashioned work of art turns out to be a living woman, the boundaries dissolve and "the art itself is Nature" (4.4.97). But the magic of the final scene is more than a trick or reverse illusion whereby art that appears totally lifelike is revealed to be life that resembles art; the crossover suggests ways in which life needs art if it is to be realized triumphantly or manifested in its completeness. At its best art does not pervert or tamper with nature, as Perdita fears when she converses with Polixenes on the topic. Rather, the beauty of artistic form shows off the full radiance of life, returning spectators in the theater to the natural world with a renewed sense of "wonder."

"Great creating Nature" (4.4.88) informs the whole play, which moves in a seasonal cycle from sterility and destruction at the court of Leontes, through regeneration in Bohemia, and finally to renewed life in Sicily. Paulina first tries to make Leontes see the work of the "good goddess Nature" (2.3.102), the continuity of generations, when she shows him the newborn princess. But Leontes rejects nature's "work of art,"[41] the child who is perfectly modeled on her parents, by cruelly dismissing Perdita as a "bastard" and Paulina as a "witch" (72, 66). Ironically it is Perdita and her future husband, Florizel, "begetting wonder" when they arrive in Sicily (5.1.133), who reawaken in Leontes not only the pain of his loss but a sense of future promise. And in the denouement it is again Paulina's task to display the work of "great Nature" (2.2.59)—the living Hermione.

In the statue as in the play itself, art serves life, revealing nature without disfiguring it. Earlier, though, the play has shown us the harmful repercussions of artfulness and illusion. Courtly sophistication discourages frankness and invites elaborate game-playing at the Sicilian palace, while Leontes, an artist of negation, falls victim to the elaborate fantasy that he himself has constructed out of "nothing" (1.2.295). In act 4 Autolycus exploits others with his "trumpery-art,"[42] counterfeit treasures and ballads that are also associated with "nothing" (4.4.618). It is art as harmful sophistication that Perdita shuns when she repudiates striped carnations and pinks as "bastards" (83) and equates the art of grafting with the use of cosmetics. Purebred without knowing it, Perdita refuses to admit that "great creating Nature" can be improved in any fashion.

Yet Polixenes is also correct when he defends the partnership of art and nature. Since hybrids occur in the wild, cross-breeding or grafting is also an "art, /That Nature makes" (92). The skill[43] of the gardener can "mend" or remold nature (93–96) but never move outside it, for "Nature is made better by no mean / But Nature makes that mean" (89–90).[44] Indeed many Renaissance contexts, rather than associating art with artificiality and deception, stressed its civilizing force as a way to remedy fallen nature.[45] George Puttenham's *The Arte of English Poesie,* in a passage close to the argument of Polixenes, discusses art as an "ayde" or helpmate to "nature"—"peradventure a meane to supply her wants."[46] Art in this sense may encompass not only the work of the painter, craftsman, or poet, but those social or cultural institutions that help to shape "natural man" into "harmony."[47] Perdita, Florizel muses, might paradoxically achieve a highly civilized "ord'ring" of her "affairs" through the spontaneous act of singing (139–40). And when she gracefully distributes her flowers, she turns the occasion into an ordered ritual,[48] though it is one that reinforces the natural cycle of the seasons. What is more, she herself comments that her artful role as the goddess Flora, however reluctantly she plays it, may actually "change [her] disposition" (135). Echoing Polixenes's observation on how art can "change" nature (96), this alteration is not a perversion of Perdita's nature but a fuller realization of what she has always been—a true royal.

If good art facilitates and shows off to advantage, even transfigures, what is natural, it must be more than just a clever imitation of reality. Sheer technical skill in the service of mimetic realism was much admired in the Renaissance.[49] Yet in any contest of verisimilitude, nature will always be the winner. Even sculpture, the most representational of the arts, can never outdo the living substance with its shadow, just as painting cannot truly be "livelier than life" (*Timon of Athens,* 1.1.38).

Leontes gradually apprehends this as he gazes at the statue of Hermione. When he notes that the sculpted image looks more "wrinkled" and "agèd" than the young Hermione (5.3.28–29), he is acknowledging the marks of time that "negate the timeless perfection of mimetic art,"[50] bringing the figure back into the world of flux and change. Now the statue strikes Leontes as so lifelike that he exclaims

> The fixure of her eye has motion in't,
> As we are mocked with art. (67–68)

His second line suggests that representation alone would be a sterile mockery, both in the sense of a lifeless imitation and a taunting of the spectator; a little later, desiring to kiss the statue, Leontes asks "Let no man mock me" (79).[51] But the sculpture *will* defer to life, as Paulina hints in preparing the king "To see the life as lively mocked, as ever / Still sleep mock'd death" (19–20). It has gone one better than anything that even Julio Romano—the celebrated Renaissance artist who can almost "put breath into his work"[52]—could create. For in the last resort, this sculptor is only the "ape" of nature (5.2.106–7). Likewise Shakespeare must bow to nature in using a living actor to project Hermione. Set against a breathing human being, any mimetic version simply pales, for "What fine chisel / Could ever yet cut breath?" (5.3.78–79).

The role of art in *The Winter's Tale* is therefore not to rival nature but to help us perceive afresh the "marvel" of life (100). As Rosalie Colie puts it, when the statue transforms to a living woman "illusion itself is abandoned in the claim that reality is more startling, more miraculous, than any contrivance of art."[53] But art has served its purpose, since it has awakened the king's imagination and thus changed his perception of reality.[54] It seems essential that Leontes respond to the "stone" as a radiant image of life before he can accept the living Hermione. The harmonious and economical form of the statue, appearing perfectly proportioned and gracefully set in the "natural posture" (23) of the queen, recreates for Leontes Hermione's actual "life of majesty" (35), allowing him to apprehend and appreciate her more fully than he was able to do in the past. And while the artform reveals itself as the natural woman, there is still a vital interchange between art and nature. For the living Hermione is in some respects a work of art—not simply the handiwork of a divine creator but, within the playworld, a supremely civilized woman, now lovingly prepared to reenter the social institution of marriage. In her gesture of forgiveness to Leontes, she confirms herself as a "royal piece" (38).

As it turns out, neither Polixenes nor Perdita has been bested in their debate on art versus nature. By the terms of the final scene they are both "precious winners" (131). In the passage where he praises the art of the gardener, Puttenham goes on to assert that art may be an "alterer" of nature, but only in helping to make nature herself appear "more beautifull or straunge and miraculous." Thus the gardener's skill is able to produce enhanced fruits, such as a cherry without a stone, which "nature could not doe without mans help and arte."[55] This kind of "change" as a route to "perfection" or completeness is also what Nature defends in her debate with Mutability in Spenser's *The Faerie Queene*. Through metamorphoses, she contends, natural things are "not changed from their first estate; / But by their change their being doe dilate."[56] In Shakespeare's play nature's change, or expansion into completion, comes through the transforming power of art.

Art has not distorted or masked nature at the end of *The Winter's Tale*. Nor has it been able to "outwork nature," as often seems to be the case with Shakespeare's artifice-loving queen Cleopatra (*Antony and Cleopatra,* 2.2.201). Perdita, who earlier shunned the mask of cosmetics as unnatural, is the first to beg to kiss the hand of the "stone" that is supposedly enhanced with "oily painting" (5.3.83). In "Lady, / Dear queen, that ended when I but began, / Give me that hand of yours to kiss" (44–46), she addresses the form not as if it were an "image" but as her living mother. Intuiting the reality of what is happening, the princess privileges nature over art. Yet soon afterward, without fully realizing it, Polixenes reinforces his conviction that the two powers can achieve a synthesis—that "the art itself is Nature"—when he responds to the creative energy of the statue-as-woman, woman-as-statue, with his admiring "Masterly done! / The very life seems warm upon her lip" (65–66).

In *The Tempest,* Prospero's "so potent art" can actually raise up dead bodies from graves (5.1.50). Paulina of *The Winter's Tale,* however, is neither a white magician nor a witch; she relies on magic that is as "lawful as eating" (5.3.111), because it entails no supernatural transformation of the dead but simply a revelation of life itself.[57] But while Paulina is no necromancer, the mere hint that she may be reviving a corpse ("I'll fill your grave up" [101]), plus Polixenes's anxiety that Hermione may have been "stol'n from the dead" [115]), serves to generate an aura of magic and supernatural mystery. Paulina acts as a surrogate for the playwright who could, as Stephen Greenblatt points out, "appropriate for the stage the intense social energies" associated with witchcraft or the conjuring up of spirits, practices that were themselves "under attack as theatrical."[58] In another linking of theater and the numinous, this time religious worship, the statue is briefly identified with a graven image when Perdita moves to kiss it and ask for its blessing. Caught up in Perdita's reverie, we become complicit with a form of "idolatory"[59]—the idea that religious images were not mere representations but possessed magical properties, a form of icon worship that Protestants attacked as part of the older Catholic faith.

Shakespeare is harnessing the power of supernatural mysteries to create his most compelling stage illusion. For the kind of "faith" awakened in Leontes by his imaginative response to the statue, and in the audience who participates in a ritual reawakening, is enabled by theatrical performance. Exploiting what Prospero calls the "art to enchant" (*The Tempest*, Epilogue), the dramatist connects actors with audience in a powerful circuit. The "amazement" (87) that Paulina generates within her "chapel" (86) resembles a religious rite but can more properly be viewed as the magic of theater.[60]

Even if the audience is by now half-expecting it, "You perceive she stirs" (103) is an electrifying moment on stage. A reviewer of Helen Faucit's "entrancing" performance in 1848 wrote of how the gradual reanimation of the statue suspended "the blood" and took "the breath away." At the instant that Faucit's Hermione turned her head, "the whole house started as if struck by an electric shock, or as if they had seen the dead arise."[61] Before this magical climax, the words spoken by the onstage spectators suggest that the "statue" and onlookers are trading places[62] in a two-way metamorphosis. Recalling Hermione's "warm life," Leontes feels himself chided by the statue "For being more stone than it" (35–38), while the "admiring" Perdita is "Standing like stone" (41–42) in front of the image of her mother. Even Leontes's "sorrow," which could not "dry" in 16 summers (49–51), finds a parallel in the paint lavished on the "newly fixed" statue, where "the color's / Not dry" (47–48). The effect created by the work of art is wonder or astonishment, where the spectators are literally "a-stonied,"[63] or turned to stone. Yet even as Leontes, with his "Would I were dead" (62), remains locked in grief, the statue appears to thaw.[64] The depetrification has been foreshadowed by the Third Gentleman's account of the offstage reunions, where "Who was most marble there changed color" (5.2.96–97). Slowly the statue's veins, eyes, and lips all appear to bear life, until Leontes, sensing that "an air comes from her" (5.3.78) and recalling for the audience Paulina's earlier vow that the king can remarry only when his first wife is "again in breath" (5.1.83), must be restrained from kissing the image.

The king's renewed wooing revives his own heart. Paulina's invocation to Hermione, "be stone no more … Bequeath to death your numbness" (99, 102), thus applies as much to Leontes as to the queen. He is the one whose heart, like Othello's, was "turn'd to stone" (*Othello*, 4.1.182–83) when he falsely accused his wife and whose "woes" and repentance, according to Paulina, could never "stir" or remove the heaviness of his misdeeds (3.2.206–7). Now, as the woman Leontes turned into an inanimate statue "stirs" (5.3.103), the magical resurrection is reciprocal.[65] The king moves from the deadening stiffness of sorrow, through the silent petrification of "wonder" (22), and finally to the keen "pleasure" (73) of believing that the image "lives" (117). Simultaneously Hermione, who has remained dead to her husband for 16 years, is revived to warmth by his "faith" (95) and her own trust in "Dear life" (103).

"Strike all that look upon with marvel," Paulina commands the statue (100).[66] Her words apply to the larger audience in the theater, brought "by degrees to a passionate readiness"[67] to accept the stone's reanimation. There is a sense in which these spectators, guided by music after the silence of wonder, participate in a "rite of communion"[68] as they "imagine into being"[69] the statue. Paulina has offered them the chance to depart from the magic circle; if not, they must "stand still" and help bring Hermione back to life. "It is required / You do awake your faith" (94–95) now becomes an invocation to the audience as well as to Leontes.[70] Just as the Chorus to *Henry V* asks the audience to contribute with their imaginations to conjure up the spectacle of glorious war from the stage's "flat unraised spirits," so Paulina needs the "faith" of all present to bring about the triumph of "dear life." So powerful is the connection between stage and outer society, art and reality, that the spectators, while knowing that this is all a stage illusion[71]—they are watching an actor play a statue changing back to a woman—willingly suspend their disbelief.

As readers or audience members, we choose to believe that art and illusion can open windows, transforming for the better our vision of human life. Drawn into the spectacle, we not only apprehend that Hermione has miraculously returned within the world of the play but are encouraged to believe in the truth of second chances and renewal within our own relationships—the magical possibilities that inhere in the world outside the theater.[72]

## NOTES

1. Roy Battenhouse, "Theme and Structure in *The Winter's Tale*," *ShS* 33 (1980): 123–38, 123.

2. Felperin, "Tongue-tied Our Queen?": The Deconstruction of Presence in *The Winter's Tale*," in *Shakespeare and the Question of Theory*, ed. Patricia Parker and Geoffrey Hartman (London and New York: Methuen, 1985), pp. 10, 14.

3. In fact several critics, such as Kay Stockholder, *Dream Works: Lovers and Families in Shakespeare* (Toronto, Buffalo, London: University of Toronto Press, 1987), p. 185, note the "erotic coloring" suggested in the words "loving embassies" and "embrac'd" (1.1.29–30, 32) that appear in Camillo's report of the continued relationship between the kings. These "homoerotic impulses" are more pronounced in the later "twinned lambs" speech (1.2.67–75).

4. In "Parenthood: Hermione's Statue," in *Shakespeare and the Loss of Eden: The Construction of Family Values in Early Modern Culture* (New Brunswick, N.J.: Rutgers University Press, 1999), Catherine Belsey positions Leontes's jealousy within the cultural history of the early-modern period. She contends that when Leontes "rounds on affection," he reveals the underlying cause of his torment to be "passionate love," the "very basis of romantic marriage" that was gaining ground in this era (107).

5. Burton, *The Anatomy of Melancholy,* vol. 1, introd. Holbrook Jackson (Dent: London, 1932), pp. 254, 258.

6. Discussed by David Ward, "Affection, Intention, and Dreams in *The Winter's Tale,*" *MLR* 82 (1987): 545–54, 546–47.

7. Graham Holderness, *"The Winter's Tale:* Country into Court," in *Shakespeare Out of Court,* ed. Holderness, Nick Potter, John Turner (New York: St. Martin's Press, 1990), observes that in the elaborate discourse of courtly entertainment, "relationships of friendship and affection" may inevitably attract the "language of desire and fulfilment" (203). A.L. French, "Leontes' Jealousy," in *Shakespeare and the Critics* (Cambridge: Cambridge University Press, 1972), also notes how elaborate courtly games may make it impossible "to express deeply felt respect or affection except in terms which contaminate the very qualities they are supposed to mediate" (135–36).

8. A.F. Bellette, "Truth and Utterance in *The Winter's Tale,*" *ShS* 31 (1978): 65–75, 70.

9. Maurice Hunt, *Shakespeare's Romance of the Word* (London and Toronto: Associated University Presses, 1990), describes Leontes as a "despotic speaker" (87) who "continually refuses to acknowledge and share verbal contexts that could promote a good understanding" (81).

10. Carol Thomas Neely, "The Triumph of Speech in *The Winter's Tale,*" *SEL* 15, no. 2 (Spring 1975): 321–38, 324.

11. In "Knowledge and Belief in *The Winter's Tale,*" *SEL* 41, no. 2 (Spring 2001): 317–34, Walter S.H. Lim discusses the play's "subtle interrogation of the premise that knowledge can be absolute and truth certain" (328). Aaron Landau, "'No Settled Senses of the World Can Match the Pleasure of that Madness': The Politics of Unreason in *The Winter's Tale,*" *Cahiers Élisabéthains* 64 (Autumn 2003): 29–42, discusses in detail how "disastrous consequences of analytical reason" in the play's first half give way to the "redemptive faculties of irrational faith" (38).

12. R.P. Draper, The Winter's Tale*: Text and Performance* (Basingstoke and London: Macmillan, 1985), points out that because Perdita justifies Florizel's total commitment to her, Florizel's "madness" can be accepted by the audience

"as a superior form of rationality, rather than something sub-rational" (35). Fitz-roy Pyle, The Winter's Tale*: A Commentary on the Structure* (New York: Barnes and Noble, Inc., 1969), also comments on how the "anti-rational faith" of both Leontes and Florizel is "rewarded with wonderful good fortune" (121).

13.  Peter G. Platt, *Reason Diminished: Shakespeare and the Marvelous* (Lincoln and London: University of Nebraska Press, 1997), notes how in *The Winter's Tale* the marvelous is a means of overcoming the "tyranny of the rational" (153).

14.  Michael Taylor, "Shakespeare's *The Winter's Tale:* Speaking in the Freedom of Knowledge," *CritQ* 14 (1972): 49–56, finds that Leontes moves to a "higher kind of knowledge" once the sight of the statue prompts a "sensual re-awakening" in him (55).

15.  Bruce W. Young, "Teaching the Unrealistic Realism of *The Winter's Tale,"* in *Approaches to Teaching Shakespeare's* The Tempest *and Other Late Romances,* ed. Maurice Hunt (New York: The Modern Language Association of America, 1992), notes how the play "challenges us to exercise faith, to break beyond the narrow bounds of our fears and preconceptions and dare to believe in our own and others' possibilities" (93).

16.  Gerard Legh, *The Accidens of Armory* (London, 1562), cited in Mervyn James, "English Politics and the Concept of Honour, 1485–1642," in *Society, Politics and Culture: Studies in Early Modern England* (Cambridge: Cambridge University Press, 1986), p. 332.

17.  In his "Introduction" to *The Tempest,* The Arden Shakespeare (London: Methuen, 1954; 1971), Frank Kermode discusses the etymology of *nobile* and *non vile* in relation to refined "courtier-stock" (p. xlvii).

18.  Baldassare Castiglione, *The Book of the Courtier,* Book 1, trans. Sir Thomas Hoby (1561), intro. W.B. Drayton Henderson (London: J.M. Dent and Sons, Ltd.), p. 32.

19.  Castiglione, *The Book of the Courtier,* Book 4, p. 267.

20.  Castiglione, *The Book of the Courtier,* Book 1, p. 68.

21.  Norman Council, *When Honour's at the Stake: Ideas of Honour in Shakespeare's Plays* (London: George Allen and Unwin, Ltd., 1973), p. 12.

22.  Castiglione, *The Book of the Courtier,* Book 1, p. 34.

23.  Ibid., p. 32.

24.  Castiglione, *The Book of the Courtier,* Book 4, p. 297.

25.  "Of Honour and Reputation," in Francis Bacon, *Essays,* intro. Oliphant Smeaton (London: Dent, 1906; 1968), p. 160.

26.  Frank Kermode, *Shakespeare's Language* (London and New York, 2000), summarizes this traditional view as "Gentle birth predisposes one to virtue, the strong bring forth the strong" (283).

27.  Castiglione, *The Book of the Courtier,* Book 1, p. 44.

28.  Jennifer Richards, "Social Decorum in *The Winter's Tale,"* in *Shakespeare's Late Plays: New Readings,* ed. Jennifer Richards and James Knowles (Edinburgh: Edinburgh University Press, 1999), p. 82.

29.  In *Ambition and Privilege: The Social Tropes of Elizabethan Courtesy Theory* (Berkeley, Los Angeles, London: University of California Press, 1984), Frank Whigham discusses ways in which "courtesy literature," while coming to terms with and absorbing the "more modern notion that the individual creates himself by his own actions," also reinforces the "received sense of personal identity … as founded on God-given attributes such as birth" (xi–xii).

30.  Foster Watson (intro.), Thomas Eloyt, *The Governour* (London: J. M. Dent & Sons Ltd., 1907; 1937), p. 128. Spelling has been modernized.

31.  Virgil B. Heltzel (ed.), Henry Peacham, *The Complete Gentleman* (1622; 1634; Ithaca, N. Y.: Cornell University Press, 1962), p. 12.

32.  Legh, *The Accedens of Armory,* cited in James, "English Politics and the Concept of Honour," p. 312.

33.  See Aaron Kitch, "Bastards and Broadsides in *The Winter's Tale,*" *ShakS* 27 (1999): 43–71, 53.

34.  Ibid., p. 56.

35.  Stephen Greenblatt, *Hamlet in Purgatory* (Princeton and Oxford: Princeton University Press, 2001), p. 202, comments that while the audience is "amply warned not to credit the ghost of Hermione, it is at the same time strongly induced to do so" after being disarmed by Antigonus's skeptical "Dreams are toys."

36.  Kitch, "Bastards and Broadsides," p. 62.

37.  Mary Livingston, "The Natural Art of *The Winter's Tale,*" *MLQ* 30 (1969): 340–55, discusses the "inverse relationships" between the art of Autolycus and *The Winter's Tale* itself, which promise that the play "will image a truth beyond the appearances of this world" (351).

38.  David N. Beauregard, "Shakespeare against the Skeptics: Nature and Grace in *The Winter's Tale,*" in *Shakespeare's Last Plays: Essays in Literature and Politics,* ed. Stephen W. Smith and Travis Curtwright (New York and Oxford: Lexington Books, 2002), also discusses how Shakespeare "validates the sense of wonder and discredits suspicion and skepticism" in the final scene (65).

39.  Stanley Cavell, "Recounting Gains, Showing Losses: Reading *The Winter's Tale,*" in *Disowning Knowledge in Seven Plays of Shakespeare* (Cambridge: Cambridge University Press, 1987; 2003), points out that Shakespeare is "claiming the superiority of theater" as being able to secure "full faith and credit in fiction" (199).

40.  Jean E. Howard, "Introduction" to *The Winter's Tale,* in Stephen Greenblatt (ed.), *The Norton Shakespeare* (New York: W. W. Norton & Co, Inc., 1997), notes how fiction (art) in the play becomes a means to "correct old mistakes and forge new realities" (2880).

41.  See Robert Egan, "The Art Itself Is Nature: *The Winter's Tale,*" in *Drama within Drama: Shakespeare's Sense of His Art in* King Lear, The Winter's Tale, *and* The Tempest (New York and London: Columbia University Press, 1975), p. 66.

42.  Howard Felperin, *Shakespearean Romance* (Princeton, N.J.: Princeton University Press, 1972), p. 236.

43.  Leo Salingar, "Shakespeare and the Italian Concept of 'Art,'" in *Shakespeare and the Jacobeans* (Cambridge: Cambridge University Press, 1986), pp. 1–18, notes that the "skill of grafting" defended by Polixenes is a "craft" or scientific technique rather than art in its modern aesthetic sense (16).

44.  J.H.P. Pafford (ed.) *The Winter's Tale,* The Arden Shakespeare (London: Methuen, 1963; 1966), also thinks that "nature" includes the grafter himself as the "means" by which nature is improved, "since man and his powers are also natural" (93).

45.  See Northrop Frye, "Recognition in *The Winter's Tale,*" in *Essays on Shakespeare and Elizabethan Drama in Honour of Hardin Craig,* ed. Richard Hosley (Columbia: University of Missouri Press, 1962), pp. 190–91, and Edward W. Tayler, *Nature and Art in Renaissance Literature* (New York: Columbia University Press, 1964), pp. 11–37.

46.  Gladys Doidge Willcock and Alice Walker (eds.), George Puttenham, *The Arte of English Poesie* (1589; Cambridge: Cambridge University Press, 1936), p. 303 (spelling modernized). Derek Attridge, *Peculiar Language: Literature as Difference from the Renaissance to James Joyce* (Ithaca, N.Y.: Cornell University Press, 1988), discusses how Puttenham mediates an inherent contradiction; nature represents both a "total self-sufficiency" and "that which is necessarily incomplete and in need of repair" (28).

47.  Peter Berek, "'As We Are Mock'd with Art': From Scorn to Transfiguration," *SEL* 18 (1978): 289–305, 305.

48.  See Egan, "The Art Itself Is Nature," p. 69.

49.  René Girard, "'To Your Shadow Will I Make True Love,' *The Winter's Tale* (act 5, scenes I and 2)," in *The Theater of Envy: William Shakespeare* (New York: Oxford University Press, 1991), notes that an obsession with verisimilitude was the "major principle of art" in Shakespeare's period (331), but finds some muted satire of "mimetic realism" in the final scene of *The Winter's Tale* (333).

50.  Pauline Kiernan, *Shakespeare's Theory of Drama* (Cambridge: Cambridge University Press, 1996), p. 81.

51.  See Berek, "'As We Are Mock'd with Art,'" pp. 290–95.

52.  Leonard Barkan, "'Living Sculptures': Ovid, Michelangelo, and *The Winter's Tale,*" *ELH* 48 (1981): 639–67, cites an epitaph from Vasari's *Lives* (1550; 1568) on how Jupiter "saw sculpted and painted bodies breathe … through the skill of Guilio Romano" (656). Julio Romano, who died in 1546, was better known for his painting than his sculpture and more mannerist than realist in style. John Greenwood, *Shifting Perpectives and the Stylish Style: Mannerism in Shakespeare and His Jacobean Contemporaries* (Toronto, Buffalo, London: University of Toronto Press, 1988), compares Romano's *trompe d'oeil* effects in the Palazzo del Té in Mantua ("two-dimensional painting masquerading as three-dimensional sculpture") to the statue of Hermione moving out of its niche, refusing "to be confined by the bounds of its art" (13).

53.  Rosalie Colie, "Perspectives on Pastoral: Romance, Comic and Tragic," in *Shakespeare's Living Art* (Princeton, N.J.: Princeton University Press, 1974), p. 280.

54.   Frederick O. Waage, "Be Stone No More: Italian Cinquecentro Art and Shakespeare's Last Plays," *BucknellRev* 25, no. 1 (1980): 56–87, also finds in these plays a vision in which "art no longer imitates nature but transfigures it" (57).

55.   Puttenham, *The Arte of English Poesie,* pp. 303–4.

56.   "Two Cantos of Mutabilitie," in J.C. Smith and E. De Selincourt (eds.), *Spenser: Poetical Works* (London, New York, Toronto: Oxford University Press, 1912; 1965), p. 406.

57.   Gareth Roberts, "'An Art Lawful as Eating'?: Magic in *The Tempest* and *The Winter's Tale,*" in *Shakespeare's Late Plays: New Readings,* ed. Richards and Knowles (Edinburgh, Scotland: Edinburgh University Press, 1999), discusses the careful distinction in the statue scene between a divine miracle, which does not happen, and the "benevolent deceit" that turns out to be natural (140–41).

58.   Stephen Greenblatt, "Shakespeare Bewitched," in *New Historical Literary Study,* ed. Jeffrey Cox and Larry Reynolds (Princeton, N.J.: Princeton University Press, 1993), pp. 108–35, 118.

59.   Michael O'Connell, *The Idolatrous Eye: Iconoclasm and Theater in Early Modern England* (New York and Oxford: Oxford University Press, 2000), comments on how this "quasi-religious enactment … presses an audience into idolatry" (141). Landau, "'No Settled Senses of the World … ,'" goes further in finding in this scene a Counter-Reformation appeal to the "mysteries and irrationality of Catholic worship" (38). See also Thomas Rist, *Shakespeare's Romances and the Politics of Counter-Reformation* (Lampeter: The Edwin Mellen Press, Ltd., 1999), pp. 143–44.

60.   Stephen Orgel (ed.), *The Winter's Tale,* The Oxford Shakespeare (Oxford: Oxford University Press, 1996), also notes how magic in the final scene is less a link to religion than a foregrounding of theater's "therapeutic catharsis … through the marvels of representation and spectacle" (62).

61.   Review of *The Winter's Tale, Glasgow Citizen,* April, 1848, cited in Dennis Bartholomeusz, The Winter's Tale in *Performance in England and America 1611–1976* (Cambridge: Cambridge University Press, 1982), p. 74.

62.   T.G. Bishop, *Shakespeare and the Theater of Wonder* (Cambridge: Cambridge University Press, 1996), discusses the "exchange of properties" here and how "mutual desire and mutual attentiveness are alike required" for the reanimation of the statue (164).

63.   Platt, *Reason Diminished,* p. 168.

64.   Abbé Blum, "'Strike all that look upon with mar[b]le': Monumentalizing Women in Shakespeare's Plays," in *The Renaissance Englishwoman in Print,* ed. Anne M. Haselkorn and Betty S. Travitsky (Amherst: University of Massachusetts Press, 1990), pp. 99–118, notes that the "dead, unavailable, unfeeling woman must be re-vived, must respond to the one who has monumentalized her" (104).

65.   William C. Carroll, *The Metamorphoses of Shakespearean Comedy* (Princeton, N.J.: Princeton University Press, 1985), argues that "Leontes' awakening back into life parallels, or perhaps causes, Hermione's resurrection" (215).

Similarly, Cavell, "Recounting Gains, Showing Losses," finds that "each was stone, it remains unknown who stirs first, who makes the first move back" (220), and B. J. Sokol, *Art and Illusion in* The Winter's Tale (Manchester and New York: Manchester University Press, 1994), suggests how in this scene "powerful degrees of feeling in beholders may convey the colours of life into theatrical raw materials" (92).

66.   Garrett Stewart, "Shakespearean Dreamplay," *ELR* 11 (1981): 44–69, notes the phonetic closeness of "marvel" to "marble," completing "the theme of 'marble'-heartedness turned to wonder" (58).

67.   Egan, "The Art Itself Is Nature," p. 84. John Taylor, "The Patience of *The Winter's Tale,*" *EIC* 23, no. 4 (1973): 333–55, notes how the structure of the play, with its "unanticipated explosions" and "long lulls" (336), also schools us in a "patient faith that, in time, marvels will come" (355).

68.   Louis Montrose, "The Purpose of Playing: Reflections on a Shakespearean Anthropology," *Helios* 7 (1980): 51–74, 62.

69.   Kirby Farrell, "To Beguile Nature of Her Custom: Drama as a Magical Action," in *Shakespeare's Creation: The Language of Magic and Play* (Amherst: The University of Massachusetts Press, 1975), p. 59.

70.   Farrell, "To Beguile Nature of Her Custom," observes that just as Leontes has achieved a "capacity for wonder" (55), so we as audience need a "liberating wonderment" (52); O'Connell, *The Idolatrous Eye,* also finds that "an act of faith is required for the enactment of the seeming miracle" (141).

71.   Andrew Gurr, "The Bear, the Statue, and Hysteria in *The Winter's Tale,*" *SQ* 34 (1983): 420–25, comments that Paulina's words "it appears she lives" point to the "duality of a demonstrable truth and a stage illusion" (425). R. P. Draper, The Winter's Tale*: Text and Performance* (Basingstoke and London: Macmillan, 1985), also notes the double effect, as Shakespeare's dramatic craftsmanship "enables him to work the magic of illusion with seemingly passionate conviction, while yet retaining consciousness of it as a deliberately contrived effect" (11); and Mary Ellen Lamb, "Ovid and *The Winter's Tale:* Conflicting Views toward Art," in *Shakespeare and Dramatic Tradition,* ed. W. R. Elton and William B. Long (London and Toronto: Associated University Presses, 1989), pp. 69–87, stresses the audience's "double perception of the statue scene as miracle and fraud" (82).

72.   Bishop, *Shakespeare and the Theater of Wonder,* discusses how the end of *The Winter's Tale* delivers us back to "the world" by generating a "desire to restore or refurbish a world that has somehow gone wrong" (16). In contrast David W. Collins, "The Function of Art in Shakespeare's *The Winter's Tale,*" *BSUF* 33, no. 2 (Spring 1982): 55–59, thinks that the self-conscious theatricality of the play's ending accentuates the gap between the "illusion of an earthly paradise" and the "harsh reality of the world as we know it" (59). Kenneth Gross, *The Dream of the Moving Statue* (Ithaca and London: Cornell University Press, 1992), goes further in arguing that because it carries a "demonic, mortal threat," the "event of animation" remains mysterious and disorienting rather than encouraging a simple "faith in magic" (108–9).

# 6

# CRITICAL APPROACHES

## TRADITIONAL APPROACHES

### Character and Psychoanalysis

Neoclassical critics, favoring realism and decorum in literature, did not take kindly to *The Winter's Tale*. Echoing Ben Jonson's disdain for *"Tales, Tempests,* and Such Like Drolleries" (1614),[1] John Dryden (1672) listed *The Winter's Tale* among those plays of Shakespeare that were "grounded on impossibilities."[2] Alexander Pope, one of the earliest editors of Shakespeare (1725), simply refused to believe that more than "some characters, single scenes," or perhaps a few "particular passages" were written by the great dramatist himself.[3] Conceding that the play is "very entertaining" despite "all its absurdities," Samuel Johnson (1765) mentioned only the character of Autolycus as being "very naturally conceived and strongly represented."[4]

It was in the Romantic era that interest in *The Winter's Tale* began to burgeon. William Hazlitt (1817), having enjoyed John Philip Kemble's theater production, praised the play's language and presentation of character, noting Hermione's "patient forbearance," how Autolycus comes across as a "very pleasant, thriving rogue," and the "crabbed and tortuous style" through which Leontes's jealousy is communicated.[5] But because Shakespeare's Late Plays do not specialize in complex characterization in the way that his tragedies do, the full-blown analysis that A. C. Bradley pioneered in the early twentieth century—examining dramatic characters in great depth, as though they were creations in a novel or real people— made little headway in these plays.

The one exception to the rule, the character who has generated con-
siderable psychological commentary, is Leontes. Harold Bloom (1998),
the most recent critic sympathetic to Bradley's humanist or essentialist
approach, calls the first part of *The Winter's Tale* a "psychological novel,
the story of Leontes."[6] In the nineteenth century, S. T. Coleridge (1818)
found Leontes a remarkably accurate portrait of the jealous disposition,
pointing to the "excitability" by inadequate causes, "grossness of conception," and sense of "shame" that come through in Leontes's speeches.[7]
Not prepared to accept its sudden onset as a dramatic convention, "finally
inexplicable"[8] in realist terms, critics in the mid-twentieth century turned
to Freudian theories to account for the source of Leontes's irrational response. In 1949, J. I. M. Stewart explained Leontes's jealousy as the result of homosexual attraction to his friend Polixenes. Stewart implements
Freud's analysis of paranoid jealousy—formulated as "*I* do not love him,
*she* loves him"—to suggest that Leontes defends against his own desire
by imagining that Hermione lusts after Polixenes.[9] Discussion in the jour-
nal *American Imago* (1970s–1980s) pursued Freudian ideas much further.
Stephen Reid delves into the primary oedipal fears that result in paranoid jealousy, speculating that Leontes can fulfill his homosexual fantasy
only vicariously through the union of Perdita (Leontes's feminine self)
and Florizel (Polixenes's masculine self).[10] Murray M. Schwartz links
the jealousy to preoedipal anxieties, in which the infant's yearning for
his mother's nurturing confronts his dread of "maternal malevolence";[11]
this is what makes Leontes turn so savagely on Hermione. Just as Stewart
believes that Shakespeare's plays tap powerfully into "types of conflict
which consciousness normally declines to acknowledge,"[12] so Schwartz
justifies his approach by contending that "any critical response that denies
unconscious motives would impoverish the power of Shakespeare's over-
determined language."[13]

The fact that Leontes's irrational behavior lends itself so well to modern clinical explanation is a testament to Shakespeare's remarkable insight
into human psychology. It may even offer a window into the artist's own
psyche as well as the whole creative process. But while psychoanalyzing
dramatic characters confirms their complexity, it bypasses what is most
compelling about the play as a theatrical experience: in this case, how
jealous thoughts lead to acts that have terrible consequences.[14] In his article "'Integration' in *The Winter's Tale*" (1974), L. C. Knights turns away
from psychoanalysis of individual characters to suggest that the psychological experience takes place within the reader or audience. Showing how
the play explores "two contrasting states of the human soul"—the "unbal-
anced self-enclosure" of Leontes followed by a widening "circle of rela-

tionships" in the pastoral sequence—Knights argues that Shakespeare's drama makes us *"live through* movements of mind, feeling, sympathy, that have to be experienced as part of ourselves."[15]

## Myth, Symbol, and New Critical Approaches

Justifying the broader implications of his psychological approach, Stewart points out how close the "radical workings of the human mind" are to "myth or folk-story."[16] Indeed the "old tale" of Shakespeare's play moves from the ravages of the king's jealousy to a pastoral world that assimilates the classical myth of Proserpine. It celebrates the return of spring—to Leontes's psyche as well as to Sicily—within the framework of romance. In this respect the symbolic structure of *The Winter's Tale,* its movement toward completeness and harmony, also lends itself to Jung's theories about the primordial "workings of the human mind." In particular, Leontes's progress toward psychic wholeness calls on certain Jungian archetypes operating within the mythic process of "individuation."[17] Encountering his shadow self during his darkly jealous phase, the king is able to integrate animus and anima—the masculine and feminine sides of the psyche—once he reconnects with Perdita[18] and then Hermione at the close of the play. Moreover the audience's sense of participating in a communal ritual of renewal in the final scene may draw on rebirth archetypes deep within what Jung calls the collective unconscious. Death is followed by reprise when the statue of Hermione becomes flesh and blood; while the queen is not actually reborn, she is nevertheless wonderfully returned to life.

From the mid-twentieth century on, Northrop Frye's categorization of literary kinds in his *Anatomy of Criticism* (1957) has been most influential in showing how literature is rooted in myth and archetype. Sharing the same emphasis as the anthropologist James Frazer, whose *Golden Bough* (1890) gathered myths and rituals centering on the figure of a king who dies and is resurrected, Frye proposes that literary genres develop out of seasonal myths. Within this scheme, *The Winter's Tale* begins in the winter of tragedy, incorporates the summer of romance, and ends in the spring of comedy, whose "mythical or primitive basis" is a "movement toward the rebirth and renewal of the powers of nature."[19] Obviously there is a danger that this typology will reduce complex drama to seasonal paradigms. Nevertheless, Frye's insights into romance's quest motif, and his extended discussion of "Recognition in *The Winter's Tale*" (1962),[20] illuminate the play's dramatic structure and themes beyond its archetypal function.

Since it centers on a king who must be regenerated and presents Bohemia as the vigorous green world of pastoral, *The Winter's Tale* has invited extended analysis as a myth in which the "theme of the changing seasons" is closely interwoven with "death and resurrection."[21] F.C. Tinkler (1937) finds that Perdita and Florizel are "almost vegetation deities"[22] who have the power to restore the wasteland of Leontes. Noting the religious tenor that develops in the play's language—act 5 is replete with terms such as "saint-like," "awake your faith," and "redeem"—several mid-twentieth-century critics have explicated *The Winter's Tale* as a Christian allegory. As late as 1980, Roy Battenhouse discusses the structure of the play in terms of how "grace" is victorious over "sin" and the better instincts of mankind are "rewarded providentially";[23] he is also quick to adduce biblical parallels, such as the link between the three Gentlemen reporting the royal reunions in act 5 and the Three Wise Men who marked the birth of Christ.[24] Certainly Shakespeare's audience was more alert than most modern readers are to New Testament allusions. Most likely, when they heard the First Gentleman declare that "Every wink of an eye some new grace will be born" (5.2.118–19), early modern audiences would recall St. Paul's words to the Corinthians on how, at the "last trump" we shall all be changed to become immortal "in the twinkling of an eye" (1 Corinthians 15:52). Still, it is unwise to foist a homiletic message or a point-by-point allegory on this richly textured drama. J.A. Bryant, Jr. offers just such a theological scheme when he claims that Hermione is a "type" of Christ the "redeemer" and Leontes the figure of the Jew who needs to be saved with the help of Paulina (St. Paul).[25] In a subtler discussion of the "allegorical lines" of the play that does not overschematize its developing human relationships, Alastair Fowler finds that *The Winter's Tale* centers on the "repentance" of Leontes. Through a natural process of grace, the king gradually recovers the "moral harmony" that Hermione represents.[26]

G. Wilson Knight, whose study *The Crown of Life* was published in 1948, is even more eclectic. His interpretation embraces the nature symbolism of *The Winter's Tale* as well as its "deeply Christian" overtones, concluding in semimystical fashion that the play is a testament to "life itself," the "creating and protecting deity whose superhuman presence and powers the drama labors to define."[27] Although he never identified himself with one school of critics, Knight's sensitivity to metaphoric language, and his theories on how image clusters feed into the "spatial unity" of poetic drama, align him with the New Critics working mainly in the 1940s, '50s, and '60s. Under practitioners such as Cleanth Brooks and W.K. Wimsatt, New Criticism declines to analyze poetry as a product of its cultural context or drama in terms of the "more easily extractable elements of 'plot' and 'character.'"[28] Instead, as L.C. Knights points out, "linguistic vitality" and image patterns[29] become keys to unlock the "urgent personal themes" of a Shakespearean play.[30] F. R. Leavis, a member of the *Scrutiny* group of critics, rejects Bradley's focus on character and analyzes instead how the "concrete fulness" of Shakespeare's language in *The Winter's Tale* points to a "profundity" of theme that belies the play's fairy-tale situations.[31] Similarly, Derek Traversi's close reading of the play (1953) responds to the texture and music of the poetry, finding that it reflects the rhythms of human experience as the play's action moves from "tragic breakdown" to "inclusive harmony." Plot as such disappears, "assimilated to the interplay of imagery." Traversi thus analyzes the final scene not as a theatrical triumph but as "the crown of an intricate development of poetic resources."[32]

## Genre

The New Critics bypassed dramatic plot and conventions. But more historically and formally minded critics have chosen to explore *The Winter's Tale* not only through its structure (binary or tripartite, with linking parallels between sections) but in terms of its genre. The purpose of this approach is not to put the play in a "critical straightjacket."[33] Rather, it is to explore the generic conventions that Shakespeare enjoys defying as much as utilizing or remolding. While the play belongs chronologically to the group of Shakespeare's four Late (often called Last) Plays, and draws heavily on Robert Greene's prose romance *Pandosto*,[34] *The Winter's Tale* has proved resistant to simple classification.[35] Its blend of pastoral and romantic adventure qualifies it for the category of romance, charted historically by critics such as E. C. Pettet (1949)[36] and Hallett Smith (1972).[37] But the "conventional romance model" does not account for the play's openness to "irony and travesty."[38] Impressed with its mix, Harold Bloom wryly suggests labeling *The Winter's Tale* "grotesque comedy" rather than "pastoral romance."[39] Because it comes close to tragedy in the first three acts but ends happily with the restoration of Perdita and Hermione, the play is often discussed as tragicomedy. Again, though, it far outstrips Marvin T. Herrick's broad definition of the English form of tragicomedy as "tragedy with a happy ending" (1955),[40] and it blithely bypasses Guarini's late Renaissance specifications for how pastoral tragicomedy should be constructed.

E. M. W. Tillyard (1938) was influential in considering *The Winter's Tale* a completion of Shakespeare's tragic pattern along the lines of Dante's *Divine Comedy*.[41] In this model the final comic reconciliation retains vestiges of the somber movement that precedes it, so that, as Wilson Knight also notes, tragedy is "contained, assimilated, transmuted."[42] Rosalie A. Colie

(1972), immersed in the theory of kinds, discusses the drama's "mixture of comedy with tragedy" as part of the "pastoral mode." She finds that the play, which flouts verisimilitude in its "naked, disillusionary dramaturgy," conducts a "frontal examination of the structural and thematic limits" of pastoral tragicomedy.[43] Its self-conscious artifice is an invitation to the audience to perceive the convention of the "marvelous" being pushed to the limits, until illusion is finally stripped away in the statue scene and art gives way to life.[44]

Earlier critics often found this mix of realist and mannerist styles disconcerting—a sign that Shakespeare was only gradually rising to the challenge of turning romantic narrative into drama and had not yet mastered the art of segueing from tragedy into comedy. S. L. Bethell (1947),[45] who contends that the play's deliberately archaic dramaturgy alerts the audience to the play's deeper meanings, is an early exception. In contrast, Arthur Quiller-Couch (1918) deplores its "serious scampings of artistry,"[46] while the dry observation of Lytton Strachey (1922), that Shakespeare was half "bored to death"[47] when he composed his idyllic romances, went largely unchallenged for decades. Later critics, though, have almost universally praised the experimental, risky nature of *The Winter's Tale*. Like Colie, Joan Hartwig (1972) finds a purpose in this tragicomedy's unsettling of perceptions through sudden shifts in mode. The technique of dislocation, making the audience "simultaneously involved and removed" from the action, is more than an exciting end in itself. Rather, we are invited to "look though the artistic illusion, with its patently theatrical devices, into a level of reality toward which we have yearned without knowing it."[48] In Howard Felperin's more succinct phrase (1972), this turns out to be "art for life's sake."[49] Barbara A. Mowat (1976) also defends the "open form dramaturgy" of *The Winter's Tale,* with its "thematic discontinuities" and "character dislocations," as both Shakespeare's "mature reflections" on his dramatic art and a means of presenting "life in its full complexity—tragic and comic, wonderful and terrible, real and unreal."[50] Among postmodernist critics writing after the 1980s, Kiernan Ryan (1999) goes furthest in proposing that Shakespeare's romances break from mimetic realism to offer instead a "discourse of the future." Demonstrating within Time's speech a "template of provisionality," Ryan explains how Shakespeare in this part of *The Winter's Tale* projects a vision of the "future perfect" (or "what *will have been*"), thereby expanding the "scope of the possible."[51]

## Theatrical

We know that Shakespeare's company began using the private Blackfriars Theatre as their winter venue after 1608. Some historians of the theater, such as G.E. Bentley (1948),[52] have deduced from this that *The Winter's Tale* and Shakespeare's other tragicomic romances were written for a coterie audience. Designed to suit the tastes of playgoers more sophisticated than those who frequented the public Globe Theatre, the plays would also be crafted to meet the requirements of a smaller stage in an indoor playhouse. Other scholars, such as Alfred Harbage (1941),[53] were quick to challenge such theories. They pointed out that romance material had a long-standing appeal and that these Late Plays could accommodate easily to both public and private theaters. What is more, F.P. Wilson (1945) notes that because *Pericles* was produced at the Globe before Beaumont and Fletcher's tragicomic *Philaster* (1610), Shakespeare does not appear unduly influenced by the work of his younger contemporaries.[54]

Theater scholars call attention to the material conditions within which *The Winter's Tale* was first produced. It is salutary to remember, when analyzing dramatic characters or studying patterns of myth and image, that Shakespeare's play had to come alive on stage. Part of the King's Men's repertoire, it also made its mark when performed in James's court. The king and his audience presumably enjoyed the offbeat dramaturgical devices, such as the pivotal scene with the bear, that Nevill Coghill defends in his influential article "Six Points of Stage-Craft in *The Winter's Tale*."[55] One of the most prolific of the stage-based critics, J.L. Styan (1967), emphasizes how the play's "dramatic score" is always conditioned by the kind of theater for which it was originally created. Thus the actor of Leontes could utilize the sheer size of the stage to "draw apart and remain critically silent" during the 53 lines in which the actors representing Hermione and Polixenes converse alone. Attuned to clues for tempo and pacing, Styan notes how the statue's coming to life "is prolonged with intensity for almost five minutes" (more than 80 lines), in which "precisely placed theatrical gestures" reach their climax when Hermione silently embraces her husband.[56]

Styan constantly draws attention to the nonillusionary aspects of Shakespeare's theater—a dimension that was lost in the detailed naturalism of William Macready's and Charles Kean's nineteenth-century productions. When Granville Barker produced *The Winter's Tale* in 1912 he did not return to the exact conditions of the Elizabethan playhouse that William Poel championed at the beginning of the twentieth century. But Barker rejected distracting spectacle in favor of stylized sets and fast-moving dialogue; and his comments in his *Preface*—for instance on the "perfect sufficiency" of Hermione's eight lines in the finale—are firmly grounded in his experience of directing the play in the theater.[57] In the twenty-first century, Alan C. Dessen's *Rescripting Shakespeare* (2002) suggests how the modern director can learn something by returning to the original text. The

Folio's stage direction "silence," after Hermione is summoned to trial, is now usually turned into a speech act in which the Officer commands "silence" in court. But Dessen argues that it could be an "electric moment" on stage if it signals Hermione's reluctance to appear or to communicate when she is first called into court. It would also foreshadow her silence in the statue scene.[58]

Stage-based critics suggest how a producer can sensitively draw on the prompts built into the dramatic score and how the audience builds impressions from this "visual, aural and kinetic orchestration."[59] Charles Frey (1978) aims to be more inclusive—to develop a "multidimensional" and "temporal-affective" interpretation of *The Winter's Tale* that does justice to it both as dramatic literature and as theater.[60] He believes that the attentive reader or spectator reacts to the drama as a "structure of ideas" as well as "moment to moment revelations" as the play moves forward in time. Accordingly Frey concentrates on how "clusters of scenic rhythms, features of style, patterns of action" mark out the distinctive "orchestration" and "drive" of the play.[61] In his book *Shakespeare's Vast Romance: A Study of* The Winter's Tale (1980), he succeeds, to a large extent, in reconciling the interests of the literary reader with those of the playgoer.

### Metadramatic

It is no secret that Shakespeare's drama is often self-referential. At certain points *The Winter's Tale* reminds audience members that they are in a theater watching a play, encouraging them to make connections between the dramatic illusion and their own world. Since the production of Ann Righter's seminal *Shakespeare and the Idea of the Play* (1962) and James Calderwood's *Shakespearean Metadrama* (1971), critics have speculated on the effects—aesthetic and emotional—of this theatrical self-consciousness. Even earlier, in her *Shakespeare's Wordplay* (1957), M.M. Mahood analyzes Leontes's tortured awareness of different meanings of play (harmless amusement versus harmful role-playing and deceit) in his "go play, boy, play" speech (1.2.187–90). Thomas F. Van Laan (1978) also shows how Leontes develops "the idea of the playlet," becoming a "wilful playwright-director" both here and in Hermione's trial scene.[62] By pondering the semantic ambiguity of "play," the king conveys his deep sense of alienation from a secure domestic world, as when he reaches out to include the theater audience in his obsession that most wives are adulterous (1.2.192–96). Similarly, Hermione's vision of herself as participating in a stage performance "devis'd / And played to take spectators" (3.1.35–36) expresses her humiliation at being forced to defend herself publicly. As Righter points out, Perdita is also a Player Queen, conscious of herself acting an aristocratic role at the sheep-shearing, unaware that she "is what she plays." The effect here is not one of alienation. Rather, "life and the play are essentially indivisible"; Perdita is revealed as the true princess, just as when the statue turns out to be Hermione, "What had seemed illusory was real all the time."[63]

Metadramatic critics have also probed the complex relationship between art and nature as a key concern in *The Winter's Tale,* since the play examines not only the opposing claims of courtly sophistication and country life but how far Shakespeare's highly mannered dramatic art images reality beyond the theater. Peter Egan (*Art within Art* [1975]), was one of the first of these critics to find within *The Winter's Tale* an "aggressive artistic manifesto" concerned to "define the aesthetic and moral relevance" of Shakespeare's "art" to "reality" by forging connections between moral renewal in the playworld and in the lives of the audience.[64] Theater also trades on the marvelous and generates wonder in its spectators. Ways in which *The Winter's Tale* self-consciously draws on ideas about magic and promotes the shared experience of amazement, especially in the statue scene, have been explored more recently in several studies.[65]

## RECENT APPROACHES (1980 TO THE PRESENT)

### New Historical and Cultural Materialist

New Historicism, along with much postmodern critical theory, rejected the essentialist view of literature—the notion that it centers on the individual and provides universal, ahistorical insights into human nature. Instead of focusing on the humanist concerns of character, language, or form, New Historicists have discovered discourses on power in dramatic literature of the early modern period. They uncover strategies by which texts may subvert the dominant ideology of the age but eventually reinscribe it once any socially transgressive elements are contained. Cultural Materialists, the left-wing British flank of New Historicism, have examined more closely how literary representations arise out of the material conditions of a particular society. Shakespeare's plays can thus be seen as firmly embedded in the political, cultural, and economic contexts of the late sixteenth and early seventeenth centuries. As discourses, they may interrogate rather than automatically affirm the "absolutist ideology"[66] of the court. Paying attention to marginalized voices, as cultural materialists do, shows how these texts often resist the dominant culture, opening the way to possible social change.

The genre of romance has not proved as fruitful an area for ideological analysis as have Shakespeare's tragedies. Nevertheless, *The Winter's Tale* raises several issues of interest for New Historicists and materialist critics. Evidently a hit at the Jacobean and Caroline courts, it was performed seven times there before 1640; yet at first it appears quite politically daring. Constance Jordan (1997) finds that the play, which features a tyrannical king, contributes to political discourse on the "abuse of rule" at a time when James's drive toward absolutism was challenging the idea of a more constitutional or "mixed monarchy."[67] Other scholars, such as Donna B. Hamilton, "*The Winter's Tale* and the Language of Union, 1604–11," and Stuart M. Kurland, "'We Need No More of Your Advice': Political Realism in *The Winter's Tale*," have examined how the play, without being too inflammatory and thus risking censorship, touches on issues current at James's court.[68] In "*The Winter's Tale* and Religious Politics" (2003), James Ellison argues in detail that the play's ending, a uniting of Protestant Bohemia and Catholic Sicily, comments on James's wish to bring together moderate Protestant and Catholic states in Europe. Certainly act 5, with its securing of a dynasty, reestablishes the status quo at the court of Sicily.[69] David M. Bergeron (1985) points out how the "stability" of the royal family is foregrounded here,[70] while Ellison concludes that the drama is ultimately "pro-government" without succumbing to "outright flattery."[71] Drawing on the New Historicist paradigm of how hegemonic norms are ultimately confirmed in early modern drama, Leonard A. Tennenhouse (1986) contends that *The Winter's Tale,* along with the other Late Plays, "reinscribe[s] the self-enclosed family" within the "particular style of patriarchal rule" that James promoted—the king's "sole authority" as father.[72]

In a sophisticated analysis, "*The Winter's Tale:* Country into Court" (1990), Graham Holderness discovers more subversiveness, arguing that deconstruction takes place on several levels in the play. In the sheep-shearing episode, where an "amateur court masque" infiltrates a "boisterous, popular festival," courtly values are interrogated by being incorporated into pastoral romance. And because Paulina stage-manages the denouement, the play also "subverts the priorities of a patriarchal polity by problematizing masculine authority and endorsing female power."[73] Although Howard Felperin's focus in "'Tongue-Tied, Our Queen?': The Deconstruction of Presence in *The Winter's Tale*" (1985) is not primarily ideological, he contributes to poststructuralist discussion of *The Winter's Tale* by analyzing how its language deconstructs any secure "resting-point for reference." Even the voice of the oracle is open to question, just as Leontes's suspicions cannot be categorically confirmed or disproved. Linguistic ambiguity and instability means that authoritative meaning is "re-peatedly deferred" in the text.[74]

The other area of *The Winter's Tale* that lends itself to historical and materialist analysis is the socioeconomic stratum in Bohemia. While pas-toral conventions preclude a fully realistic presentation of country life, this part of the play offers much more than literary shepherds and rogues; Bohemia proves to be early modern England by another name. The Marx-ist critic C.L. Barber (1964), writing 20 years before New Historicists took the field, stole some of their thunder when he observed that "the play is about the process of social change in seventeenth century England." He generalizes the resulting themes fairly broadly as the "toughness of traditional rural life in the face of political change" and the "hope for a regenerated England through a reunion of court with cottage."[75] In con-trast comes Richard Wilson's searching historical analysis and refusal to gloss over specific material conditions and conflicts in "*As You like It* and the Enclosure Riots" (1993). Relevant to *The Winter's Tale* and its sheep-shearing festival is Wilson's discussion of the strategies that James's gov-ernment used to control insurrections in country areas, "neutralizing the rites of collective action" against private ownership of land by reviving "old rural games" and sports.[76]

The Old Shepherd, now grown to an "unspeakable estate" after 16 years, has obviously converted his windfall of "fairy gold" into the profit-able investment of sheep farming (4.2.42–43, 3.3.122). While he does not appear to be a "covetous"[77] landlord who exploits his poorer neighbors by enclosing their land for pasture, he may, as Michael D. Bristol (1991) suggests, represent the tension in Jacobean society between "an ethos of subsistence or redistribution" and "an ethos of accumulation and social mobility typical of a market economy."[78] Alternatively, in line with Wil-son's theory of how the lower classes were contained within early modern drama, this shepherd could feature as a depoliticized "carnival"[79] figure who welcomes "all" social ranks to his annual festival (4.4.57).

To New Historicists and cultural materialists, the figure of Autolycus is also a site of contesting discourses. At the Globe Theatre in 1611 he caught the eye of Simon Forman, who associated him with one of the "feigning beggars" scavenging in the countryside, or possibly a conman operating in Jacobean London.[80] Sensitive to the "struggle between in-fracontexts" in *The Winter's Tale,* Barbara A. Mowat (1994) outlines the different figures that Autolycus might represent. On one level a celebra-tion of the resourceful trickster, he could also incarnate the "unemployed vagrant"—a figure either "scandalously evil" in his guise as a dissembling beggar or "truly pitiable," a destitute victim of the enclosure movement.[81]

This last claim is questionable, however, since Autolycus is no authentic rustic but a displaced servant of the court who effortlessly transforms back into a courtier when he dons Prince Florizel's robes in act 4, scene 4. Still another of Autolycus's roles that Mowat does not consider is that of capitalist entrepreneur. He peddles ballads and trinkets as his commodities, a liminal figure who finds his "market" in what Bristol calls the "edges and interstices of organized economic activity."[82]

Several critics have gone further in speculating on whether the "rogue" Autolycus is envisaged as truly subversive, or whether his energies are contained by the social hierarchy at the end of the play. In *Shakespearean Subversion: The Trickster and the Playtext* (1992), Richard Hillman thinks that Autolycus, for all his "carnivalesque subversiveness" is "integrated, vices and all, into the new dispensation."[83] Certainly the trickster is now dependent on the patronage of the newly knighted shepherds to pursue an "honest" (5.2.167) career at court. But he is given no role in the offstage reunions or in the statue scene, with its spectacular reinstatement of sovereignty. This exclusion from royal revelry could suggest that he is still situated as an outsider rather than co-opted by the ruling class. His promise to be a "tall fellow" of his "hands" (175) also leaves open the possibility that he will return to "dangerous marginality"[84] by reverting to stealing from courtiers in his new environment. If the implication is that he will remain "constant" to what he previously called his profession of "knavery" (4.4.686–87), then he could embody what Ronald W. Cooley, "Speech versus Spectacle in *The Winter's Tale*" (1997), calls the "failure of Jacobean England's historical attempt … to assimilate those it has defined as unassimilable."[85]

### Feminist

Since the early 1980s, feminist critics have found much to discuss in *The Winter's Tale*. After all, the play has "three female roles of the first importance"[86]—Hermione and Perdita are strong women and Paulina is an unconventional one—plus a main protagonist whose misogynistic cruelty brings the play close to tragedy. Not only is Leontes obsessed with the idea of women's promiscuity ("no barricado for a belly"), but Paulina's husband, Antigonus, oddly threatens to "geld" his daughters, punishing females indiscriminately if an icon of chastity such as Hermione proves "honor-flawed" (2.1.147, 142). Paulina draws attention to obsessive male anxieties over paternity when, with pronounced illogic, she sarcastically hopes that Perdita will not grow up to "suspect," as her father does, "Her children [are] not her husband's" (2.3.105–6).[87] Several feminist critics have used a Freudian psychoanalytic model to argue that Leontes's anxieties stem from the infant's preoedipal needs, or have viewed the jealousy in Lacanian terms, a symptom of a culture in which women are "constructed by men as Other"[88] and feared for their "unknowable 'feminine' otherness."[89] Other commentators have analyzed sexual attitudes toward women, as well as the ways in which gender is constructed, within the patriarchal context of the playworld.

In 1983, Marilyn French's appropriately named *Shakespeare's Division of Experience* somewhat ahistorically and schematically analyzed the dynamics of the play in terms of masculine and feminine "principles." She emphasizes how the male world of "power" is partly subordinated to female values; Leontes finally accepts Hermione as an "incarnation of the inlaw feminine principle," which comprises "love, harmony, the joy of nurturance."[90] Carol Thomas Neely (1993), employing a "compensatory"[91] mode of feminist criticism in "*The Winter's Tale:* Incest and Issue," is also upbeat about the role of women as nurturers in the play and their ability to transform the men of *The Winter's Tale*. Once his "possessive misogyny" has dissipated, Leontes can respect the "new autonomy" of Hermione in the statue scene; not only are the women released from the males' "rigid conceptions" of them, but the men are "also freed ... to regenerate themselves."[92]

Neely also touches on the "innocent presexual boyhood" that Polixenes introduces in his "twinned lambs" speech, which serves the two kings as a defense against women, fueling their misogyny.[93] Other feminist critics have used a Freudian model to account for the men's distrust, even hatred of women. Coppélia Kahn (1981) finds in the idealization of asexual boyhood a repudiation of mature sexuality—in Freudian terms, "an effort to repeat the mother-child symbiotic unity and to avoid male identity." Perdita, who combines the "qualities of the chaste preoedipal mother" with the "sexually desirable oedipal mother," is the channel through which Leontes can reconcile his divided attitudes toward women.[94] Ruth Nevo (1987) also finds that "infantile fears of isolation, separation and abandonment" underlie Leontes's "seizure" of jealousy.[95] Janet Adelman (1992) more thoroughly analyzes how this sense of "primal loss," being abandoned by the mother, is reactivated by the "sexualized female body" of a very pregnant Hermione. Like Neely, Adelman discovers some healing at the close of *The Winter's Tale,* a "radical recuperation of the maternal body" mediated by both Perdita and Paulina.[96]

Adelman does not gloss over tensions in the play's finale. She concedes the "return of a masculine authority," pointing out that the power of "maternal presence" is contained in this particular society because Hermione is past childbearing age, and the "promised generativity" of Perdita is deferred until the future.[97] Other feminists are more dubious about any rewriting of patriarchal assumptions at the end of *The Winter's Tale*. Hermione is maternal when she focuses on her daughter (her "issue"), which may suggest a "female continuity and generativity outside the sphere of male desire."[98] But while she embraces Leontes she does not speak to him.[99] Is she once again "tongue-tied," silenced by the male? Examining the parallel between Leontes and Ovid's Pygmalion, who wills his image of a woman into life, Lynn Enterline (1997) considers that "Pygmalion's … fantasy so narrowly constricts female speech that there is, quite literally, *nothing* Hermione can say to Leontes."[100] It is true that Leontes participates in the reanimation of the statue—astonished by its lifelike appearance, he takes on Hermione's petrification, briefly becoming more "stone" than she before both husband and wife soften into living warmth. Yet he effectively "killed" Hermione 16 years earlier (5.1.17), turning her into a static, "chastened" object, her "erotic power curtailed."[101] Questions linger that qualify the romantic reunion. When Hermione returns to life at the end of the play, is she still monumentalized (to use Abbé Blum's term [1990]),[102] subjected to the male gaze[103] within a patriarchal society that remains essentially unchanged? Lori Humphrey Newcomb (2001) points out that the use of boy actors to represent women in Shakespeare's theater would contribute to a monolithic, conventional view of female gender— another way in which "the monumentalization of women" is achieved in *The Winter's Tale*.[104]

Peter Erickson (1985) begins his chapter "The Limitations of Reformed Masculinity in *The Winter's Tale*" by proposing that the patriarchal power established at the play's conclusion is a more "benevolent one, capable of including and valuing women." But as his discussion progresses, several concessions undercut this optimism. He notes that whereas "male bonds" are reinforced, women suffer a "contraction of power," so that to some extent the play's ending reinstates a "traditional conception of polarized sexual roles."[105] Valerie Traub (1992) is more decisive in arguing that the play "perpetuates defensive structures of dominance instituted by men"; the anxieties that caused Leontes to impose "stasis" on Hermione remain "inherent in their relationship." Thus the finale of *The Winter's Tale* functions more as "wish-fulfilment for Leontes" than liberation of the queen. It restores his "kingly command" over "social relations," as shown by his quickly containing the unruly Paulina by marrying her off to Camillo.[106] Still, the play offers the union of Florizel and Perdita, which Traub does not discuss. Unlike the older generation of males, Florizel shows no signs of jealous possessiveness or incipient misogyny toward his betrothed, while the princess-as-shepherdess commands respect in the pastoral sequence. There is some hope that she will establish a strong matriarchal presence when the kingdoms of Sicily and Bohemia are united. Ruth Vanita (2000) observes that the play's "mother-daughter bonding" is cast in matrilineal terms, transmitting a "moral power" that may overrride the males' "economic and political" power.[107]

Paulina returns authority to Leontes when she resumes the traditional role of wife in a marriage arranged by him. Assimilated into a conventional comic ending, co-opted by the male regime, she has nevertheless acquired significant power during the course of the play. Her character incorporates the shrew and the scold but goes beyond these comic stereotypes;[108] refusing to be silenced, she uses the power of her "tongue," a "trumpet" to "red-looked anger" (2.2.32–34), against the tyranny of Leontes. A subversive woman who wants to appropriate masculine authority,[109] she is accused by the king of being a "mankind witch" who should be "burned" (2.3.66, 112). It is noticeable that King Polixenes, finding Perdita sexually and politically threatening because the prince has fallen in love with her, resorts to the same stereotype of disorderly women as witches when he calls the princess a "fresh piece / Of excellent witchcraft" (4.4.426–27). Although Paulina does not assist at the birth of Perdita, when she brings the child to Leontes she is a midwife by association—a role that, as Richard Wilson (1993) notes, came under surveillance in the early modern period because it challenged patriarchy's need to "impose mastery on the female body."[110] Yet once Paulina replaces Camillo as the confidant and conscience of Leontes, she increasingly takes on the conventionally male roles of his "most influential counsellor"[111] and his physician. In addition, she gains some political clout when she makes the king swear not to seek out a new wife to provide an heir for the kingdom. As Neely comments, Paulina serves both as "defender" of Hermione and "surrogate"[112] during the queen's absence; in the final scene she adds the roles of stage-manager and magician when she practices her "lawful" magic to reintroduce the queen-as-statue. Admittedly this is a clever masquerade—in contrast to Prospero in *The Tempest* she has no control over spirits, nor is she responsible for an actual resurrection—but she does, as Patricia Southard Gourlay (1975) points out, parlay fears about females as witches into a recognition of women's beneficent, "life-giving" powers.[113]

## NOTES

1.   Edward B. Partridge (ed.), "Induction" to Ben Jonson, *Bartholomew Fair,* Regents Renaissance Drama Series (London: Edward Arnold, 1964), p. 10.

2. John Dryden, *An Essay on the Dramatique Poetry of the Last Age* (1672), included in Brian Vickers (ed.), *Shakespeare: The Critical Heritage,* vol. 1, 1623–1692 (London and Boston: Routledge & Kegan Paul, 1974), p. 145.

3. Alexander Pope, *The Works of Shakespeare* (1725), included in Vickers (ed.), *Shakespeare: The Critical Heritage,* vol. 2, 1693–1733, p. 413.

4. W. K. Wimsatt (ed.), *Dr. Johnson on Shakespeare,* vol. 1 (Harmondsworth, Middlesex: Penguin, 1960; 1969), p. 109.

5. Duncan Wu (ed.), *The Selected Writings of William Hazlitt,* vol. 1 (London: Pickering and Chatto, 1998), pp. 232–33.

6. Harold Bloom, *Shakespeare: The Invention of the Human* (New York: Riverhead Books, 1998), p. 639.

7. Thomas Middleton Raysor (ed.), Samuel Taylor Coleridge, *Shakespearean Criticism,* vol. 3 (London: Dent, 1960), pp. 110–12.

8. R. A. Foakes, *Shakespeare: The Dark Comedies to the Last Plays* (London: Routledge and Kegan Paul, 1971), p. 119.

9. J.I.M. Stewart, *Character and Motive in Shakespeare* (London: Longman's, Green and Co., Ltd., 1949), pp. 33–35. See also C. L. Barber, "'Thou That Begetst Him That Did Thee Beget': Transformation in *Pericles* and *The Winter's Tale,*" ShS 22 (1969): 59–67, 65.

10. Stephen Reid, "*The Winter's Tale,*" AMIAA 27, no. 3 (1970): 263–78, 274.

11. Murray M. Schwartz, "Leontes' Jealousy in *The Winter's Tale,*" American Imago 30, no. 3 (1980): 250–73, 273.

12. Stewart, *Character and Motive,* p. 37. Kay Stockholder, *Dream Works: Lovers and Families in Shakespeare's Plays* (Toronto, Buffalo, London: University of Toronto Press, 1987), also employs a Freudian methodology, viewing the play's action as a "negotiation" between the protagonist's unconscious and conscious drives (15) as Leontes works out his "dreamlike compulsions" (191).

13. Schwartz, "Leontes' Jealousy," p. 251.

14. In contrast, Maydee G. Lande, "*The Winter's Tale:* A Question of Motive," AMIAA 43, no. 1 (1986): 51–65, finds that Leontes's speech acts, and not "psychoanalytic theory," are the clue to his "anger and his vulnerability" (64). Meredith Skura, *The Literary Uses of the Psychoanalytic Process* (New Haven and London: Yale University Press, 1981), also concedes that there is "no room" for purely "unconscious" motives in the "fully explained world" of *The Winter's Tale* (40).

15. L. C. Knights, "'Integration' in *The Winter's Tale,*" SeR 84 (Fall 1974): 595–613, 608, 606, 604.

16. Stewart, "Character and Motive," p. 36.

17. Elizabeth Bieman, *William Shakespeare: The Romances* (Boston: Twayne Publishers, G. K. Hall & Co., 1996), discusses the "puer-senex" archetype developed in Leontes (86).

18. L.A.G. Strong, "Shakespeare and the Psychologists," in *Talking of Shakespeare,* ed. John Garrett (London: Hodder and Stoughton, 1954), suggests that Perdita represents Leontes's feminine side. Once Leontes has welcomed her

back, the statue of Hermione can be unfrozen (202–3). In her Jungian interpretation, Diane Elizabeth Dreher, *Domination and Defiance: Fathers and Daughters in Shakespeare* (Lexington: University of Kentucky Press, 1986), also discusses Leontes's "spiritual rebirth in the regeneration of the *anima,* his acceptance of the life-giving woman's part in himself" (153).

19.  Northrop Frye, *A Natural Perspective: The Development of Shakespearean Comedy and Romance* (New York and London: Columbia University Press, 1965), p. 119.

20.  In Richard Hosley (ed.), *Essays on Shakespeare and Elizabethan Drama in Honor of Hardin Craig* (Columbia: University of Missouri Press, 1962), pp. 235–46.

21.  F. David Hoeniger, "The Meaning of *The Winter's Tale,*" *UTQ* 20, no. 1 (1950): 11–26, 23.

22.  F. C. Tinkler, *"The Winter's Tale" Scrutiny* 5 (1936–37): 344–64, 358.

23.  Roy Battenhouse, "Theme and Structure in *The Winter's Tale,*" *ShS* 33 (1980): 123–38, 123.

24.  Ibid., 126.

25.  J. A. Bryant, Jr., "Shakespeare's Allegory: *The Winter's Tale,*" *SeR* 63, no. 2 (1955): 202–22, 213–14, 217.

26.  Alistair Fowler, "Leontes' Contrition and the Repair of Nature," *E&S* 13 (1978): 36–64, 39, 60–61.

27.  G. Wilson Knight, *The Crown of Life: Essays in the Interpretation of Shakespeare's Final Plays* (London: Methuen & Co., 1948), pp. 91, 128.

28.  L. C. Knights, "On Some Contemporary Trends in Shakespeare Criticism," in *Some Shakespearean Themes and an Approach to* Hamlet (Harmondsworth: Penguin Books, 1960), p. 13.

29.  As in Caroline Spurgeon, *Shakespeare's Imagery and What It Tells Us* (Cambridge: Cambridge University Press, 1935), and Wolfgang Clemen, *The Development of Shakespeare's Imagery* (London: Methuen, 1951).

30.  Knights, "On Some Contemporary Trends," p. 14.

31.  F. R. Leavis, "The Criticism of Shakespeare's Late Plays," in *The Common Pursuit* (Harmondsworth: Penguin Books, 1962), p. 175.

32.  Derek Traversi, *Shakespeare: The Last Phase* (Stanford, Calif.: Stanford University Press, 1953), pp. 106–7, 188.

33.  Bill Overton, The Winter's Tale, *The Critics Debate* (Atlantic Highlands, N.J.: Humanities Press International, Inc., 1989), p. 34.

34.  In The Winter's Tale*: A Commentary on the Structure* (New York: Barnes and Noble, Inc., 1969), Fitzroy Pyle discusses how the play is a "transmutation of its primary source" (p. xi).

35.  Alison Thorne (ed.), *Shakespeare's Romances,* New Casebooks (Houndmills, Basingstoke: Palgrave Macmillan, 2003), comments on how in these plays Shakespeare seems to be searching for a "syncretic framework" free from the "cognitive limitations" of traditional generic distinctions (3).

36.  E. C. Pettet, *Shakespeare and the Romance Tradition* (London and New York: Staples Press, 1949).

37.  Hollett Smith, *Shakespeare's Romances* (San Marino, Calif.: The Huntingdon Library, 1972).

38.  Simon Palfrey, *Late Shakespeare: A New World of Words* (New York: Oxford University Press, 1997), p. 39.

39.  Bloom, *Shakespeare: The Invention of the Human,* p. 660.

40.  Marin T. Herrick, *Tragicomedy: Its Origin and Development in Italy, France, and England* (Urbana: University of Illinois Press, 1955), p. 317.

41.  E.M.W. Tillyard, *Shakespeare's Last Plays* (London: Chatto and Windus, 1938), p. 84.

42.  Knight, *The Crown of Life,* p. 127.

43.  Rosalie A. Colie, "Perspectives on Pastoral: Romance, Comic and Tragic," in *Shakespeare's Living Art* (Princeton, N.J.: Princeton University Press, 1972), pp. 244, 243, 267.

44.  Ibid., pp. 281–82.

45.  S. L. Bethell, The Winter's Tale*: A Study* (London: Staples Press Ltd., 1947).

46.  Arthur Quiller-Couch, *Shakespeare's Workmanship* (Cambridge: Cambridge University Press, 1934), p. 241.

47.  Lytton Strachey, "Shakespeare's Final Period," in *Books and Characters* (London: Chatto and Windus, 1922), p. 60.

48.  Joan Hartwig, *Shakespeare's Tragicomic Vision* (Baton Rouge: Louisiana State University, 1972), pp. 7, 31.

49.  Howard Felperin, "Our Carver's Excellence," in *Shakespearean Romance* (Princeton, N.J.: Princeton University Press, 1972), p. 244.

50.  Barbara A. Mowat, *The Dramaturgy of Shakespeare's Romances* (Athens: The University of Georgia Press, 1976), pp. 117, 119.

51.  Kiernan Ryan (ed.), *Shakespeare: The Last Plays* (London and New York: Longman, 1999), pp. 16–18.

52.  G. E. Bentley, "Shakespeare and the Blackfriars Theatre," *ShS* 1 (1948): 38–50.

53.  Alfred Harbage, *Shakespeare's Audience* (New York: Columbia University Press, 1961), points out that Shakespeare worked mainly at the Globe Theatre, where the audience was "both genteel and plebeian" (90).

54.  E. P. Wilson, *Elizabethan and Jacobean* (Oxford: Oxford University Press, 1945), p. 126.

55.  Nevill Coghill, "Six Points of Stage-Craft in *The Winter's Tale*" *ShS* 11 (1958): 31–41.

56.  J. L. Styan, *Shakespeare's Stagecraft* (Cambridge: Cambridge University Press, 1967), pp. 81, 135.

57.  *Preface* to *The Winter's Tale* (1912), in *More Prefaces to Shakespeare,* ed. Edward M. Moore and Harley Granville-Barker (Princeton, N.J.: Princeton University Press, 1974), p. 22.

58.  Alan C. Dessen, *Rescripting Shakespeare: The Text, the Director, and Modern Productions* (Cambridge: Cambridge University Press, 2002), pp. 229–30.

59.  Jean E. Howard, *Shakespeare's Art of Orchestration* (Urbana and Chicago: University of Illinois Press, 1984), p. 136.

60.  Charles Frey, "Interpreting *The Winter's Tale*," *SEL* 18 (1978): 307–29, 312, 323.

61.  Charles Frey, *Shakespeare's Vast Romance: A Study of* The Winter's Tale (Columbia and London: University of Missouri Press, 1980), p. 114.

62.  Thomas F. Van Laan, *Role-Playing in Shakespeare* (Toronto, Buffalo, London: University of Toronto Press, 1978), pp. 227, 236.

63.  Ann Righter, *Shakespeare and the Idea of the Play* (Harmondsworth: Penguin, 1967), pp. 178–80.

64.  Peter Egan, *Drama within Drama: Shakespeare's Sense of His Art in* King Lear, The Tempest, The Winter's Tale *and* The Tempest (New York and London: Columbia University Press, 1975), pp. 89, 57.

65.  See, for instance, T. G. Bishop, *Shakespeare and the Theatre of Wonder* (Cambridge: Cambridge University Press, 1996).

66.  William R. Morse, "Metacriticism and Materiality: The Case of Shakespeare's *The Winter's Tale*," *ELH* 58 (1991): 283–304, 283. Morse offers a reminder that a nation's culture can never be identified with one "totalizing" hegemony (299).

67.  Constance Jordan, *Shakespeare's Monarchies: Ruler and Subject in the Romances* (Ithaca and London: Cornell University Press, 1997), pp. 30, 33.

68.  Donna B. Hamilton, "*The Winter's Tale* and the Language of the Union, 1604–11," *ShStud* 21 (1993): 228–50. Stuart M. Kurland, "'We Need No More of Your Advice': Political Realism in *The Winter's Tale*," *SEL* 31 (1991): 365–86.

69.  Martin Orkin, "A Sad Tale's Best for South Africa," *Textual Practice* 11, no. 1 (1997): 1–23, finds that "seventeenth-century notions of hierarchy" are replicated by the end of the play (9).

70.  David M. Bergeron, *Shakespeare's Romances and the Royal Family* (Lawrence: University Press of Kansas, 1985), p. 178.

71.  James Ellison, "*The Winter's Tale* and Religious Politics," in *Shakespeare's Romances,* ed. Alison Thorne (Houndmills, Basingstoke: Palgrave Macmillan, 2003), pp. 171–204, 196.

72.  Leonard A. Tennenhouse, "Family Rites," in *Power on Display: The Politics of Shakespeare's Genres* (New York: Methuen, 1986), p. 174.

73.  In Graham Holderness, Nick Potter, John Turner, *Shakespeare: Out of Court* (New York: St. Martin's Press, 1990), p. 235.

74.  In Patricia Parker and Geoffrey Hartman (eds.), *Shakespeare and the Question of Theory* (London and New York: Methuen, 1985), p. 15.

75.  C. L. Barber, "*The Winter's Tale* and Jacobean Society," in *Shakespeare in a Changing World,* ed. Arnold Kettle (New York: International Publishers Co., 1964), p. 251.

76.  In Richard Wilson, *Willpower: Essays on Shakespearean Authority* (Detroit, Mich.: Wayne State University, 1993), p. 79.

77.   Barbara A. Mowat, "Rogues, Shepherds, and the Counterfeit Distressed: Texts and Infracontexts in *The Winter's Tale*," *ShakS* 22 (1994): 58–76, 68.

78.   Michael D. Bristol, "In Search of the Bear: Spatiotemporal Form and the Heterogeneity of Economies in *The Winter's Tale*," *SQ* 42, no. 2 (1991): 145–67, 164. Craig Horton, "The Country Must Diminish: Jacobean London and the Production of Pastoral Space in *The Winter's Tale*," *Paragon* 20, no. 1 (2003): 85–107, also finds the Old Shepherd's "great estate" a cultural anomaly, combining "rural subsistence" with "mercantile success" associated with the city (102).

79.   Wilson, *Willpower,* pp. 80–81.

80.   Social misfits in Shakespeare's time are discussed in Lee Beier, *Masterless Men: The Vagrancy Problem in England, 1560–1640* (London and New York: Methuen, 1985).

81.   Mowat, "Rogues, Shepherds and the Counterfeit Distressed," p. 69.

82.   Bristol, "In Search of the Bear," p. 163.

83.   Richard Hillman, *Shakespearean Subversions: The Trickster and the Playtext* (London and New York: Routledge, 1992), pp. 223–24.

84.   Ronald W. Cooley, "Speech versus Spectacle: Autolycus, Class and Containment in *The Winter's Tale*," *Ren&R* 21, no. 3 (1997): 5–23, 18.

85.   Cooley, "Speech Versus Spectacle," p. 5.

86.   Overton, The Winter's Tale, *The Critics Debate,* p. 46.

87.   Derek Cohen, "Patriarchy and Jealousy in *Othello* and *The Winter's Tale*," *MLQ* 48 (1987): 207–23, points out that "in a patriarchy the fidelity of wives is the major prop and condition of social order" (207).

88.   Mark Breitenberg, *Anxious Masculinity in Early Modern England* (Cambridge: Cambridge University Press, 1996), p. 181.

89.   Yoko Takakuwa, "Diagnosing Male Jealousy: Woman as Man's Symptom in *The Merry Wives of Windsor, Othello,* and *The Winter's Tale*," in *Hot Questrists after the English Renaissance: Essays on Shakespeare and His Contemporaries,* ed. Yasunari Takahashi (New York: AMS Press, Inc., 2000), p. 25.

90.   Marilyn French, *Shakespeare's Division of Experience* (New York: Summit Books, 1981), pp. 290–91, 311.

91.   The term is used by Carol Thomas Neely in "Feminist Modes of Criticism: Compensatory, Justificatory, Transformational," *WS* 9 (1981): 3–15, to define an approach which gives full weight to, and even amplifies, female voices in a text (6).

92.   Carol Thomas Neely, "Incest and Issue in *The Winter's Tale*," in *Broken Nuptials in Shakespeare's Plays* (Urbana: University of Illinois Press, 1993), pp. 207, 209.

93.   Ibid., p. 194.

94.   Coppélia Kahn, *Man's Estate: Masculine Identity in Shakespeare* (Berkeley, Los Angeles, London: University of California Press, 1981), p. 219.

95.   Ruth Nevo, *Shakespeare's Other Language* (New York and London: Methuen, 1987), pp. 105–6.

96. Janet Adelman, *Suffocating Mothers: Fantasies of Maternal Origin in Shakespeare's Plays,* Hamlet *to* The Tempest (New York and London: Routledge, 1992), pp. 224, 221, 228.

97. Ibid., pp. 194, 236.

98. Ibid., p. 234.

99. Joyce Wexler, "A Wife Lost and/or Found," *Ucrow* 8 (1988): 106–17, finds reconciliation impossible, for "no wife" could forgive Leontes for what he has done (116).

100. Lynn Enterline, "'You Speak a Language That I Understand Not': The Rhetoric of Animation in *The Winter's Tale,*" *SQ* 48 (1997): 17–44, 43.

101. Valerie Traub, *Desire and Anxiety: Circulations of Sexuality in Shakespearean Drama* (London and New York: Routledge, 1992), p. 45.

102. Abbé Blum, "Strike all that look upon with mar[b]le': Monumentalizing Women in Shakespeare's Plays," in *The Renaissance Englishwoman in Print,* ed. Anne M. Haselkorn and Betty S. Travitsky (Amherst: University of Massachusetts Press, 1990), pp. 110–11. H.W. Fawkner, *Shakespeare's Miracle Plays: Pericles, Cymbeline, and* The Winter's Tale (London and Toronto: Associated University Presses, 1992), also raises the question of Hermione's "self-silencing" and "self-petrification" once she is converted to a masculine ideal (114).

103. Joel Davis, "Paulina's Paint and the Dialectic of Masculine Desire in the *Metamorphoses, Pandosto,* and *The Winter's Tale,*" *PLL* 39, no. 2 (2003): 115–43, analyzes ways in which the statue is positioned as "an unthreatening object of voyeuristic desire" (139).

104. Lori H. Newcomb, "'If That Which Is Lost Be Not Found': Monumental Bodies, Spectacular Bodies in *The Winter's Tale,*" in *Ovid and the Renaissance Body,* ed. Goran V. Stanivukovic (Toronto, Buffalo, London: University of Toronto Press, 2001), p. 245.

105. Peter Erickson, *Patriarchal Structures in Shakespeare's Drama* (Berkeley, Los Angeles, London: University of California Press, 1985), pp. 148, 167, 162, 172.

106. Traub, *Desire and Anxiety,* pp. 45, 48, 49.

107. Ruth Vanita, "Mariological Memory in *The Winter's Tale* and *Henry VIII,*" *SEL* 40, no. 2 (2000): 311–37, 316, 312. M. Lindsay Kaplan and Katherine Eggert, "'Good queen, my lord, good queen': Sexual Slander and the Trials of Female Authority in *The Winter's Tale,*" *RenD* 25 (1994): 89–118, also find that the play interprets positively "the nexus of female sexuality and authority" (104) by presenting women as "integral and morally reliable caretakers of the patriarchal project of lineal inheritance" (110).

108. Overton, The Winter's Tale: *The Critics Debate,* p. 66.

109. See Holderness, "*The Winter's Tale:* Country into Court," p. 217. Jane Tylus, *Writing and Vulnerability in the Renaissance* (Stanford, Calif.: Stanford University Press, 1993), also discusses Paulina as a "vivid example of a female unruliness that evades patriarchal control" (165).

110. Wilson, "Observations on English Bodies: Licensing Maternity in Shakespeare's Late Plays," in *Willpower,* pp. 169, 171.

111. See Carolyn Asp, "Shakespeare's Paulina and the *Consolatio* Tradition," *ShakS* 11, (1978) pp. 145–58, 155. Asp points out that there are "no parallels" for Paulina's "position" as counselor in the political or social context of Shakespeare's age (146). In contrast, Amelia Zurcher, "Untimely Monuments: Stoicism, History, and the Problem of Utility in *The Winter's Tale* and *Pericles," ELH* 70, no. 4 (2003): 903–27, finds that as "Stoic exemplar" Paulina offers a "moral but not a truly political challenge" (913–14).

112. Neely, "Incest and Issue in *The Winter's Tale,"* p. 199.

113. Patricia Southard Gourlay, "'O My Most Sacred Lady': Female Metaphor in *The Winter's Tale," ELR* 5 (1975): 375–95, 393. David Schalkwyk, "'A Lady's "Verily" Is as Potent as a Lord's': Women, Word, and Witchcraft in *The Winter's Tale," ELR* 22, no. 2 (1992): 242–72, also notes in the final scene a "gradual exorcism of the specter of witchcraft" associated with the female (265). Kristie Gulick Rosenfield, "Nursing Nothing: Witchcraft and Female Sexuality in *The Winter's Tale," Mosaic* 35, no. 1 (2002): 95–112, discusses how Leontes finally connects Paulina's "witchcraft to the power of art" instead of seeing her as a "demonized sorceress" (106).

# 7

# THE WINTER'S TALE *IN* PERFORMANCE

*The Winter's Tale* is full of frank experimentation and theatrical risks. But like the statue of Hermione, it can come alive only on stage, where it usually does so triumphantly. Speculations aside, we can never be sure exactly how the play was staged in Shakespeare's time at the public Globe or the private Blackfriars Theatre. The eyewitness account of Simon Forman, who saw it at the Globe in 1611, is disappointing. He recounts most of the plot and reacts strongly to Autolycus, but we hear nothing about the bear or the statue. After its initial popularity—it was performed at court six times between 1611 and 1634[1]—*The Winter's Tale* was not staged for about 100 years. With its sprawling action and bold improbabilities it did not suit the Restoration's increasingly neoclassical tastes. When revived in the eighteenth century it was in a much-adapted form that concentrated on the young lovers' romance in Bohemia: Macnamara Morgan's *Sheep-Shearing: or, Florizel and Perdita* (1754) was succeeded in 1756 by David Garrick's popular *Florizel and Perdita, a Dramatic Pastoral* in three acts. In this "lop'd, hack'd, and dock'd" version,[2] Leontes and Hermione (as a statue) do not appear until the final act. No wonder, then, that at least one reviewer found the resurrection of Hermione "childish" and irrational.[3]

While the more tragic part of the play was restored in John Philip Kemble's production of 1802, the text he used was by no means complete; the excision of Time, for instance, caused some narrative confusion. Even as late as 1887, Mary Anderson, tailoring the text for the Lyceum Theatre, confidently asserted that "no audience of these days would desire to have *The Winter's Tale* produced in its entirety."[4] Her own script left out much that had been cut previously, including the knotty "Affection" speech of

Leontes in act 1, scene 2; the debate on art and nature in act 4, scene 4; and chunks of the reported reunions in act 5, scene 2. Such extensive pruning of the text phased out soon after the turn of the century. William Poel's experiments in staging Shakespeare's plays on a reconstructed Elizabethan stage, focusing attention on the verse, were one inspiration for Harley Granville Barker's virtually uncut presentation of *The Winter's Tale* at the Savoy in 1912. Meanwhile productions in the second half of the twentieth century, while forging strong design concepts, have respected the integrity of the playtext, giving equal weight to the tragic and tragicomic parts in Sicily and the romantic pastoral in Bohemia.

Rather than analyzing productions from the last three centuries in their totality, what follows will focus on sets and costumes, categories that are crucial in any theatrical interpretation, and on those features of *The Winter's Tale* that have required special handling on stage. Time, the bear, and the statue are all unique to this play. A production may accentuate the strangeness of these phenomena, jolting the audience into a fresh awareness of the implausible, tragicomic "old tale" they are witnessing. Or the director may blend these figures (Time and the bear, at least) into the overall stage illusion. The play poses particular challenges for the actors too. These include whether the actress playing Hermione can encompass the varied facets of the role, how quickly Leontes reveals his jealousy in act 1, scene 2, and how effectively the Bohemian characters, especially the comic, Autolycus, counterbalance the Sicilian ones.

## SETS AND COSTUMES

The history of stage production reveals just how closely the choice of sets and costumes mirrors the tastes of the age. Whereas Shakespeare's company worked with minimal props and wore contemporary costumes, Kemble (1802) used painted "flats" to conjure up detailed, sometimes jarring, locations. Those representing a Grecian square in the first scene of *The Winter's Tale* slid back to reveal the palace of Leontes against a "background of open Gothic arches";[5] act 4 created the illusion of English countryside, with a cottage, an arbor, and a village green. The quest for authentic antiquarian detail in setting and costumes peaked in Charles Kean's production of the play in the second half of the nineteenth century. While Samuel Phelps's long run of the play at Sadler's Wells (1845–1860) had been consistently Grecian in its decor, Kean (1856) went further. He set the first part of the play in the wealthy Sicilian city of Syracuse around 330 B.C., when Apollo was worshipped throughout the ancient Hellenic world, and changed Bohemia to Bithynia (Persia), not only to make the seacoast legitimate but to forge a contrast between a "classically Greek Sicilia and a more romantically Asiatic Bohemia/Bithinia."[6] While Mrs. Kean's Hermione looked distinctly Victorian with her "layer upon layer" of bunched petticoats,[7] the costumes overall were carefully modeled on Greek vase paintings. This was the age of pictorial realism and spectacular effects in the theater. Hermione's trial was stupendous, with an effect of "colossal proportions" in the "dense assembly of auditory and officials"[8] as the queen was carried in on a litter. Interestingly, several pieces of stage business that Kean introduced were assimilated into theatrical conventions of future years. Vestiges of a Pyrrhic dance urging Polixenes to stay, performed by 36 young women dressed as "warlike" youths,[9] could still be found in the Baccanalian dance that Anthony Quayle used in his 1948 production at Stratford-upon-Avon. A hymn to Apollo, preceding the Pyrrhic dance in Kean's production, was heard in triplicate—at the play's opening, just before the oracle was disclosed, and at the end—in Beerbohm Tree's elaborate staging of *The Winter's Tale* in 1906;[10] such a hymn, now sung during the oracle scene (3.1), even made its way into Ronald Eyre's 1981 Stratford production.[11]

By the time Tree put on his truncated version of the play, sound effects such as fanfares and orchestral themes had become an integral part of the show. And the passion for naturalistic illusion—slow-moving spectacle that inevitably altered the rhythm of Shakespeare's scenes and detracted from his verse—was fully indulged by Tree. His pastoral scene featured a stream that Florizel had to cross before throwing flowers up at the window of Perdita's cottage, while Autolycus washed his face in the stream, and the Clown's donkey drank from it.

It was Granville Barker's production of *The Winter's Tale* at the Savoy, opening in September 1912, that broke this mold of realism. Evening performances ended after only six weeks; yet this piece of theater jolted audiences into a new way of seeing and hearing Shakespeare's play. Bypassing the picture frame stage, the director placed the main action on a platform, 12 feet in depth, built over the orchestra pit. Behind this a few steps led up to a shallow proscenium stage with a small inset stage slightly above and to the back of that. As George Bernard Shaw enthused, having a thrust stage instead of the old footlights "apparently trebled the spaciousness of the stage";[12] it also resembled Shakespeare's playhouse in helping to connect the actors more closely with the audience. Strong, even harsh lighting that came from the auditorium itself as well as the playing area—cylinder lights placed in front of the dress circles and bright white arc lights above and across the main stage—increased this sense of space.[13] The set was also predominantly white, with pilasters on the inner stage to sug-

gest rather than fully represent a Grecian palace during the first half of
the play. A depiction of a thatched cottage, also placed on the inner stage,
signaled a Bohemia that had a Cotswold flavor. Many of the scenes took
place in front of drop curtains that were painted in various nonnaturalistic
designs, such as the "black and silver geometrically patterned"[14] curtain
that framed the statue scene. Instead of providing detailed illusion like
Beerbohm Tree's, Norman Wilkinson's "post-Impressionist"[15] sets were a
stimulus to audience imagination. They also allowed for continuous staging (with no complicated changes of scenery) and fast-paced delivery of
the lines, providing a space where the conventions of Shakespeare's own
theater, such as Leontes's direct address to the audience or the disguise of
Camillo, who simply holds a mask in front of his face during much of act
4, scene 4, could come into their own. Accentuated against the pale, abstract set were the gorgeous and often extravagant costumes, designed by
Arthur Rothenstein in shades of emerald, lemon, and scarlet. The immediate inspiration for them was not classical Greece but the late Renaissance,
mannerist period of Julio Romano. But they were also eclectic, with mod-
ernist touches; Perdita's costume seemed a "blend of Botticelli and Beard-
sley."[16] The satyrs, stylized in conception, were horned creatures sporting
huge masks and garlands of flowers.

    Although Granville Barker was determined to scrap the ornate scen-
ery and extraneous spectacle of the Victorian stage in order to do justice
to Shakespeare's language and development of character, his production
of *The Winter's Tale* was still a highly individual interpretation, never a
"museum reconstruction"[17] of the play. Twentieth-century theater has increasingly acknowledged that there is no such thing as unmediated Shakespeare. Whether within the confines of a picture frame stage, or utilizing
a more open space that can fully accommodate boldly symbolic sets, the
most successful modern productions have offered clear interpretations
of the play. Since the role of the actors, "the chemistry of relationships
created by casting,"[18] is an all-important part of the developing interpretation, it is usually unfair to term this enterprise exclusively "director's
theater."[19] The governing idea, arising from a careful study of the text, can
emerge fully only through the art of collaboration—the director working
closely not only with the actors, but with lighting crews, choreographers,
and set and costume designers. At its worst, the resulting design concept
may stifle the drama or prove merely trendy. At its best it will clarify and
illuminate the play for contemporary audiences.

    On the original proscenium stage of the Shakespeare Memorial The-
atre in Stratford, the scenic tradition died hard. Peter Wood's 1960 setting
for *The Winter's Tale* was frankly picturesque: for Sicily a Renaissance

palace with black arches; a starlit sky, with sparkling trees, for the sheep-shearing scene; and a whole gallery of statues for the final sequence. A clear break in tradition came with Trevor Nunn's production for the Royal Shakespeare Company (RSC) in 1969, which decisively exchanged realism for symbolism. The play opened in what looked like a stark white box (white tiles enclosed by colorless walls), in which "ice white cubes" opened to reveal the playthings of a child's nursery. The dominant prop on stage was a giant rocking horse. Father and son, clad in pale clothes,[20] rode on this horse, while Polixenes played with a yo-yo and later with an eerily humming top[21] that was prompted, perhaps, by Leontes's reference to a "schoolboy top" in act 2, scene 1 (103). When Leontes delivered his tortured asides, there was a sudden shift to blue strobic lighting in which Hermione and Polixenes, whose suit turned from brown to "lurid red"[22] under the lights, appeared to be striking lecherous poses. This briefly allowed the audience to view the couple from the point of view of the jealous husband. Overall the set and special effects made the situation at once more "personal and more archetypal"[23] than had been the case in previous productions by suggesting that the jealousy of Leontes was rooted in the Freudian conflicts of childhood—an interpretation that gained ground with psychological critics in the 1980s. But the stage metaphor also pointed to the theme of recreation, as nostalgic childhood dream turns into a nightmarish game before playful Bohemia restores a sense of sanity.

The energetic pastoral scenes, completely different in style, were an essential part of this positive recreation. Envisaged in terms of late 1960s culture, the shepherds looked like a "tribe of hippies" wearing bits of Carnaby Street gear, while Perdita's role as Flora lent itself to the concept of flower power.[24] Critics saw shades of the popular musical *Hair* in the hirsute satyrs (one a green man) who romped enthusiastically to Guy Wolfenden's rock music. I recall a very spirited arrangement of the three-part "Whither" song by Mopsa, Dorcas, and Autolycus. By presenting rural Bohemia in colorfully contemporary terms, Nunn's production woke the audience to the restorative energy of this society in contrast to the relatively timeless, claustrophic world of the king's infantile jealousy.

Some subsequent productions rooted the Sicilian part of the play in a more specific time period. In his 1988 version of *The Winter's Tale* for The National Theatre in London, Peter Hall successfully foregrounded the idea of King Leontes having absolute power by placing him in the Caroline court of the 1630s, where his family and entourage resembled figures out of a Van Dyck painting. But most productions soon after 1969 chose symbolic sets or nonnaturalistic devices to bring out key aspects of the play. In 1976, Trevor Nunn collaborated with John Barton at the

RSC to create a northern, "arctic" world[25] that accentuated the "old tale" as well as the wintry nature of Leontes's delusions. Sicily/Lapland was represented by a circular floor scattered with Nordic rugs, while encircling dark panels carried designs that told parts of the story through what looked like primitive cave drawings. The set and its props helped to draw the audience into the "two-dimensional world of make-believe."[26] In such a setting Hermione's trial was a simple nomadic gathering where her attendants squatted informally on the floor around her—an effect very different from the "imposing appearance of the king on his throne, with sages and councillors ranged behind and on each side of him" in Kean's "colossal" mid-nineteenth-century version.[27] Bohemia presented an only slightly warmer version of this arctic world. In contrast, the countryside in Ronald Eyre's 1981 production at Stratford-upon-Avon was that of Victorian England, with Autolycus an all-purpose festival entertainer. The opening set, however, remained unlocalized, part of a "chamber"[28] theater style where the stage was a square surrounded by plain panels. Tailor's dummies, used to accommodate the actors' fancy dress costumes, were placed in full view of the audience,[29] further breaking any illusion by emphasizing the "play" world. Through large double doors and into this neutral setting burst a gaudy pageant, featuring Father Time as an old man from under whose skirts Mamillius materialized. In emblematic terms this stressed Time as creator and revealer as well as destroyer, while immediately setting up a contrast between these New Year festivities and the wintry gloom to follow.

## THE FIGURE OF TIME

This pageant in Eyre's production was a clever way of introducing the significance of temporal process early in the play. The character of Time in act 4 is a frankly narrative convention to bridge the gap of 16 years, and the director's challenge is to make him an arresting visual link without too much distracting spectacle. In Shakespeare's day Time might have been portrayed emblematically as an old man carrying an hourglass and perhaps a scythe. Directors now may decide to project Time in an even more stylized way, as part of a complex allegory. Or, as was the case at Stratford, Connecticut, in 1958, where Time wore a business suit and carried an umbrella, he can be transformed into the audience's contemporary.

Not surprisingly, Victorian Charles Kean made Time an excuse for a grandiose "classical allegory."[30] Chronos (Time) spoke his lines from an enormous globe, which was preceded on stage by the moon and her stars and followed by a tableau of the sun god Apollo, sitting in a chariot led by "exquisitely sculpted" horses.[31] Some critics were enchanted, but at least one reviewer considered this pageant a time-wasting piece of "precious nonsense."[32] Less pretentious but also stylized was the appearance of Time in Hall's 1988 production, in which the advancing figure was accompanied by the sound of loud ticking and framed by the circular golden model of the Copernican heavens slowly released from above.[33] In an imaginative transition away from the winter of death, Time in Peter Brooks's 1951 Stratford-upon-Avon production made his way through a whirling snowstorm that gradually subsided to reveal the figures of Florizel and Perdita in all the brightness of a Bohemian summer. In keeping with the central image of Leontes boxed in by jealousy and a prisoner of time, Nunn's 1969 production linked Leontes and Time by having each make his first appearance from inside a silver-sided cubicle. Before the main action began, Time's sonorous words "I that please some, try all" accompanied the sight of the "helpless figure" of Leontes, arms outstretched, "spinning in a transparent box."[34] Time himself stepped out of this box to deliver his speech in act 4, while Hermione, encased in the cubicle as a statue before she returns to life, emerges to complete the sense of Time's purposes being fulfilled in act 5.

## "EXIT PURSUED BY A BEAR"

Using an ingenious twist, the 1976 Nunn-Barton production doubled the parts of Time and the bear. An actor wearing a bear mask and carrying a staff "decorated with human skulls"[35] rapped out "an awful death-summons"[36] as he escorted off Antigonus; a little later he took off the mask to deliver his speech on Time. Perhaps anticlimactic in the theater, such a nonnaturalistic way of presenting the bear was prepared for by the ubiquitous motifs within this Nordic-style production: the primitive animal designs; the bear skin that became a prop when Polixenes playfully draped it over Hermione; a mock bear hunt game that Mamillius played with Polixenes;[37] and the way that even the later dance of satyrs turned into a "ritual ballet-hunt."[38]

Resorting to artifice is one way of dealing with "exit pursued by a bear," the most notorious stage direction in the whole of Shakespeare. Some scholars have speculated that since the bear-baiting arena was close by, the original Globe Theatre might have employed the real thing, or possibly (based on a description of the white bears featured in Jonson's masque *Oberon*) have used a reasonably tame polar bear, if such a creature existed.[39] But Shakespeare's company was more likely to have played it safe by using an actor in a bearskin or bearsuit for the animal supposed to kill

Antigonus offstage, as must have been the case in the popular play *Muce-dorus,* revived around the time that *The Winter's Tale* made its debut.[40] In recent productions the question has become how realistic and ferocious to make the pretend bear and whether to downplay the grotesque dimension of an elderly male being carried off by a mock predator. Although Peter Hall, whose bear did attack Antigonus and dragged him off stage, claimed that it didn't matter if a few uneasy titters were heard in the audience because that would signify "shock";[41] most productions have not wanted to risk laughter. Kemble created the convincing illusion of a bear at a distance, "roaring horribly."[42] Kean's bear was a "masterpiece of the zoological art"[43] and, perhaps more surprisingly, Granville Barker's was presented in realistic style.[44] Nunn's 1969 production, for all its symbolism, created a huge, lifelike bear. The actor wore eight-inch-high boots to make the creature appear more formidable as it lumbered along on its hind legs to envelop Antigonus, while blue strobic lighting foregrounded the strangeness of the attack. The shaggy black bear in Adrian Noble's production for the RSC in 1992 actually sniffed at the baby "as if pondering an appetiser," before a phantasm of billowing white silks, vaguely representing the ghostly but maternal figure of Hermione, descended from the flies to distract the creature.[45]

One of the most theatrically effective presentations of the bear was non-naturalistic. Instead of an actor in costume, Eyre's 1981 production created the terrifying silhouette of a bear glimpsed between flashes of lightning. The effect was "nightmarish,"[46] both "uncanny and frightening."[47] In the RSC production directed by Terry Hands in 1986, a huge bearskin that had been draped on the nursery floor in act 1 now rose up, suspended on wires, so that its head seemed about to devour Antigonus.[48] A production at the University of Toronto in 1993 almost bypassed the bear altogether. It nevertheless created an appropriately grotesque effect for this tragicomic turning point when, after a quick glimpse of three bear heads accompanied by "hungry slurping noises," three pairs of "red-gloved hands" reached out from a V-shaped opening in the stage floor to pull Antigonus down into it.[49]

## THE STATUE

The culminating theatrical surprise, the statue that turns out to be Hermione, is almost always "overwhelmingly moving" in performance.[50] In his commentary on "The Statue in the Theatre," Stephen Orgel provides nine visual representations that show how closely the costuming and decor of the statue mirror their specific eras. In Garrick's adaptation, Mrs. Pritchard wears "classical drapery,"[51] while the stylishly dressed Elizabeth Farren, who later played the role, leans on a monument engraved with putti and figures from Greek drama. Mrs. Siddons (1802) is dressed more simply, looking like one of Jane Austen's heroines in an unadorned Regency dress of white muslin. Her elbow rests on a covered cylinder. This convention of having the "statue" lean on something—so much easier for the actress to hold a monumental pose that way!—was maintained until the early twentieth century. Ellen Terry is photographed in 1906 wearing a white gown with sculpted folds, her right hand resting on a cylinder. In an original touch at Stratford, Ontario (1958), the statue was recumbent, so that Hermione's rising up at Paulina's request emphasized the resurrection motif.[52]

The moment when the statue comes to life should be magical. Critics applauded the sudden movement of Mrs. Siddons's head after "music strikes."[53] Particularly impressive was the slow turn (so that her eyes finally rest on Leontes) and majestic descent of Helen Faucit's Hermione in William Macready's production (1835). Faucit describes how her own composure was almost destroyed by the charge of intense emotion, the "passionate joy" of Macready's Leontes as he frantically embraced her, caressing and kissing her hair. She must have cried out involuntarily, for Macready had to whisper "Control yourself"—all this "during a tumult of applause that sounded like hail."[54]

Where the statue is positioned will also affect audience response. If it is placed well upstage, as in Macready's and Kean's productions, the focus is likely to be on the stationary Hermione, since Leontes and his entourage will also be gazing at her with their backs or profiles turned toward the audience. If the statue is further downstage, as in the Nunn-Barton production of 1976, where it was encased in a cubicle downstage left, then the audience will be watching the facial reactions of the onstage spectators. The effect was similar in Hall's 1988 production. There the statue, placed in a veiled recess center stage, had its back toward the audience. This meant that the focus stayed on the court's responses until, at the crucial moment, Hermione turned around, drew back the curtain, and walked downstage to face her husband and the audience.[55] The postmodernist performance at Toronto University in 1993 went further in actually placing the statue offstage right to suggest how "unimaginable" the whole transformation was. A shadow across the lighted stage signaled the moment that the statue moved, and when Hermione actually walked on stage (shocking the spectators) she couldn't quite bring herself to touch her husband. Instead she began to cry uncontrollably. This interpretation emphasized the darker subtextual possibilities emerging from Hermione's failure to speak to Leontes while ignoring the warmth implied by "She

hangs about his neck" (5.3.112). But it was part of an "exciting" production that responded to the text's "startling contrasts in tone."[56]

In Nunn's 1969 production, where Dame Judi Dench doubled as
Hermione and Perdita, Nunn wanted to keep her performing both parts
in the final sequence rather than finding a different actress to play Perdita throughout the scene, as had been the case when Mary Anderson
doubled the parts in 1887. Nunn managed this through a "mechanical,
quick-change"[57] device that several critics condemned as too distracting.[58]
Longing to "kiss" the hand of the statue, Dench as Perdita rushed behind
the cubicle containing it. But at that point the glittering perspex sides of
the cubicle closed, allowing Dench a little time to substitute herself for the
actress posing in there, who then unobtrusively slipped back onstage to
represent the silent Perdita.

## HERMIONE AND PAULINA

Doubling the parts of Hermione and Perdita is a challenge for any actress.
Dench, though, had no difficulty romping energetically as the 16-year-old
after projecting sprightliness combined with dignity and integrity in her
role as the queen. I still recall her perfect timing as she hesitated fraction-
ally to underline the gravity of "as they do" after the lines "if powers divine
/ Behold our actions" in the trial scene. Like Mary Anderson (1887), whose
crash to the marble floor at the news of Mamillius's death was praised as
a "magnificent moment,"[59] Dench's slow-motion fall after moving toward
Leontes with outstretched arms at this point (once again counterpointed
by the blue strobes) struck the audience as "marvellously timed."[60] According to Hazlitt, Mrs. Siddons (1802) achieved "monumental dignity" as
Hermione,[61] but *The Times* critic found her too stiff and serious in the early
scenes: in other words, too statuesque too soon.[62] Mrs. Yates, in Garrick's
eighteenth-century production, had a stately physique but was deemed
good *only* as the statue, for "when she had to speak the charm was broken
and the spectators wished her back on her pedestal."[63] In William Burton's
New York production (1881), Amelia Warner, "playful, graceful, dignified, and majestic,"[64] captured the light and shade of Hermione's character,
while Ellen Terry (1906) evoked dignified graciousness without appearing
too cold. Inevitably, of course, critics will perceive the same performance
differently. Some found Lillah McCarthy in Granville Barker's production
(1912) "delightfully unstagey."[65] Rebecca West, however, thought her too
"nerveless and stolid," lacking "poise and significance" as the statue.[66]

As a rigorous truth-teller, Paulina is virtually failure-proof on stage.
Still, the actress must decide how far to develop the comic dimension

of the character—she is branded by Leontes as a shrew in the second act—or whether to accentuate the dignity, at times severity, of her moral stand. The Paulina of Mrs. Kemble (1807) was thought to be too "vulgar,"[67] but that of Mrs. Warner, in Phelps's Victorian production, remained respectably "earnest" and "firm."[68] The "immense inner dignity"[69] and sanity of the character was captured in Brooks's 1951 Stratford production by Flora Robson, who stayed sensitive to the cadences of the poetry. She also endowed the character with a "spiritual dimension," as did the imposing Elizabeth Spriggs in 1969.[70] Peggy Ashcroft (1960) brought out the complexities of the character, managing to "combine an iron strength of character with mature grace and sweetness."[71] Sheila Hancock (1981) was much less "stridently aggressive" than some Paulinas, more the "compassionate friend" than the "tart scold";[72] her sudden apology for reminding Leontes of his crime at the end of the trial scene seemed genuine. In handling this sequence an actress must decide whether or not Paulina actually knows Hermione is alive when she lambastes the king; if she does, and has decided to guide Leontes to repentance the hard way, this will lend an edge of contrivance to her impassioned speeches. The Paulina of Eileen Atkins in Hall's 1988 production, while justly indignant, was nevertheless sensed to be "deliberately inducing a breakdown in Leontes."[73] At Stratford, Ontario, in the same year, Susan Wright presented a Paulina who really believed the queen was dead.[74] Accordingly, her speeches to Leontes were more single-minded, their tone more intense.

## LEONTES

The greatest challenge for the actor of Leontes is how to portray the king's jealousy—whether to build slowly or make it explosive. The text, as opposed to any subtextual nuances, gives warrant for suddenness, but some actors have chosen to make the king already jealous when the play opens. Charles Kean's Leontes "anxiously" watched his wife with Polixenes from the start,[75] while John Gielgud's (in Brooks's 1951 production) entered trying to control his smouldering jealousy in order to maintain his dignity.[76] Whichever path is chosen, the actor must generate some passion in the scene. Kemble (1802) played the king in classical style, but he rose to an impressive "classical phrensy"[77] of jealousy and despair. With his talent for "emotional realism," Macready (1823) presented the jealous rage of Leontes as a "gradually ripening"[78] process, fed by his obvious unease ("At my request he would not") when Polixenes agrees to stay after Hermione's entreaties.

"Ideal Home" cottage (Bohemia) in Granville Barker's 1912 production of *The Winter's Tale*. Copyright © V and A Images/Victoria and Albert Museum.

The Royal Shakespeare Company's production of *The Winter's Tale* (directed by Trevor Nunn, 1969); Hermione (Judi Dench); Leontes (Barrie Ingham), and Polixenes (Richard Pasco). Joe Cocks Studio Collection, Copyright © Shakespeare Birthplace Trust.

The Royal Shakespeare Company's production of *The Winter's Tale* (directed by Trevor Nunn, 1969); The Old Shepherd (Sydney Bromley); Polixenes (Richard Pasco), Perdita (Judi Dench), and Florizel (David Bailie). Tom Holte Theatre Photographic Collection, Copyright © Shakespeare Birthplace Trust.

The Royal Shakespeare Company's production of *The Winter's Tale* (directed by Trevor Nunn and John Barton, 1976); Polixenes (John Woodvine), Leontes (Ian McKellen), Paulina (Barbara Leigh-Hunt), and Hermione (Gemma Jones) in the statue scene. Joe Cocks Studio Collection, Copyright © Shakespeare Birthplace Trust.

The BBC/Time Life production of *The Winter's Tale* (directed by Jane Howell, 1980). Polixenes (Robert Stephens) and Hermione (Anna Calder-Marshall) together near the beginning of the play. Copyright © BBC.

The BBC/Time Life production of *The Winter's Tale* (directed by Jane Howell, 1980). Perdita (Debbie Farrington) and Florizel (Robin Kermode) in pastoral Bohemia. Copyright © BBC.

The BBC/Time Life production of *The Winter's Tale* (directed by Jane Howell, 1980). Perdita (Debbie Farrington), Leontes (Jeremy Kemp), and Hermione (Anna Calder-Marshall) at the end of the play. Copyright © BBC.

In keeping with what the editors of the 1931 New Cambridge edition surmised, the Leontes of Eric Porter, in Wood's 1960 production, heard only the end of the long exchange between Polixenes and Hermione that concludes with "If you first sinned with us." He therefore misinterpreted Hermione's welcoming embrace of the Bohemian king when she declares he will be "for some while" her "friend." In Hall's 1988 production, Tim Piggott-Smith's king also left the stage during most of that conversation and then misconstrued Hermione's repartee to Polixenes. At "Too hot, too hot" his mask of warm friendliness instantly dropped as he succumbed to jealousy in a strikingly physiological way. "Tremor cordis" for him meant literal heart palpitations, a convulsing disease that disappeared, leaving him drained, only at the end of the trial scene.[79] Similarly, Henry Ainsley (1912) played the jealousy with a "spasmodic fierceness"[80] that took up director Granville Barker's suggestion that Leontes is a "drunkard of passion."[81] At Ashland, Oregon (1965), James Edmondson's king was an "impassioned animal," a "lion without control."[82] The Leontes of Ian McKellen (1976) suddenly contorted with jealousy, becoming anguished and insecure, regaining moments of sanity only as he roughhoused with Mamillius.[83] True to the "old tale" emphasis of that Nunn-Barton production, this Leontes appeared "spell-struck."[84] In Nunn's 1969 version, Barrie Ingham experienced jealousy as a "demented breakdown"[85] into lurid fantasy, underscored by the distorted tableaux of Hermione and Polixenes embracing. Patrick Stewart (1981) showed a "dangerous geniality"[86] in his almost manic welcoming of Polixenes, where he actually addressed the "Too hot, too hot" speech to his friend in a semijoking manner. But this mask soon cracked to reveal the jealousy underlying his "barely controlled hysteria."[87]

The roles that Leontes plays in the last act, when he is chastened by Paulina and then mesmerized by the statue, are less challenging for an actor because less open to conflicting interpretations. Macready's "truth and depth of passion"[88] in the final scene made for riveting theater. An engraving from 1837, freezing what was presumably a marvelous moment on stage, shows his startled gesture, arms raised, when Paulina unveils the statue;[89] and in performance he was said to have drawn back instinctively from Hermione before slowly advancing, trembling, to touch her hand. Phelps (1858) uttered a "wild cry of transport"[90] when the statue moved. Gielgud's particular style of acting—"romantic dignity"[91] coupled with restrained, sensitive articulation of the verse—was particularly suited to the king's moving repentance. He made "O, she's warm!" a moment of "breathless awe."[92] Patrick Stewart's expression of yearning in that half-line, heard on the videotape *Playing Shakespeare* (1982),[93] was also a high point in his progression toward reclaiming Hermione.

## BOHEMIA: PERDITA AND AUTOLYCUS

Since audiences need to feel the regenerative energy of the pastoral world, productions are most successful when they clearly contrast Bohemia with Sicily, in style as well as tone. Despite too much emphasis on spectacle, Kean's Bithynia/Bohemia generated some wild Baccanalian spirit; up to 300 extras swelled the dance of the satyrs into a "revel of organized confusion."[94] Granville Barker's pastoral romp (1912) was felt to be the "real life and soul of the play,"[95] while Nunn's Bohemia (1969) parlayed the novelty of 1960s counterculture into a vibrant community totally at odds with the white sterility and claustrophobia of Sicily. Carrying on the tradition of a Victorian English village fete established by Eyre in 1981, Noble's RSC production in 1992 created the warm atmosphere of an English country festival in the 1930s or '40s, complete with a brass band and red, blue, and yellow balloons down which Autolycus parachuted.

While she is far from a bumpkin, Perdita is better played as countrified in this setting than as too courtly. Earlier Perditas suffered from being overrefined. Miss Hickes (1802) was too "delicate"[96] and "languid";[97] Mrs. West (1823) too cold;[98] and Miss Phillips (1833) too "ladylike."[99] But Judi Dench (1969) found the business of transforming rural Bohemia into a new hippie world "wonderfully exciting,"[100] and her earthy Perdita reflected that. Granville Barker (1912) continually urged his Perdita, played by Cathleen Nesbitt, to keep up the pace and be natural, not too "poetical."[101] Certainly Perdita is down-to-earth and frank in wanting Florizel to be buried in her arms; yet her character also embodies the kind of "spritual innocence"[102] that Cheri Lunghi projected in the 1976 RSC production.

Autolycus is a star part and a demanding one. Shakespeare must have designed the role for Robert Armin, purveyor of fools and sophisticated clowns, who took over as lead comedian in Shakespeare's company after 1599. As singer, pickpocket, and peddler, Autolycus threads his way through the Bohemian scenes, so much so that some critics feel he has outstayed his comic welcome by the end of act 4.[103] Certainly an actor playing Autolycus must be an energetic and versatile comedian. Three of the early ones undoubtedly were: Ned Shuter (1756), whom Garrick considered a comic genius; Joseph Munden, praised for his "buoyancy"[104] and brilliant impersonations in both Kemble's and Macready's productions (1802, 1823); and John Bannister (1802), whom Hazlitt found entirely convincing as the "sturdy" beggar roaring in counterfeit pain in act 4, scene 3. Donald Wolfit (1937) was full of "contagious gaiety and picked purses like a professional."[105] The vagabond trickster who wanders "here and there" (4.3.17) has lent himself to some lively contemporary incarnations. Derek Smith (1969) played Autolycus as a "discotheque co-median"[106] with a blonde Afro hairdo, jazzing up his songs and executing his comic routines, such as the dislocated shoulder he fakes for the Clown, with "burlesque energy."[107] Geoffrey Hutchins (1981) presented Autolycus as a seedy Victorian impresario and master of disguise, suggesting now "a butler, now a music-hall comedian, now a travelling showman in a moustache and top hat."[108]

To keep the audience engaged in his various improvisations, Autolycus needs to establish some rapport with them, as did William Burton in his New York production of 1857 by nodding and winking confidentially to the audience.[109] In his National Theatre production, though, Peter Hall (1988) wanted Autolycus to be less ingratiating and more a disturbing "figure of anarchy."[110] Accordingly actor Ken Stott played down the comedy but ended up alienating the audience. Since Autolycus the conman definitely has a hard, exploitative edge to him, actors must decide whether to foreground that socially subversive element or to settle for playing him as the lovable rogue. In Granville Barker's production (1912), Arthur Whitby provided a "rich bit of roguery" on stage but also conveyed a "lurking suggestion of the sinister."[111] Burton (1857) endowed the character with some sophistication—a reminder that Autolycus was a courtier at one time—and an edge of depravity,[112] while David William, directing *The Winter's Tale* in Stratford, Ontario (1988), urged Joseph Ziegler to portray Autolycus as a criminal as well as an artist.[113]

## *THE WINTER'S TALE* ON VIDEOTAPE: THE BBC/TIME LIFE PRODUCTION (1980)

Producing a play on television obviously means downsizing it. The medium specializes in talking heads, and *The Winter's Tale* contains plenty of two-person conversations that lend themselves to that. The small screen, though, is less successful in presenting a full stage picture, or situations in which it is important to view the actions and reactions of characters simultaneously. Unlike in the theater, where the audience is at liberty to look at any part of the action on stage, the television camera chooses the angle for us, so that our perspective on the action is inevitably reduced and manipulated by the choice of shot.[114] The BBC/Time Life production of *The Winter's Tale*, directed by Jane Howell, nevertheless capitalizes on the opportunities that the medium affords, using versatile camerawork and choreography tailored to the two-dimensional screen. It selects studio sets flexible enough to suggest both Sicily and Bohemia while forging significant contrasts between the two locations. The casting is good, with actors using the intimacy of the medium to establish their characters naturalistically, through quiet vocal delivery and the nuances of expression revealed through closeups.

Although head-and-shoulders shots dominate, the blocking and camerawork are far from static. Characters sometimes move around one another, as when Polixenes is anxiously questioning Camillo about his loss of favor in act 1, scene 2. Crosscutting between closeups on the face of the speaker and reaction shots from the listener, with both heads at times remaining in the frame, turns what could be static and pictorial into a dynamic encounter. And while television finds it difficult to convey the sense of space and depth that is always obtained in the theater, this production switches between long, mid, and close shots to provide different angles on the drama as it unfolds. Our first view of the Sicilian court is in long shot. A red ball, which turns out to belong to Mamillius, is suddenly tossed out of a glacial corridor before the small figures of Camillo and Archidamus emerge through the tunnel, smiling as they proceed toward the front of the set. This economically establishes the wintry vastness of the court, introduces the "play" metaphor through the appearance of the ball, and provides a cue for the topic shift to the prince when Mamillius runs in to retrieve his toy.

At the beginning of act 2, when Leontes interrupts the banter between the prince and his mother, the camera cuts between two groups: to the left, the women clad in soft beige and cream colors; and to the right, Leontes and his six courtiers dressed in black.[115] As Hermione explains to the courtiers her "honorable grief," the camera pulls back and lifts slightly to show the whole scenario, two groups framed by the three-quarters profile of the king at left foreground. This technique, in which the camera moves back and up to capture an entire group, is particularly helpful in Hermione's very public trial scene. After a head-and-shoulder shot of Hermione, her eyes wearily closed, the camera pans around and up to provide a bird's-eye view of the whole court: Leontes sitting in state upstage, surrounded by about 14 courtiers also in black robes; Hermione standing at the very center, with her women and Paulina behind her; and the backs of a few more spectators in the immediate foreground. After this establishing shot the focus narrows to Hermione in order to concentrate, through closeups, on her dignified defense. Breaking up the static composition, Leontes paces angrily toward her on "You had a bastard" before he strides back to resume his throne after proclaiming, "so thou / Shalt feel our justice."

Much of the sheep-shearing scene consists of personal encounters that this televised version handles with some variety. The twosome of Perdita and Florizel later expands to three when they discuss their predicament with Camillo and to four when they are joined by Autolycus. Five characters—the lovers, the Old Shepherd, Camillo, and Polixenes—are included in several of the frames depicting the showdown between prince and king. While the open stage would afford a wider perspective on the dance of shepherds and shepherdesses and on the peddler Autolycus touting his wares, this BBC production manages to convey the impression of a crowded, festive occasion by utilizing both mid-length and long shots. Perdita is surrounded by country folk who offer support and sympathetic laughter when she gives flowers to Polixenes and Camillo. There is physical movement, too, when the camera tracks the rivals Dorcas and Mopsa surging forward and almost falling on top of the Clown after singing "Thou hast sworn my love to be." The play's final scene also provides a sense of depth as well as "chamber drama" when the royal procession files into Paulina's room, and in the foreground a chastened Polixenes silently embraces his son Florizel.

This production uses television's specialty, the tight shot, to define character or persona more sharply. All the soliloquies and asides of Leontes are pitched directly at the camera, just as they would be addressed to the audience around the stage in Shakespeare's Globe Theatre. Now, though, there is the added benefit of the viewer being able to observe each detail of facial expression—the wide-eyed anguish of jealousy that Jeremy Kemp's Leontes conveys—and to hear every whispered confession of his inner torment. We feel the full force of his solipsistic fantasy when he turns away from a public scene with his courtiers to confess "I am a feather for each wind that blows" (2.3.152) and "No, I'll not rear / Another's issue" (190–91)—comments that are not usually delivered as asides. It is Autolycus, of course, who benefits most from this strategy of becoming complicit with the camera and thus the audience beyond it. He not only addresses cynical asides such as "what a fool Honesty is!" (4.4.599) to the camera, but often glances at it while gulling his victims. During his impersonation of a courtier for the shepherds, the rogue looks knowingly in our direction, encouraging us to relish his talent in manipulating those less sophisticated than he is.

## SETS AND COSTUMES

The main studio set, designed by Don Humfray under Jane Howell's direction, is flexible enough to represent both Sicily and Bohemia. Like Granville Barker, Jane Howell wanted to avoid "explicit scenery"[116] or realism of setting; instead she opted to stimulate the audience's imagination with a "semi-abstract" design that suggested the "never-never land"[117] of fairy tale but could also create a strong impression of seasonal change. As the play opens we observe an almost glacial construction: two "white conical towers" situated in front of two huge, "iceberg-like"[118] wedges through which characters make their entrances. Behind them the backdrop is a "monochromatic, evenly lit cycloramic curtain."[119] To the right of the set stands a bare tree, nonnaturalistic in being entirely white; along with the colorless background, it clearly symbolizes winter. The impression of cold is heightened by the costumes of both Leontes and Hermione, he in dark, fur-lined robes and a Russian hat, she in a long beige gown with an elegant sheepskin vest and a matching cap. The fade to a blank white screen before we see Mamillius tugging his mother through the white wedges to begin act 2 reinforces the wintriness.

The slender cones are gone but the wedges remain, now gray and weathered, for the transition to the seacoast of Bohemia in act 3, scene 3. Antigonus sits beside a cairn of gray stones on a shallow platform before he puts down the baby's basket and suddenly encounters the bear. The following shot is of the Old Shepherd sitting in an almost identical spot by the stones, though now, thanks to a shift in cyclorama, the sky is a deep, tranquil blue. Another lighting change gives a new definition to the set when the pastoral proper begins with the entrance of Autolycus in rural Bohemia. Here the white cones have been replaced by stone urns filled with staves of hay, while the pale wedges are suffused with a glow from the deep yellow backdrop. In keeping with the ambiance of summer, the wintry tree has turned brown and sprouted a few golden leaves. (While gold may seem somewhat autumnal, the green leaves of spring are being reserved for the return to Sicily in act 5.) Brown is also the dominant color of Autolycus's garb and the Old Shepherd's tunic and hat, while the younger rustics wear beige clothes over white shirts and blouses.

The summerized tree serves as a useful focal point for the characters. Autolycus sits under it with his pack in act 4, scene 3, explaining his role as rogue and thief, and at the end of the sheep-shearing scene, when he excuses himself to "look upon the hedge," sound effects suggest that he is relieving himself behind the tree while rejoicing over his latest lucky break. Perdita is first introduced at the beginning of that scene crafting her garlands of flowers under the tree. She and Florizel recline there when Polixenes comes over to grill his son. Within this stylized setting, where the floor of the set is simply painted green to represent summer grass, the crowded country sequences are played naturalistically. The dance of shepherds and shepherdesses, for instance, is relaxed rather than formal; and, perhaps because of its sheer size and staginess, this production leaves out the demanding dance of the satyrs.

With its striking seasonal variations, this one basic set serves for all the play's outside scenes. Interior ones are arranged somewhat differently. For Hermione's trial the circular space is extended to include iron railings in front of the white wedges; a table with a red cloth on it for the judges; and a red carpet leading up to the reddish-gold throne, with matching canopy, on which Leontes sits. The prison scene (2.2) takes place in darkness, with warm side-lighting on the faces of Paulina and Emilia. The scene where Paulina brings the baby to Leontes (2.3) is a gloomy interior within the royal palace. It begins with a shot of the king slowly raising his head from a table on which a candle burns to deliver his "Nor night nor day no rest" speech, and it ends with a matching shot of his face next to the candle. Transitions between scenes are handled well. As Leontes gazes straight ahead, the sound of knocking accompanies a fade into the next scene (3.1). Someone is hammering the indictment of Hermione onto the wintry tree; we are back in the outside world, where Dion and Cleomenes have just returned with news from the oracle. More sharp knocking at the end of this scene, with a fade onto the queen's exhausted face, turns out to be the ominous sound of the judge's gavel announcing the beginning of the trial.

For the final scene, "a chapel in Paulina's house," the royal procession enters through an ornamental archway into a dark, candle-lit hall. At the far end stands the curtained cubicle containing Hermione's statue. The final frame, though accompanied by a musical arrangement of Renaissance pipes and tambourines slightly too rollicking for a tragicomedy, provides a vista of hope and renewal by again incorporating the larger space of the main set. As the characters proceed through the dark archway, suddenly they are back in the bright courtyard. The final shot is of the backs of three hurrying figures with Hermione, in the middle, holding up the hands of the two kings as they all stride exuberantly past the tree. Now it is no longer winter; the tree sports a few green leaves, and even the white wedges through which the royal party exits are appropriately tinged with green and set against a bright blue backdrop.

## TIME, THE BEAR, AND THE STATUE

Time is presented as a pivotal figure between wintry Sicily and the summer of Bohemia. He appears against a dead white backdrop (similar to that of Sicily), clad in a beige tunic with a fur collar; but he is sunburned and wears a straw hat that is more rustic than royal. Providing continuity, he is the last of the old men that we have seen in quick succession: Antigonus with his white hair and beard, the Old Shepherd, and now gray-bearded Time. Speaking evenly and with authority, Time appears to be the most venerable of these antique figures, present "ere ancient'st order was." In traditional, emblematic fashion he carries a large brown hourglass that he tips at "I turn my glass." As he asks the audience to imagine him in "fair Bohemia," the camera gradually tightens the shot from mid to closeup, so that by the time he utters his final couplet his whole face fills the screen. Since Time remains static against a neutral backdrop, we are encouraged to focus carefully on his choric, thematically charged words.

Some reviewers noted a link between King Leontes, a tall figure huddled in dark furs, and the shaggy, dark brown bear of Jane Howell's production.[120] Indeed a few suggestions in the text do link the two, for the Clown compares "authority" to a "stubborn bear" (4.4.808–9) while Antigonus, killed by the ferocious animal, is felt to be a victim of Leontes's cruel tyranny. Staying on the level of suggestion, the BBC version avoids a realistic treatment of "exit pursued by a bear." In fact it shows no pursuit at all.[121] Instead a lightning flash heralds a "savage" clamor, with the sound of horns and hunting dogs coming from the right. Antigonus then turns to face what we briefly see at the left of the screen—the towering silhouette of a huge bear, mouth open and roaring, foreleg raised and with claws extended. The next shot is angled up at the bear's head and teeth. After a closeup of Antigonus declaring "This is the chase," a lunging, roaring bear head fills the whole frame, its incisors the one flash of white before the screen turns totally dark. Howell clearly did not want to risk the potentially ludicrous spectacle of an elderly man being chased off stage by a simulated bear. Instead the sudden terror of the attack, the bear engulfing Antigonus, is cleverly suggested through brief flashes of the creature followed by a dark brown screen.

What is lacking in the statue scene is the wider perspective afforded by a stage production. At first we are given the impression of a fairly large assembly of spectators gathered by Paulina—one frame as she welcomes them to her "house" includes nine figures—but as the scene progresses the camera more often cuts between shots of the statue and of Leontes's emotional face reacting to it. He is visibly moved, evincing both regret and rapture. Closeups allow the viewer to glimpse his tear-stained cheek when he asks, "Would you not deem it breathed?" Clad in white (even her hair beneath her matronly cap appears to be white) and standing in an illuminated cubicle, Hermione as a statue looks almost unearthly; perhaps to enhance the supernatural overtones, the cubicle's pale curtains part of their own accord when Paulina asks the court to "behold" the sculpture. The queen leans forward slightly with her hand extended in a gracious gesture of supplication. When the camera lingers on her as she pauses and looks imploringly at Leontes during the nearly five lines that follow Paulina's "'Tis time," we notice a faint tremor. Then she very slowly extends her hand and walks, arm outstretched, toward her immobile husband; several seconds later his fingers tremulously clasp hers. The couple kisses in silence after his words "lawful as eating" until, with a gasp, she throws her arms around his neck. This is a moving reunion, as is Hermione's with Perdita, where mother and daughter are surprised into delighted laughter. Still, as Stanley Wells notes, "the focus on individuals denies us the sense of simultaneous involvement, the thrill of ritual participation as the stone is made flesh."[122] We miss the opportunity to watch all the beholders registering shock when the statue begins to move, or to assimilate the whole stage picture, both figures in view, as Hermione moves slowly toward the hesitant Leontes.

## HERMIONE AND PAULINA

The slow coming to life of the statue accentuates Hermione's majesty and dignity. It also highlights her warmth—she "hangs" about her husband's "neck" and is ecstatic at having found Perdita—and her graciousness, for when she gazes beseechingly at Leontes, she reveals not a trace of resentment. Warmth, dignity, and grace define Anna Calder-Marshall's portrayal of Hermione throughout. In the opening scene she is both affectionate and spirited, amused at Polixenes's "verily" and enjoying the challenge of making him stay. This becomes something of a courtly contest, for she curtsies on "kind hostess" once he is won, enjoying applause from the onstage spectators. Her devotion to her husband is apparent in her earnest "'Tis Grace indeed" after his account of their courtship; the closeup on her serious, almost somber face as she gives him her hand to kiss anticipates the moment when she reaches out to him in the final scene. But since she also generously offers her hand to Polixenes, who kisses it as she appoints him "for some while a friend," we can understand how Leontes might perceive them as a newly forged couple.

In act 2, scene 1, Calder-Marshall's Hermione makes a convincing transition from easy warmth with Mamillius to shock and chagrin when Leontes accuses her of infidelity. Closeups show her horrified at the word "adult'ress," wincing at the fresh blow of being called "traitor." She shows compassion toward her deluded husband in "how will this grieve you" and continued respect for him, quite devoid of bitterness, when she curtsies to confirm "the king's will be done."

Though physically petite, Calder-Marshall's Hermione combines regal demeanor with vulnerability during her trial. A diminutive figure in the midst of a large assembly, she looks and sounds exhausted at the beginning but gains strength as she warms to her defense. The queen's integrity comes through in refusing to "acknowledge" faults that are not hers and her tenderness and vulnerability when her voice cracks in remembering the love of her husband that she now feels is "lost." Quickly regaining her "aristocratic self-control"[123] as she recapitulates the wrongs done to her, this Hermione sternly points a gloved hand at Leontes to demand "hear this" and to denounce his "rigor." Her indignation is tempered by her wish that her father could observe her with "eyes / Of pity, not revenge!"— words that are appropriately spoken in an aside pitched to the side of the camera since she, unlike Leontes, has never used the convention of confiding in the audience.

Paulina's most forceful moments in this production come after Hermione has been carried off the stage, apparently lifeless. But Margaret Tyzack was praised for her "powerful, deeply felt"[124] presentation of Paulina as the "strongest personality at the Sicilian Court" throughout.[125] Dressed in mauve and wearing a tall headdress that makes her appear imposingly magisterial by extending her gray hair upward, Tyzack's Paulina commands attention. Even in the private prison scene she is peremptory in insisting that Leontes "*must* be told" about the birth of his child. Boldly entering the king's private chambers, she speaks in stentorian tones while the male courtiers timidly try to shush her. Stern rather than scolding, she avoids any hint of the comic shrew, courageously standing up to the king with her retort "I care not" when he threatens to have her "burned." The actress also offsets the danger of playing Paulina as an overbearing virago (the "bossy hospital matron")[126] by injecting sudden moments of tenderness. In the prison scene she melts when she thinks of how the baby's "pure innocence" may soften Leontes, and she is tender when she carries the basket containing Perdita up to Leontes. Mesmerized, the male attendants cluster around her as she delightedly shows off the newborn.

When she reenters at the end of the trial scene, crying "Woe the while!" a long shot shows Tyzack's Paulina clutching her throat, almost crushed with grief and outrage. She is deeply angry as she begins her "What studied torments?" speech. Sarcastically dismissing Leontes's earlier trespasses as "nothing," she builds to a "thrilling" climax[127] in which she almost shrieks "Cry woe" to announce the queen's death. Yet her apology for being insensitive ("I am sorry for't") seems utterly sincere[128] as she moves over to Leontes and kneels to deliver the gently spoken "Do not receive affliction at my petition." As Leontes raises her up, the concluding shot is of her leading him out by the hand, two allies preparing for mourning.

The opening frame of act 5 shows Paulina's face against a dark background, anxiously observing Leontes before the camera moves behind her to take in a group of courtiers urging the king to "forgive" himself. She remains intransigent in promoting the oracle and chastises the messenger who praises Perdita, instead of Hermione, as "peerless." But although Tyzack's Paulina is pleased to gain a tactical advantage over the males—she relishes their consternation when Leontes swears not to take another wife—she is now gentle and humane with the king himself. And in the final scene she is almost self-effacing. A skillful choreographer rather than a proud miracle worker when she displays the statue, she sensitively controls the reactions of the onlookers without putting herself center stage. Correspondingly the camera hugs Leontes's face more closely than hers, even though she speaks a few more lines than he does in this scene.

## LEONTES

Several reviewers found Jeremy Kemp's Leontes too "understated."[129] Forgoing the broad strokes and high-toned delivery of a stage performance, Kemp's enactment of jealousy is concentratedly quiet and introverted, geared to the intimacy of the television medium with its close attention to aural as well as visual detail. It stands in clear contrast to the more mannered acting style of Robert Stephens, who plays Polixenes (the Sicilian king's counterpart) as somewhat theatrical, even dandyish. Kemp's presentation of Leontes is not entirely low-key, however. He projects his lines more forcefully and moves purposefully when he packs Hermione off to prison and in the trial scene where he accuses her of having a "bastard" by Polixenes.

Kemp's miniaturist portrait of Leontes in the early part of the play is finely etched. He appears entirely cordial when he urges Polixenes to "Stay your thanks awhile," and warmly compliments his wife with "Well said, Hermione." Following one theatrical tradition, he stays off to the side talking with Camillo during the long exchange where Hermione asks Polixenes about the boyhood of the kings, coming back only in time to hear part of his wife's ambiguous "slipped not / With any but with us" comment. Still, his full-blown jealousy comes as a shock. It is first hinted at when he turns to the camera to register the surprise of "At my request he would not" and then confides his whispered "Too hot, too hot!" speech to the audience. His private fantasy is briefly interrupted by an interchange with Mamillius, enabling him to speak the contorted "Affection" speech in tight shot, over Mamillius's shoulder, as he embraces his uncomprehending son. Only when Hermione and Polixenes suddenly appear at a distance in the right of the frame, puzzled by the king's withdrawal, must he revert to behaving sociably.

Kemp's king is again shown in closeup, counterpointed by shots of Camillo's nonplussed reaction, when he spits back his councillor's ill-chosen word "satisfy" and gives a nasty nuance to the sibilance in "My wife is slippery." That he is in the grip of a private fantasy even when accompanied by his courtiers in act 2 is underlined when the camera zooms in on his words "How blest am I / In my just censure" until his face fills the whole screen at the conclusion of "I have drunk, and seen the spider." By now the camera has become the confidant of all his soliloquies and asides; in this way the audience shares in the horror of his delusion. R. P. Draper finds that this technique generates pity for Kemp's Leontes, "making him a tragic, rather than a deranged, figure."[130] Shown at more distance, though, the king's petty tyranny is revealed when Leontes bends back Antigonus's finger to make him "feel" an anguish equivalent to his own about Hermione, and when the camera lingers on him sitting comfortably in state at the trial scene while his wife, weak after childbirth, is forced to stand.

The king's quiet remorse when he learns that Mamillius and then Hermione are dead is not a huge contrast in style from his interiorized jealousy. From this point on he is a "sadder and wiser"[131] man, willingly guided by Paulina. His understated delivery in the statue scene, where he is entranced, rueful, and hopeful by turns, captures the magic and reverence of the occasion. But at other points in act 5 Kemp's Leontes shakes off passivity, buoyantly striding off the throne and out of the chamber once he is energized by the mission of helping Florizel and Perdita. At the same time his costume change in this act, from dark furs to pale gold robes and hat, underscores his transition from wintriness to late summer. He also enjoys the ironic reversal of being able to steer Paulina into marriage in the play's finale; his low-toned "O peace, Paulina!" is both humorous and gently chiding.

## THE CHARACTERS IN BOHEMIA

Perdita, played by dark-haired Debbie Farrington, is always bathed in the mellow light that accompanies the Bohemian scenes. She plays the shepherdess-princess appropriately as an entirely unspoiled but mature 16-

year-old. Her west country accent and slightly deliberate way of speaking put her firmly in the rustic camp; while she emanates a natural courtesy and poise as she distributes her flowers, her manner is devoid of any false sophistication. Farrington's Perdita is both sweet and earnest, a principled "country lass to be reckoned with"[132] when she holds her own in the debate with Polixenes. Honest to the point of hating any deception, she gently chides Florizel for disguising himself as a shepherd, while a profile shot at the Sicilian court in act 5 shows her biting her lip uneasily when the prince spins a yarn to Leontes. Although Farrington's Perdita is not as playful as Hermione (we could never imagine her romping as Dame Judi Dench's princess did in Nunn's 1969 stage production), her down-to-earth humor shines through when she laughingly responds to Camillo's compliment on living by "gazing" with "Out, alas! / You'd be so lean that blasts of January / Would blow you through and through." She is modest rather than prudish, charmingly bashful after confessing her desire for Florizel. Small touches reveal her kind heart. Quick to comfort the Old Shepherd when he sinks to the ground after Polixenes's violent threats, she also makes a compassion-ate move toward Paulina near the end of the play when it seems as though the "old turtle[dove]" will be left out of the wedding celebrations.

For his part, Robin Kermode as Florizel makes a splendidly devoted swain, totally convincing in his passion. Always attentive toward Perdita, he cannot take his eyes off her when they dance; and he is consoling, em-bracing and gently kissing her after Polixenes has destroyed their betrothal ceremony. As he declares that he is now "heir" to his "affection" he almost weeps, quickening the pace of his lines with a desperate need to reassure her of his constant love. He actually looks like a younger version of Polix-enes; yet he is much more idealistic and spontaneous than this king who, even at the play's opening, can only sigh jadedly for his lost innocence.

At first it is hard to warm up to Rikki Fulton's Irish Autolycus. Perhaps because the character is usually played by a younger actor, the viewer expects the agility and bounce of a quick-change stage comedian; Ful-ton, though a "well-known comic personality" in his own right,[133] seems a little too static. As he is not an actor who specializes in singing, Autoly-cus's songs are downplayed, often swallowed up as exit lines. Gradually, though, the subtleties of Fulton's presentation emerge through the me-dium of the small screen. Because the actor so often addresses the camera, his Autolycus comes across as particularly shrewd and knowing, eager to share his exploits with the audience. In his first appearance he opens up his pack to show us his stolen "sheets" before hiding behind the tree to as-sess how suitable the Clown will be for fleecing. When the good-hearted rustic puts his hands under Autolycus's arms to lift him up without injuring him further and promptly gets his pockets picked, we savor the full irony of his "charitable office" to the rogue.

Disguised in fake moustache and beard, Fulton's peddler effortlessly pulls in the Bohemian crowd by promising to sell them salacious ballads. Alone afterward, he shares with us his joy in having picked the rustics' pockets (his "I could have filed *keys* off that hung on chains" is particularly gleeful) and sold all his trinkets. So shamelessly does he play to the camera that when Camillo briefly soliloquizes to it about his plans (4.4.666–71), Fulton's Autolycus looks mystified, peering over Camillo's shoulder as if to try to ascertain whether his prerogative of talking to the audience has been preempted. His impersonation of a courtier for the shepherds is swaggeringly confident. Strutting in his new sheepskin-trimmed tunic and cap, he adopts an affected accent and flamboyantly wields a toothpick—a courtly mannerism that the Clown amusingly apes as soon as he is promoted to "gentleman born" in the final act.

After listening to the report of the royal reunions in act 5, Autolycus again takes up his station under the tree, ruefully assessing his missed opportunities. Although he must now resign himself to an apparent reversal of fortune, since the shepherds have turned into courtiers he can only imitate, this rogue manages to suggest through facial expression and gestures that he is getting the last laugh. When his new "masters" have left the set, Fulton's Autolycus gives a droll smile to the camera, eyebrows raised jauntily. The gleam in his eye shows that he senses another opportunity to come out ahead. He tips his hat, and, as the camera follows him from behind, we glimpse the old spring in his step.

## NOTES

1. Dennis Bartholomeusz, The Winter's Tale *in Performance in England and America, 1611–1976* (Cambridge: Cambridge University Press, 1982), p. 12. In what follows I am indebted to Bartholomeusz's careful research and detailed accounts.

2. Theophilus Cibber, *Dissertations on Theatrical Subjects* (1756), pp. 31–35, cited in Bartholomeusz, The Winter's Tale *in Performance,* p. 38.

3. Review of *The Winter's Tale, London Chronicle,* 24 March 1757, cited in Dennis Bartholomeusz, The Winter's Tale *in Performance in England and America, 1611–1976* (Cambridge: Cambridge University Press, 1982), p. 32.

4. Mary Anderson, Preface to the acting edition of *The Winter's Tale,* quoted in Bartholomeusz, The Winter's Tale *in Performance,* p. 117.

5. Bartholomeusz, The Winter's Tale *in Performance,* p. 49.

6. R.P. Draper, The Winter's Tale, *Text and Performance* (London: Macmillan, 1985), p. 48.

7.  Noted by Ellen Terry, in *Ellen Terry's Memoirs,* ed. Edith Craig and Christopher St. John (New York: Putnam, 1932), p. 15.

8.  John William Cole, *The Life and Theatrical Times of Charles Kean, F.S.A,* vol. 2 (1859; New York and London: Garland Publishing, Inc., 1986), p. 171.

9.  Ibid., p. 170.

10.  See Bartholomeusz, The Winter's Tale *in Performance,* p. 127.

11.  See Gemma Jones, "Hermione in *The Winter's Tale,*" in *Players of Shakespeare,* ed. Philip Brockbank (Cambridge: Cambridge University Press, 1985), pp. 153–65, 157.

12.  G. B. Shaw, Interview in *The Observer,* 29 September 1912.

13.  See Batholomeusz, The Winter's Tale *in Performance,* p. 146.

14.  Dennis Kennedy, *Granville Barker and the Dream of Theatre* (Cambridge: Cambridge University Press, 1985), p. 126.

15.  A. B. Walkley, review of *The Winter's Tale, The Times,* 23 September 1912, p. 7.

16.  Batholomeusz, The Winter's Tale *in Performance,* p. 140.

17.  Kennedy, *Granville Barker and the Dream of Theatre,* p. 124. The production of Winthrop Ames, which opened in New York on March 28, 1910, was more Elizabethan in its staging.

18.  Robert Smallwood, "Directors' Shakespeare," in *Shakespeare: An Illustrated Stage History,* ed. Jonathan Bate and Russell Jackson (Oxford: Oxford University Press, 1996), p. 179.

19.  See Draper, The Winter's Tale, *Text and Performance,* p. 74.

20.  The tradition of wearing white Edwardian clothes, along with the relative youthfulness of the main protagonists, set the tone for future productions, as in Terry Hands's 1986 RSC production starring Jeremy Irons as Leontes.

21.  See David A. Male, The Winter's Tale: *Shakespeare on Stage* (Cambridge: Cambridge University Press, 1984), p. 11.

22.  John Russell Brown, *Free Shakespeare* (New York and London: Applause Books, 1997), p. 25.

23.  Roger Warren, *Staging Shakespeare's Late Plays* (Oxford: Clarendon Press, 1990), p. 11.

24.  Male, The Winter's Tale: *Shakespeare on Stage,* p. 17.

25.  Draper, The Winter's Tale, *Text and Performance,* p. 55.

26.  Richard David, *Shakespeare in the Theatre* (Cambridge: Cambridge University Press, 1978), p. 223.

27.  Cole, *The Life and Theatrical Times of Charles Kean,* p. 171.

28.  Smallwood, "Directors' Shakespeare," p. 190.

29.  See Draper, The Winter's Tale, *Text and Performance,* p. 52.

30.  Cole, *The Life and Theatrical Times of Charles Kean,* p. 172.

31.  Bartholomeusz, The Winter's Tale *in Performance,* p. 92.

32.  Review of *The Winter's Tale, Daily News,* 30 April 1856, cited in Bartholomeusz, The Winter's Tale *in Performance,* p. 92.

33.  See Warren, *Staging Shakespeare's Late Plays,* p. 129.

34. Irving Wardle, review of *The Winter's Tale, The Times,* 16 May 1969.

35. Male, The Winter's Tale: *Shakespeare on Stage,* p. 16.

36. David, *Shakespeare in the Theatre,* p. 222.

37. See Batholomeusz, The Winter's Tale *in Performance,* p. 222, and Draper, The Winter's Tale, *Text and Performance,* pp. 55–56.

38. David, *Shakespeare in the Theatre,* p. 223.

39. Teresa Grant, "White Bears in *Mucedorus, The Winter's Tale,* and *Oberon, The Fairy Prince,*" *N and Q* 48 (September 2001): 311–13, points out that Alleyn and Henslowe (working with the Lady Elizabeth's Men by 1611) were issued with a royal warrant to keep two white bears. Grant argues that these polar bears, presumably those reported captured in the arctic in 1609 and brought back to England, would have been tame enough to use in *The Winter's Tale.*

40. Dennis Biggens, "Exit Pursued by a Beare," *SQ* 13 (1963): 3–13, evaluates the different theories about the bear. Whereas J.L. Styan, *Drama, Stage, and Audience* (Cambridge: Cambridge University Press, 1975), speculates that only a real bear would "touch horror and farce at the same time" (34), George Walton Williams, "Exit Pursued by a Quaint Device: The Bear in *The Winter's Tale,*" *Ucrow* 14 (1994): 105–9, argues that an "artificial bear" would be most effective in turning the play "from tragedy to comedy" (108).

41. Warren, *The Staging of Shakespeare's Late Plays,* p. 128.

42. The British Museum copy of the Kemble promptbook, cited in Batholomeusz, The Winter's Tale *in Performance,* p. 55.

43. Review of *The Winter's Tale, The Times,* 1 May 1856, cited in Bartholomeusz, The Winter's Tale *in Performance,* p. 91.

44. Bartholomeusz, The Winter's Tale *in Performance,* p. 161.

45. Benedict Nightingale, review of *The Winter's Tale, The Guardian,* 3 July 1992.

46. Draper, The Winter's Tale, *Text and Performance,* p. 71.

47. Male, The Winter's Tale: *Shakespeare on Stage,* p. 17.

48. Reviewers did not all react favorably to this dramatic shorthand. In *Today,* review of *The Winter's Tale,* 5 May 1986, David Shannon called it "merely silly."

49. Alexander Leggatt, "*The Winter's Tale* Retold," *SQ* 44 (1993): 483–87, 485.

50. Stephen Orgel (ed.), *The Winter's Tale,* The Oxford Shakespeare (Oxford: Oxford University Press, 1996), p. 62.

51. Ibid., p. 67.

52. Bartholomeusz, The Winter's Tale *in Performance,* p. 188.

53. James Boaden, *Memoirs of the Life of John Philip Kemble, Esq.,* vol. 2 (New York: Wilder and Campbell, 1825), p. 314.

54. Helen Faucit, "Shakespeare's Women," *Blackwood's Magazine,* 1 January 1891, pp. 34–37.

55. Warren, *The Staging of Shakespeare's Last Plays,* p. 145.

56. Leggatt, "*The Winter's Tale* Retold," pp. 487, 483–84.

57. Batholomeusz, The Winter's Talc *in Performance,* p. 220.

58.   Dench herself, in Judi Dench, "A Career in Shakespeare," in *Shakespeare: An Illustrated Stage History,* ed. Jonathan Bate and Russell Jackson (Oxford: Oxford University Press, 1996), writes "it did not work for me," admitting "I didn't feel so much moved as breathless, by the time I had swapped with the double who played Perdita" (206).

59.   Review of *The Winter's Tale, Blackwood's Magazine,* September 1890, cited in Bartholomeusz, The Winter's Tale *in Performance*, p. 119.

60.   Irving Wardle, review of *The Winter's Tale, The Times,* 3 July 1970.

61.   William Hazlitt, *The Characters of Shakespeare's Plays,* in *The Selected Writings of William Hazlitt,* vol. 1, ed. Duncan Wu (London: Pickering and Chatto, 1998), p. 233.

62.   Review of *The Winter's Tale, The Times,* 11 November 1807 and 29 November 1811, cited in Bartholomeusz, The Winter's Tale *in Performance*, pp. 51–52.

63.   Thomas Campbell, *Life of Mrs. Siddons,* vol. 2 (London: E. Wilson, 1834), p. 265.

64.   Review of *The Winter's Tale, New York Albion,* 27 September 1851, cited in Bartholomeusz, The Winter's Tale *in Performance*, p. 101.

65.   Review of *The Winter's Tale, Westminster Gazette,* 22 September 1912, cited in Bartholomeusz, The Winter's Tale *in Performance*, p. 155.

66.   Review of *The Winter's Tale, Daily Herald,* 23 September 1912.

67.   Review of *The Winter's Tale, The Times,* 11 November 1807, cited in Bartholomeusz, The Winter's Tale *in Performance*, p. 53.

68.   Helen Faucit, *Blackwood's Magazine,* 1 January 1891, p. 32.

69.   Batholomeusz, The Winter's Tale *in Performance*, p. 173.

70.   Ibid., p. 217.

71.   Ibid., p. 209.

72.   Roger Warren, "Interpretations of Shakespearian Comedy, 1981," *ShS* 35 (1982): 141–52, 148.

73.   Warren, *The Staging of Shakespeare's Last Plays,* p. 124.

74.   Ibid., p. 125.

75.   Cole, *The Life and Theatrical Times of Charles Kean,* vol. 2, p. 176. Batholomeusz, The Winter's Tale *in Performance,* notes that H. B. Irving (1895), F. R. Benson (1903), and Balliol Holloway (1937) all played Leontes as jealous from the start (197–98, 202).

76.   Batholomeusz, The Winter's Tale *in Performance,* p. 170.

77.   Hazlitt, *The Characters of Shakespeare's Plays,* in *The Selected Writings of William Hazlitt,* vol. 1, p. 233.

78.   Review of *The Winter's Tale, The Times,* 6 November 1823, cited in Bartholomeusz, The Winter's Tale *in Performance*, p. 66.

79.   Warren, *The Staging of Shakespeare's Late Plays,* p. 105, p. 122. Samuel Phelps (1845) also acted on Coleridge's observation that Leontes was constitutionally jealous; see Bartholomeusz, The Winter's Tale *in Performance*, pp. 77–78.

80.   Review of *The Winter's Tale, Referee,* 22 September 1912, cited in Bartholomeusz, The Winter's Tale *in Performance*, p. 151.

81.  Granville Barker, Preface to *The Winter's Tale,* p. 20.

82.  Bartholomeusz, The Winter's Tale *in Performance,* p. 192.

83.  Ibid., p. 232.

84.  David, *Shakespeare in the Theatre,* p. 223.

85.  Gordon Parso, review of *The Winter's Tale, Morning Star,* 17 May 1969. Batholomeusz, The Winter's Tale *in Performance,* found instead a "curious lack of intensity" in Ingham's performance here (216).

86.  Warren, "Interpretations of Shakespearian Comedy, 1981," p. 148.

87.  Draper, The Winter's Tale*: Text and Performance,* p. 59.

88.  Review of *The Winter's Tale, Morning Chronicle,* 29 October 1833, cited in Bartholomeusz, The Winter's Tale *in Performance*, p. 67.

89.  Orgel (ed.), *The Winter's Tale,* p. 70.

90.  Review of *The Winter's Tale, Weekly Despatch,* 10 October 1858, cited in Bartholomeusz, The Winter's Tale *in Performance*, p. 79.

91.  Bartholomeusz, The Winter's Tale *in Performance,* p. 170.

92.  W. Moelwyn Merchant, *Shakespeare and the Artist* (London: Oxford University Press, 1959), p. 213.

93.  This televised workshop was directed by John Barton and acted by members of the Royal Shakespeare Company.

94.  Cole, *The Life and Theatrical Times of Charles Kean,* vol. 2, p. 173.

95.  A. B. Walkley, review of *The Winter's Tale, The Times,* 23 September 1912.

96.  Review of *The Winter's Tale, Theatrical Repertory,* 25 March 1802, p. 409, cited in Bartholomeusz, The Winter's Tale *in Performance*, p. 58.

97.  Review of *The Winter's Tale, The Times,* 26 March 1802, cited in Bartholomeusz, The Winter's Tale *in Performance*, p. 58.

98.  Review of *The Winter's Tale, Imperial Gazette* (1823), p. 316, cited in Bartholomeusz, The Winter's Tale *in Performance*, p. 75.

99.  Review of *The Winter's Tale, Sunday Herald,* November 1833, p. 85, cited in Bartholomeusz, The Winter's Tale *in Performance*, p. 75.

100.  See Dench, "A Career in Shakespeare," p. 205.

101.  Kennedy, *Granville Barker and the Dream of Theatre,* p. 133.

102.  Batholomeusz, The Winter's Tale *in Performance,* p. 224.

103.  See Warren, *Staging Shakespeare's Late Plays,* p. 138.

104.  Review of *The Winter's Tale, The Guardian,* 9 November 1823, cited in Bartholomeusz, The Winter's Tale *in Performance*, p. 56.

105.  Review of *The Winter's Tale, Manchester Guardian,* 25 April 1937, cited in Bartholomeusz, The Winter's Tale *in Performance*, p. 202.

106.  Ronald Boyden, review of *The Winter's Tale, Observer,* 18 May 1969.

107.  Draper, The Winter's Tale*: Text and Performance,* p. 66.

108.  Warren, "Interpretations of Shakespearian Comedy, 1981," p. 148.

109.  *Critical Opinions,* p. 6 *(Daily Tribune),* cited in Bartholomeusz, The Winter's Tale *in Performance,* p. 107.

110.  Warren, *Staging Shakespeare's Late Plays,* p. 132.

111.  Review of *The Winter's Tale, The Times,* 23 September 1912, cited in

Bartholomeusz, The Winter's Tale *in Performance*, p. 159.

112.    *Critical Opinions,* p. 15 *(Sunday Times),* cited in Bartholomeusz, The Winter's Tale *in Performance*, p. 107.

113.    Warren, *Staging Shakespeare's Late Plays,* p. 132.

114.    See Sheldon P. Zitner, "Wooden O's in Plastic Boxes," *UTQ* 51 (Fall 1981): 1–12.

115.    This patterning supports what Susan Snyder, "Mamillius and Gender Polarization in *The Winter's Tale*," *SQ* 50, no. 1 (1999): 1–8, sees as an important part of the later trial scene: Leontes's imposing of a "pattern of gender groups in formal, hostile encounter" (7).

116.    Quoted in Susan Willis, *The BBC Shakespeare Plays: Making the Televised Canon* (Chapel Hill and London: The University of North Carolina Press, 1991), p. 165.

117.    Joseph McLellan, review of *The Winter's Tale, Washington Post,* 8 June 1981.

118.    Draper, The Winter's Tale*: Text and Performance,* p. 56.

119.    Willis, *The BBC Shakespeare Plays,* pp. 167–69.

120.    G. M. Pearce, review of *The Winter's Tale,* BBC Shakespeare, *Cahiers Elisabéthains* 20 (October 1981): 97–99.

121.    Donald K. Hedrick, "Shakespeare Plays on TV, *The Winter's Tale*," *SFNL* 6, no. 1 (1982): 4–6, wished for a "lively chase" within a less-restrained production and found the presentation of the "shabbily costumed" BBC bear "too tame" (4).

122.    Stanley Wells, "Goes Out, Pursued by a Furry Animal," *TLS* (20 Feb. 1981): 197.

123.    Draper, The Winter's Tale*: Text and Performance,* p. 62.

124.    Wells, "Goes Out, Followed by a Furry Animal," p. 197.

125.    Draper, The Winter's Tale*: Text and Performance,* p. 64.

126.    Ibid.

127.    Anthony Masters, review of *The Winter's Tale,* BBC Shakespeare, *The Times,* 9 February 1981.

128.    Hedrick, "Shakespeare Plays on TV, *The Winter's Tale*," comments on the "bitter sincerity" here (4).

129.    Kenneth Rothwell, "The Shakespeare Plays: *Hamlet* and the Five Plays of Season Three," *SQ* 32, no. 3 (1981): 395–401, 401. Willis, *The BBC Shakespeare Plays,* also felt that Kemp's Leontes failed to strike the necessary "spark" (223), and Wells, "Goes Out, Followed by a Furry Animal," finds that his "anguished utterances" lack "air" (197).

130.    Draper, The Winter's Tale*: Text and Performance,* p. 60.

131.    Ibid.

132.    Wells, "Goes Out, Followed by a Furry Animal" (197).

133.    Draper, The Winter's Tale*: Text and Performance,* p. 67.

# BIBLIOGRAPHICAL ESSAY

To avoid overlap, especially with the material of chapter 6 on "Critical Approaches," this essay concentrates on what the Guide has not already reviewed—editions, book-length studies, and anthologies that contain important essays on *The Winter's Tale*. Readers interested in sources and related texts should start with the commentary and excerpts in Geoffrey Bullough, *Narrative and Dramatic Sources of Shakespeare,* vol. 8 (London: Routledge, 1975). They may also consult the notes to chapter 2 which, along with chapter 6, refer to recent articles on the cultural and political contexts of *The Winter's Tale.* As well as discussing cultural materialist work, chapter 6 covers a spectrum from older psychological and image/myth approaches to feminist studies of the play. The notes to chapter 3 direct readers toward further consideration of the generic horizons of the play—its affinities with romance, pastoral, and tragicomedy. Chapter 5 refers in detail to studies that touch on key themes of the play, while chapter 7 covers significant reviews and performance criticism of *The Winter's Tale.*

## EDITIONS

As the 1623 Folio contains the only early printed version of *The Winter's Tale,* modern editions do not vary much in their textual choices. This Guide uses the *Signet Classic Shakespeare* edition (London and New York: Penguin Books, 1963), carefully prepared by Frank Kermode and updated in 1998—a widely accessible text that includes six excerpts from essays, old and recent, offering critical interpretations of the play. The

196

pocket-sized *New Penguin Winter's Tale* (London and New York: Penguin Books, 1986), edited by Ernest Schanzer, also offers a helpful introduction and notes. J.H.P. Pafford's *Arden Shakespeare* edition (London: Methuen, 1963; 1966) remains useful, especially in explaining the text's transmission and providing longer notes; the *New Arden,* edited by John Pitcher, is scheduled for publication in March 2006. Most comprehensive and up-to-date is Stephen Orgel's 1996 *Oxford Shakespeare* edition (Oxford: Oxford University Press), which contains an 83-page introduction with insights into the play's cultural contexts and an illustrated commentary on its theatrical history. While *Signet* includes the most relevant parts of Greene's *Pandosto,* Shakespeare's major source, an appendix in the *Oxford* version prints the complete text of this novella. An edition that takes risks in restoring "some of the nuances of Renaissance punctuation" and "the flexibility of Renaissance spelling" is the *Everyman Shakespeare's* Winter's Tale (London: J.M. Dent; Vermont: Charles Tuttle, 1995); this probably makes it more suitable for the advanced student. It has the advantage of easy access to the extensive notes and glossary, placed on the left-hand pages facing the text, and it boasts excerpts from no less than 29 important commentaries on the play. All of these editions are available in paperback.

## BOOK-LENGTH STUDIES AND KEY CHAPTERS ON *THE WINTER'S TALE*

S.L. Bethell, in The Winter's Tale: *A Study* (London: Staples Ltd., 1947), was one of the first critics to recognize that the play's apparently unsophisticated structure was designed to jolt audiences into thought. Yet like many commentators in the 1940s and '50s, such as E.M.W. Tillyard in *Shakespeare's Last Plays* (London: Chatto and Windus, 1938; 1954), Bethell finds the underlying themes of the play to be traditionally Christian. Reluctant to allegorize it, A.D. Nuttall provides a balanced analysis of the play in his short study *Shakespeare:* The Winter's Tale (London: Edward Arnold, 1966). Fizroy Pyle, The Winter's Tale: *A Commentary on the Structure* (New York: Barnes and Noble, Inc., 1969), astutely examines both the dramatic development of scenes and how they modify material from Greene's *Pandosto.* In *The Winter's Tale,* Twayne's New Critical Introductions (Boston: Twayne Publishers, 1987), Wilbur Sanders focuses mainly on character interactions and dramatic nuances; Charles Frey, *Shakespeare's Vast Romance: A Study of* The Winter's Tale (Columbia and London: University of Missouri Press, 1980), more comprehensively examines how the play moves "in time," gauging its impact on a theater audience as well as its literary merit. Bill Overton's The Winter's Tale, *The Critics Debate* (Atlantic Highlands, N.J.: Humanities Press Inc., 1989), offers a good overview of the play as well as assessing significant critical approaches to it.

G. Wilson Knight's "Great Creating Nature": An Essay on *The Winter's Tale,* in *The Crown of Life* (London: Methuen and Co., Ltd., 1948), is bursting with insights, especially into the imagery and texture of the play. More recently Frank Kermode covers several of the play's linguistic features in his *Shakespeare's Language* (London and New York: Allen Lane, The Penguin Press, 2000). Among studies of the play's formal distinctiveness in relation to received genres, the most notable are Rosalie A. Colie, *Shakespeare's Living Art* (Princeton, N.J.: Princeton University Press, 1974), which discusses the play as tragicomic pastoral, as does David Young, *The Heart's Forest: A Study of Shakespeare's Pastoral Plays* (New Haven and London: Yale University Press, 1972). See also chapters in Howard Felperin, *Shakespearean Romance* (Princeton, N.J.: Princeton University Press, 1972), in R. S. White, *"Let Wonder Seem Familiar": The Endings of Shakespeare's Romances* (Atlantic Highlands, N.J.: Humanities Press, 1985), and in Robert M. Adams, *Shakespeare: The Four Romances* (New York and London: W. W. Norton and Co., 1989). Northrop Frye's tying of the romance genre to seasonal myth, as in *A Natural Perspective: The Development of Comedy and Romance* (New York and London: Columbia University Press, 1965), remains seminal for *The Winter's Tale.* Joan Hartwig analyzes the play's tragicomic features in *Shakespeare's Tragicomic Vision* (Baton Rouge: Louisiana State University, 1972), while Barbara A. Mowat, *The Dramaturgy of Shakespeare's Romances* (Athens: The University of Georgia Press, 1976), convincingly explores the play as innovative "open drama." In *William Shakespeare: The Romances* (Boston: Twayne Publishers, G. K. Hall and Co., 1990), Elizabeth Bieman interprets the drama through a Jungian viewpoint.

Owing more to postmodern and cultural materialist methodology are Graham Holderness, *"The Winter's Tale:* Country into Court," in *Shakespeare: Out of Court,* ed. Holderness, Nick Potter, John Turner (New York: St. Martin's Press, 1990), and Howard Felperin's provocative essay, "'Tongue-tied Our Queen?': The Deconstruction of Presence in *The Winter's Tale,"* in *Shakespeare and the Question of Theory,* ed. Patricia Parker and Geoffrey Hartman (London: Methuen, 1985). H. W. Fawkner's reading of the play in *Shakespeare's Miracle Plays:* Pericles, Cymbeline *and* The Winter's Tale (London and Toronto: Associated University Presses, 1992) is also frankly deconstructive.

Not surprisingly, such a theatrical play has attracted metadramatic interpretations—in particular, those of Robert Egan in *Drama within Drama: Shakespeare's Sense of His Art in* King Lear, The Winter's Tale, *and* The Tempest (New York and London: Columbia University Press, 1975)—as well as an interest in how *The Winter's Tale* generates "wonder" in the theater. Chapters in Kirby Farrell's *Shakespeare's Creation: The Language of Magic and Play* (Amherst: The University of Massachusetts Press, 1975), T. G. Bishop's *Shakespeare and the Theatre of Wonder* (Cambridge: Cambridge University Press, 1996), and Peter G. Platt's *Reason Diminished: Shakespeare and the Marvelous* (Lincoln and London: University of Nebraska Press, 1997) all illuminate this aspect of the play. The fullest study of how the play has been performed is Dennis Batholomeusz, The Winter's Tale *in Performance in England and America, 1611–1976* (Cambridge: Cambridge University Press, 1982). In The Winter's Tale*: Text and Performance* (Basingstoke and London: Macmillan Publishers, Ltd., 1985), R. P. Draper comments on four productions, three staged by the Royal Shakespeare Company (1969, 1976, and 1981) and the fourth the videotaped BBC/Time Life version (1980); David A. Male covers the same three theatrical performances, with photographic illustrations, in The Winter's Tale*: Shakespeare on Stage* (Cambridge: Cambridge University Press, 1984). A long chapter in Roger Warren's *Staging Shakespeare's Late Plays* (Oxford: Clarendon Press, 1990) examines the evolution of Peter Hall's 1988 production of the play for the National Theatre in London. The journals *Shakespeare Survey* and *Shakespeare Quarterly* continue to review recent productions of *The Winter's Tale* on both sides of the Atlantic.

## COLLECTIONS OF ESSAYS

An older anthology well worth consulting is *Shakespeare:* The Winter's Tale (London: Macmillan and Co., 1969), edited by Kenneth Muir. It contains some of the earliest criticism and theatrical reviews of the play as well as excerpts from the work of Tillyard, Bethell, Knight, and Frye. Harold Bloom's contribution to the Modern Critical Interpretations series, *William Shakespeare's* The Winter's Tale (New York, New Haven, and Philadelphia: Chelsea House Publishers, 1987), reprints several pieces referred to in this Guide. Carol Thomas Neely, "Women and Issue in *The Winter's Tale,*" and Anne Barton, "Leontes and the Spider: Language and Speaker in Shakespeare's Last Plays," are two important ones. The fullest collection of traditional essays, ranging from William Hazlitt's nineteenth-century notes to theater reviews in the late 1980s, is The Winter's

Tale*: Critical Essays* (New York and London: Garland Publishing Inc., 1995), edited by Maurice Hunt. As his introduction, Hunt offers a helpful 58-page survey of the play's "Critical Legacy."

Other critiques of *The Winter's Tale* are contained in anthologies covering all of Shakespeare's Late Plays, such as Carol McGinnis Kay and Henry E. Jacobs (eds.), *Shakespeare's Romances Reconsidered* (Lincoln and London: The University of Nebraska Press, 1978). With the exception of Hunt's anthology, the critical bias since the late 1980s has been toward cultural materialist essays; Kiernan Ryan, editor of *Shakespeare: The Last Plays* (London and New York: Longman, 1999), presents a stimulating futuristic approach to *The Winter's Tale* in his introduction. For the New Casebooks series, *Shakespeare's Romances* (Houndmills, Basingstoke: Palgrave Macmillan, 2003), Alison Thorne selects excerpts from Janet Adelman's feminist study of *The Winter's Tale* and a new historicist essay by James Ellison. As its title suggests, *Shakespeare's Late Plays: New Readings* (Edinburgh: Edinburgh University Press, 1999), edited by Jennifer Richards and James Knowles, offers feminist and materialist essays not published elsewhere, while editor Nancy Klein Maguire chooses new pieces that relate tragicomedy to political contexts in *Renaissance Tragicomedy: Explorations in Genre and Politics* (New York: AMS Press, 1987). Despite its title, a throwback to more conventional criticism comes in Stephen W. Smith and Travis Cartwright (eds.), *Shakespeare's Last Plays: Essays in Literature and Politics* (New York and Oxford: Lexington Books, 2002). David N. Beauregard, for instance, reminds readers of the religious dimension of the play's "wonder" in "Shakespeare against the Skeptics: Nature and Grace in *The Winter's Tale*."

# INDEX

148, 162–63, 164–66, 177–79, 180–82
Siddons, Mrs., 169, 170
Sidney, Sir Philip: *Arcadia*, 28, 58, 61; *Defense of Poesie*, 59, 62
Siegel, Paul, 32 n.11
Siemon, James Edward, 69 n.19
Skura, Meredith, 154 n.14
Smallwood, Robert, 190 n.18
Smith, Derek, 178
Smith, Hallett, 10 n.35, 72 n.60, 143
Smith, Jonathan, 9 n.23, 10 n.42, 109 nn.18, 21
Snyder, Susan, 76 n.117, 194 n.115
Sokol, B. J., 138 n.65
Spenser, Edmund, *The Faerie Queene*, 28, 58, 61, 130
Spriggs, Elizabeth, 171
Spurgeon, Caroline, 108 n.2
St. Paul, 24, 118, 119, 142
Stationer's Register, 1
statue, statue scene, 2, 3, 27, 29, 31, 37 nn.112, 117, 48–49, 53, 65–66, 81–82, 86, 91, 97, 100–101, 105–6, 118–19, 126–27, 129–32, 137 nn.57, 60, 64, 138 nn.66, 71, 72, 146, 147, 151, 152, 159 n.103, 161, 168, 182, 183–84, 186
Steevens, George, 5
Stephens, Robert, 186
Stewart, Garrett, 138 n.66
Stewart, J. I. M., 110 n.41, 140
Stewart, Patrick, 176
Stockholder, Kay, 133 n.3, 154 n.12
Stott, Ken, 178
Strachey, Lytton, 55, 144
Strong, L. A. G., 154 n.18
Stuart, Arabella, 14
Styan, J. L., 145

Takakuwa, Yoko, 158 n.89
Tasso, Torquato, 58, 60

Tayler, Edward W., 136 n.45
Taylor, Michael, 134 n.14
Tennenhouse, Leonard A., 32, 148
Terence, 74, n.91
Terry, Ellen, 169, 170, 190 n.7
Theocratus, 60
Third Gentleman, 65, 81, 101, 112 n.68, 119, 126, 131
Thorne, Alison, 155 n.35, 199
*Thracian Wonder*, 28, 37 n.108
Tillyard, E. M. W., 66, 70 n.38, 71 n.39, 143, 196
Time, 27, 36 n.98, 39, 41, 46, 47, 50–51, 53, 59, 70 nn.29, 30, 31, 79, 80, 108 n.8, 162, 166–67, 182–83
Tinkler, F. C., 75 n.108, 142
Toliver, Harold E., 74 n.84
Tragicomedy, 21, 47, 54, 62–66, 70 n.35, 74 nn.92, 93, 74–75 n.97, 75 n.106, 144, 195, 197, 199
Traub, Valerie, 113 n.82, 152
Traversi, Derek, 68 n.10, 74 n.88, 109 n.24, 112 nn.64, 71, 143
Tree, Herbert Beerbohm, 163, 164
Triemens, Roger J., 110 n.32
Tylus, Jane, 114 n.100, 159 n.109
Tyzack, Margaret, 185

Underdowne, Thomas, 58
Uphaus, Robert W., 71 n.38, 108 n.8

Van Doren, Mark, 9 n.21
Van Elk, Martine, 113 n.73
Van Laan, Thomas F., 146
Vanita, Ruth, 153
Virgil, 60

Waage, Frederick O., 137 n.54
Walkley, A. B., 190 n.15, 193 n.95
Ward, David, 7, 10 n.35, 133 n.6
Wardle, Irving, 192 n.60
Warner, Amelia, 170, 171
Warren, Roger, 71–72 n.52, 114 nn.95, 98, 190 nn.23, 33, 191 nn.41, 55,

192 nn.72, 73, 74, 79, 193 nn.86,
103, 108, 110, 113, 198
Weinstein, Philip M., 74 n.85
Wells, Stanley, 8 n.6, 9 n.16, 31 n.2,
34 n.45, 36 n.99, 184, 194 nn.124,
129, 132
West, Rebecca, 170
West, Mrs., 170, 177
Wexler, Joyce, 159 n.99
Whigham, Frank, 135 n.29
Whitby, Arthur, 178
White, R. S., 70 n.35, 72 n.59, 73
n.65, 197
Wickham, Glynne, 14
Wilkinson, Norman, 164
William, David, 178
Williams, George Walton, 191 n.40
Willis, Susan, 194 nn.116, 119,
129
Willson, David Harris, 33 n.28

Wilson, F. P., 145
Wilson, Harold S., 38 n.128
Wilson, John Dover, 110 n.39
Wilson, Richard, 17, 149, 153
Wimsatt, W. K., 142
Wolfenden, Guy, 165
Wolfit, Donald, 177
Wood, Peter, 164, 176
Wright, Laurence, 10 n.35
Wright, Susan, 171

Yates, Frances A., 37 n.112
Yates, Mrs., 170
Young, Bruce W., 134 n.15
Young, David, 69 n.24, 70 n.31, 73
n.77, 111 n.43, 197

Ziegler, Joseph, 178
Zitner, Sheldon P., 194 n.114
Zurcher, Amelia, 160 n.111

**About the Author**

JOAN LORD HALL is an Instructor in the University Writing Program at the University of Colorado, Boulder. Her previous books include *Henry V: A Guide to the Play* (1997), *Othello: A Guide to the Play* (1999), and *Antony and Cleopatra: A Guide to the Play* (2002), all available from Greenwood Press.